W9-BMO-834

USING

microsoft®

onenote®
2010

Michael C. Oldenburg

800 East 96th Street, Indianapolis, Indiana 46240 USA

Using Microsoft® OneNote® 2010

Copyright © 2012 by Pearson Education, Inc.

ISBN-13: 978-0-7897-4292-6

ISBN-10: 0-7897-4292-6

Library of Congress Cataloging-in-Publication Data

Oldenburg, Michael C.

   Using Microsoft OneNote 2010 / Michael C. Oldenburg.

      p. cm.

   Includes bibliographical references.

   ISBN 978-0-7897-4292-6

   1. Note-taking—Computer programs. 2. Personal information management—Computer programs. 3. Microsoft OneNote. I. Title.

   LB2395.25.O43 2011

   371.3028'1—dc23

                          2011024983

Printed in the United States of America

First Printing: September 2011

Trademarks

Warning and Disclaimer

Bulk Sales

Que Publishing offers excellent discounts on this book when ordered in quantity for bulk purchases or special sales. For more information, please contact

U.S. Corporate and Government Sales
1-800-382-3419
corpsales@pearsontechgroup.com

For sales outside of the U.S., please contact

International Sales
international@pearson.com

Associate Publisher
Greg Wiegand

Acquisitions Editor
Loretta Yates

Development Editor
Abshier House

Managing Editor
Kristy Hart

Project Editor
Betsy Harris

Copy Editor
Karen Annett

Indexer
Erika Millen

Proofreader
Williams Woods Publishing

Technical Editor
Peter O'Kelly

Publishing Coordina
Cindy Teeters

Book Designer
Anne Jones

Cover Designer
Anna Stingley

Compositor
Nonie Ratcliff

Contents at a Glance

Media Table of Contents

To register this product and gain access to the Free Web Edition and the video files, go to **quepublishing.com/using**.

Table of Contents

About the Author

Michael C. Oldenburg is a technical writer in the Office division at Microsoft Corporation. Professionally and privately, Michael is dedicated to helping people learn and enjoy what their computers can do. For the past 15 years, he has worked on a variety of software—including Microsoft FrontPage, PhotoDraw, Search Server, and OneNote. Previously, Michael worked as a network administrator in a mixed PC/Mac environment, as an international support specialist for European territories, and as a corporate trainer. His OneNote blog is currently published at blogs.office.com.

Dedication

I would like to dedicate this book to the talented program managers, developers, and testers at Microsoft, all of whom have worked hard to create and improve OneNote since its humble origins back in 2003.

Acknowledgments

Figuring out what you want to be when you grow up often depends on the level of encouragement that you receive from the people in your life. Many years ago, a family friend named Marlene Parr witnessed my then-teenage curiosity over a wondrous new invention called the IBM Personal Computer. Watching how I navigated this new device with ease only mere moments after she had given me a demonstration, Marlene allowed me the ongoing use of the PC that she had purchased for her business. I've always been grateful for this early opportunity to hear my calling, especially at a time in my youth when I could never have afforded such a wonderful machine of my own. Marlene's encouragement awakened and affirmed in me a passion for technology and software that has since become my life's work. Technology is about much more than just gadgets. It can improve the lives of millions of people all around the globe. It is my sincere hope that young people of today's generation will have similar opportunities to discover what's possible and what they're good at—no matter what the brand or tribe that may stand behind the various technologies they find exciting.

On a no less personal level, I want to express my sincere appreciation and gratitude to April Lubag Rodgers, Dale Sylvain, and Anneliese Wirth for their longtime friendship, unfailing support, and genuine encouragement—not only during this particular project, but also throughout several of the most eventful and meaningful chapters of my life.

Aside from an assumed interest in technology, the success of a technical writer is shaped by the many people that he or she meets and learns from. When I reflect on my own journey through this profession, I must immediately acknowledge Nona Allison and Holly Thomas as two of the most experienced and insightful technical editors that I have had the good fortune to meet and work with during my career. Over the years, I have never taken their generous mentorship for granted, nor will I ever forget the many valuable things that I have learned from both of them.

On the OneNote team at Microsoft, I would like to thank Olya Veselova, Alex Simmons, Daniel Escapa, and David Rasmussen for being the talented, fun, and caring people that they are and whom I've come to respect and trust over the past few years. Each of them has played an instrumental part in the original design and direction of OneNote. It's really wonderful to see the fruits of their labor rewarded by the explosive success of OneNote 2010 and through the sheer love that people all over the world continue to express for this software every day.

My sincere thanks also go out to Jessica Reading for green-lighting this project without hesitation and cheering me on; to Sonia Atchison, who thought of me when talk of a OneNote book first came up; and to my excellent acquisitions editor, Loretta Yates, for making this project a pleasant and rewarding experience right from the start.

Finally, no software product can reach its potential without the continual testing, feedback, kudos, gripes, discussions, and ideas by the millions of people who use and experience it on a daily basis. I would like to acknowledge and thank the many loyal fans of OneNote in every corner of the world, all of whom have in some way helped us to improve our favorite program.

—Michael C. Oldenburg

We Want to Hear from You!

As the reader of this book, *you* are our most important critic and commentator. We value your opinion and want to know what we're doing right, what we could do better, what areas you'd like to see us publish in, and any other words of wisdom you're willing to pass our way.

As an editor-in-chief for Que Publishing, I welcome your comments. You can email or write me directly to let me know what you did or didn't like about this book—as well as what we can do to make our books better.

Please note that I cannot help you with technical problems related to the topic of this book. We do have a User Services group, however, where I will forward specific technical questions related to the book.

When you write, please be sure to include this book's title and author as well as your name, email address, and phone number. I will carefully review your comments and share them with the author and editors who worked on the book.

Email: feedback@quepublishing.com

Mail: Greg Wiegand
Editor-in-Chief
Que Publishing
800 East 96th Street
Indianapolis, IN 46240 USA

Reader Services

Visit our website and register this book at quepublishing.com/using for convenient access to any updates, downloads, or errata that might be available for this book.

Introduction

Using Microsoft OneNote 2010 is a beginner's guide to one of the most useful and refreshingly different computer programs to be released in recent years. Considered to be somewhat of a best-kept secret since its debut in 2003, OneNote can be compared with a computerized Swiss Army knife because it has proven useful in a wide variety of situations, professions, and environments.

OneNote 2010 is the first version to be included in all of the latest Microsoft Office editions. As a result, more and more Microsoft Office users have begun to discover the many benefits of OneNote, and many users have expressed an interest in a more comprehensive introduction than what standard tutorials typically offer. This book attempts to strike a balance between providing that introduction, pointing out the program's usefulness along the way, and offering many step-by-step "Let Me Try It" instructions throughout, so you can learn OneNote through hands-on experience.

Although some features lend themselves well to written explanation, others are more compelling when demonstrated in a video. Therefore, you are encouraged to follow the instructions for unlocking the Free Web Edition of this book, which includes several free "Show Me" video tutorials that you might find worthwhile.

How This Book Is Organized

This book introduces you to the purpose of Microsoft OneNote 2010, its key feature areas, and the main program features within each of these areas.

Although some of the chapters walk you through the various tasks you can accomplish with OneNote regardless of a specific project or work environment, other chapters aim to help you understand larger usage scenarios and the options you have available to work within them. In either case, you will learn enough about individual OneNote features to let you easily apply that knowledge in a variety of real-life situations, no matter where or how you'll choose to use OneNote.

Using Microsoft OneNote 2010 provides

- Answers about what kind of program Microsoft OneNote 2010 is and what you can do with it.

- Specific examples of the various tasks and projects for which you can use OneNote and the various types of environments you can use it in.

- Information about the benefits of using OneNote 2010 over other programs.

- Guidance from a beginner's point of view; this book assumes only that you have installed the application and are ready to learn.

- Explanations of the key concepts for novice users, without resorting to the technical jargon that you might find in other training materials.

- Real-world examples that you can relate to more easily.

Using This Book

This book enables you to customize your own learning experience. The step-by-step instructions in the book give you a solid foundation in using Microsoft OneNote 2010, while rich and varied online content, including video tutorials and audio sidebars, provide the following:

- Demonstrations of step-by-step tasks covered in the book

- Additional tips or information on a topic

- Practical advice and suggestions

- Directions for more advanced tasks not covered in the book

Here's a quick look at a few structural features designed to help you get the most out of this book.

- **Chapter objective:** At the beginning of each chapter is a brief summary of topics addressed in that chapter. This objective enables you to quickly see what is covered in the chapter.

- **Notes:** Notes provide additional commentary or explanation that doesn't fit neatly into the surrounding text. Notes give detailed explanations of how something works, alternative ways of performing a task, and other tidbits to get you on your way.

- **Cross-references:** Many topics are connected to other topics in various ways. Cross-references help you link related information together, no matter where that information appears in the book. When another section is related to one you are reading, a cross-reference directs you to a specific page in the book on which you can find the related information.

 Let Me Try It tasks are presented in a step-by-step sequence so you can easily follow along.

 Show Me video walks through tasks you've just got to see—including bonus advanced techniques.

Special Features

More than just a book, your USING product integrates step-by-step video tutorials and valuable audio sidebars delivered through the **Free Web Edition** that comes with every USING book. For the price of the book, you get online access anywhere with a web connection—no books to carry, content is updated as the technology changes, and the benefit of video and audio learning.

About the USING Web Edition

The Web Edition of every USING book is powered by **Safari Books Online**, enabling you to access the video tutorials and valuable audio sidebars. Plus, you can search the contents of the book, highlight text and attach a note to that text, print your notes and highlights in a custom summary, and cut and paste directly from Safari Books Online.

To register this product and gain access to the Free Web Edition and the audio and video files, go to **quepublishing.com/using**.

This chapter provides an introduction to Microsoft OneNote 2010 and the benefits of electronic note-taking.

1

Introducing Microsoft OneNote

At first glance, it's quite easy to underestimate all that Microsoft OneNote has to offer. Compared with the complexity of the other programs in the Microsoft Office family, OneNote has a deceptively simple interface and, judging strictly by appearances, seems to have a limited arsenal of commands. As you begin to use and master it, however, you'll learn to appreciate its many capabilities. Whether you're brand new to OneNote or you have looked at it before and couldn't make heads or tails of it, I hope that by the time you finish reading this book, you will have a comprehensive overview of how to make the most of this incredibly capable program.

What Is OneNote?

OneNote is an electronic notebook that helps you to gather, manage, find, use, and share the vast amounts of information that each of us must process and make sense of during any given day (see Figure 1.1). Although most of us may already have a variety of computer programs at our disposal to help us manage information and time, OneNote is wonderfully different from the constraints of such other programs because it is not limited to any particular type of person, role, project, or place. This flexibility makes it an ideal companion for most of life's pursuits, no matter if they occur at home, at work, or at school.

With OneNote, you can

- Collect, keep, and connect to all of the things that matter to you—all in one place.

- Easily categorize the things that you keep on your computer.

- Organize information without having to learn a system or a new methodology.

- Instantly recall any part of your information whenever and wherever you need it.

- Keep private things private, but also easily share information with other people.

- Jot down simple ideas and gradually watch them take shape over time.

- Do all the things you can't do with paper—like creating more space on a page or changing your mind after you've done something.

- Replace all of the paper notebooks, sticky notes, scribbles, and sketches that are scattered around your life with a single, easy-to-use solution.

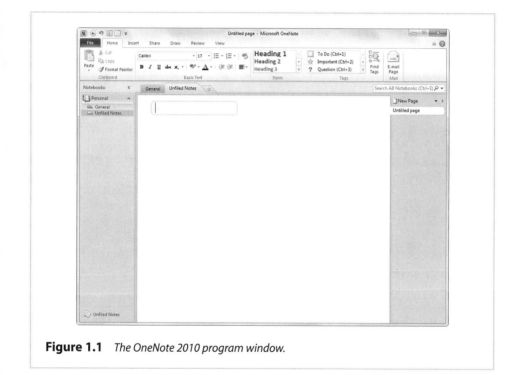

Figure 1.1   *The OneNote 2010 program window.*

OneNote has rightfully been called a lifesaver, a second brain, and the best thing to happen to computers in a long time. Spend just a few days with OneNote and this book, and I think you'll soon agree.

What Can You Do with OneNote?

We all know how to jot things down on a scrap of paper, but the limitations of paper-based notes quickly become evident when we need to find a specific piece of information again. Similarly, electronic information can be hard to find when it's trapped in an avalanche of random e-mails or in multiple versions of files, documents, and spreadsheets that are littered all over your computer's hard drive or on the Web.

Let's have a look at some of the more common benefits of electronic note-taking. Keep in mind that these lists are just a small collection of examples, but if you already spend much of your time in any of these scenarios, you should find OneNote immediately worthwhile.

OneNote at Home

Whether you're part of a small or large family, there are countless uses in which OneNote can help you stay organized around the house (see Figure 1.2).

Figure 1.2 *Examples of using OneNote 2010 at home.*

With OneNote, you can

- Keep, revise, and print your daily to-do lists.
- Plan a trip and keep comparisons of airfare, hotels, and sightseeing tours.
- Collect and share cooking recipes.
- Prioritize your family's after-work or after-school activities.
- Plan a wedding or a major new purchase like a car or a home.
- Collect ideas on the Web about gardening or another hobby you enjoy.
- Track the progress and cost of contractor jobs for a home remodel.

- Take up digital scrapbooking.

- Draft a book, write poetry, dream up song lyrics, or learn sheet music.

- Distribute a family newsletter in e-mail, on a blog, or on Windows Live SkyDrive.

OneNote at Work

OneNote is an absolutely indispensable companion in the workplace, where it adapts itself to virtually any project or team (see Figure 1.3).

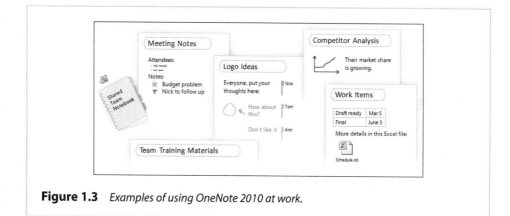

Figure 1.3 *Examples of using OneNote 2010 at work.*

With OneNote, you can

- Take meeting minutes to capture and recall important work items.

- Integrate your notes with your Outlook Calendar, Contacts, and Tasks.

- Document a project or process with a wiki-style team notebook.

- Brainstorm ideas and solve problems together with others, even if they work from home or in remote locations.

- Collaborate with others in real time without checking in and out files or waiting your turn to make edits and additions in shared documents and plans.

- Archive important e-mail conversations in their own notebook.

- Sketch out prototypes for a design project.

- Save paper by publishing corporate training materials digitally.

- Import PowerPoint slides and annotate them with detailed notes.

- Keep all files for a project together in the same notebook.

OneNote at School

At any level of school, OneNote is a wizard at keeping even the least academically inclined student organized and on track (see Figure 1.4).

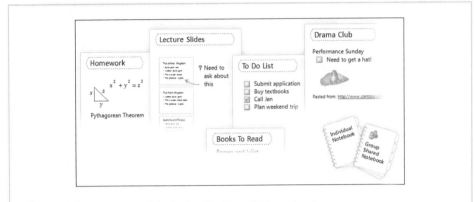

Figure 1.4   *Page examples of using OneNote 2010 at school.*

With OneNote you can

- Keep campus maps and your class schedule at your fingertips.
- Make separate sections (folders) for every class, club, activity, and semester.
- Take notes in classes, lectures, and other gatherings, on and off campus.
- E-mail your assignments and research drafts to your teachers.
- Do research in your web browser and send the information directly to OneNote.
- Create a shared notebook for everyone in your school club or study group to use.
- Test yourself and prepare for a foreign language exam.
- Use the mini translator to share notes and ideas with friends in other countries.
- Import class handouts by printing them into OneNote.
- Use quick filing to easily import information into the right class folders.

Other Benefits of Using OneNote

OneNote is the first computer program that I've come across that makes "going paperless" a realistic and achievable goal. At my work, teams now routinely store information in shared notebooks that everyone can access at any time. No more futzing with paper-based agendas and meeting minutes, no more printed-out PowerPoint slides to make annotations, and no more useless handouts that get tossed in the recycle bin five minutes after the meeting is over.

Similarly, on a larger scale, our corporate trainers have replaced the reams and reams of paper that they used to cram into the big welcome kits for new employees by migrating all of that important information into searchable OneNote notebooks. The massive amounts of reference materials are distributed as a OneNote notebook on a reusable USB thumb drive. New employees can easily search for keywords to look something up, instead of stumbling across it or spending a ton of time combing through an index.

At the individual level, OneNote is the kind of program that lets you focus on the stuff you're thinking or writing about, instead of constantly forcing you to think about the program itself or the housekeeping of your file system. It does this by removing the need to constantly save and manage your files. After you write something in OneNote, there's no Save button to click. It remembers everything you do in your notebook, so you don't have to think about it unless you want to.

New users sometimes hesitate when they first open OneNote because the obvious freedom and flexibility of the page canvas seems too good to be true. For years, computer programs have taught us to constrain information into lines of text (Word), rows and columns (Excel), text-entry boxes of various sizes and shapes (Outlook), small slides (PowerPoint), or fields and records (InfoPath and Access). The OneNote workspace is decidedly different. It's as free-form as a sheet of paper, which means you can click, write, or type anywhere you want. Unlike paper, however, you can always make more room on the page or change your mind about anything you added or edited. For other items that you place on the page—pictures or files you insert or sketches you draw—there aren't any constraints either. Best of all, everything in OneNote gets stored on your computer together.

When you're done writing, editing, or importing information into your digital notebook, OneNote will never nag you to get organized. Wasn't that one of the original ideas—the computer is *personal*, not pedantic? That idea may have gotten lost somewhere along the way, but happily, OneNote is helping to restore it.

When I first started to use OneNote, I collected random information from various sources on various pages. I knew I wanted to keep these things for reference, but I wasn't sure yet how all these things that weren't related to each other should be organized. I didn't have to worry about it and used the Instant Search function to find anything at any time. As my notebook grew in size and complexity over time, I decided one day to create a few new sections into which I moved some of the information. The great thing is that I didn't need to completely reverse course when I suddenly changed my filing habits. OneNote can instantly retrieve my information, no matter how it's been collected. The point is: There is no right or wrong way to use OneNote. Be as organized or as unorganized as you like—it's up to you!

OneNote 2010 is the first version that fully realizes the dream of universal access to your information. You can use OneNote 2010 on your desktop computer, on your laptop computer, on a Tablet PC, in a web browser with the free OneNote Web App, and on your smartphone. I'll go into more detail about some of these later in this book.

Getting Started

This discussion assumes that you've already installed OneNote 2010 on your computer and that you're familiar with basic Windows operating system tasks. If you have not installed the program, please do so before continuing. The step-by-step instructions assume that you are using any edition of Windows 7 as your operating system. If you're using an earlier version of Windows, you may need to substitute some commands here and there, but it shouldn't be too difficult to follow along.

Microsoft's free 60-day trial version of OneNote 2010 (available for download from Office.com) gives you unrestricted access to all of the program's features. If you haven't yet purchased OneNote 2010, you can use this book to guide you through the trial version and help you in evaluating whether OneNote 2010 is right for you.

 **LET ME TRY IT**

Creating Your First Notebook

When you launch OneNote 2010 for the first time after a new installation, it asks you where you want to create your first notebook. You can choose to store this notebook either on your computer's hard drive, or online with a free Microsoft service called Windows Live SkyDrive, which acts like a large hard drive that you can access over the Internet from anywhere in the world.

To keep things simple, we'll open the notebook on your computer's hard drive.

1. On the Windows taskbar, click the Start button, select All Programs, click the Microsoft Office folder, and then click the Microsoft OneNote 2010 icon.

2. When the Opening First Notebook dialog box appears, select the second option (On My Computer) and then click Continue (see Figure 1.5).

Figure 1.5   *This dialog box appears the very first time you start OneNote.*

OneNote 2010 opens the sample notebook it has just created on your computer. This notebook consists of four pages that are prefilled with information that you can read through to learn a bit more about how to use OneNote 2010. You can also use this sample notebook to experiment with, by changing its text, resizing images, and moving stuff around on the pages.

If OneNote did not prompt you to create the sample notebook, it's possible that an earlier version of OneNote or a OneNote trial version was installed previously on your computer. In that case, you can create the sample notebook manually. In Windows Explorer, navigate to the C:\Program Files\Microsoft Office\ Office14\1033 folder on your hard drive and then double-click the ONGuide.onepkg file. (If you're using a 64-bit edition of Windows, look in the C:\Program Files (x86)\Microsoft Office\Office14\1033 folder instead.) In the Unpack Notebook dialog box that appears, change the text in the Name field to *OneNote Guide* and then click Create. When the notebook opens, you can look through its four pages and experiment with the sample content.

LET ME TRY IT

Creating a New Notebook

For the remaining step-by-step practices in the rest of this book, create a blank, new notebook that you can practice in without any distractions.

1. Near the top-left corner of the OneNote program window, click the File tab. This opens the Backstage View, where you can manage your notebook files. (You learn more about the Backstage View later in Chapter 3, "A Tour of the OneNote Workspace.")

2. On the screen that opens, click New in the left navigation bar to reveal the New Notebook options on the right side of the screen.

3. In the list under Step 1 (Store Notebook On), click My Computer (see Figure 1.6).

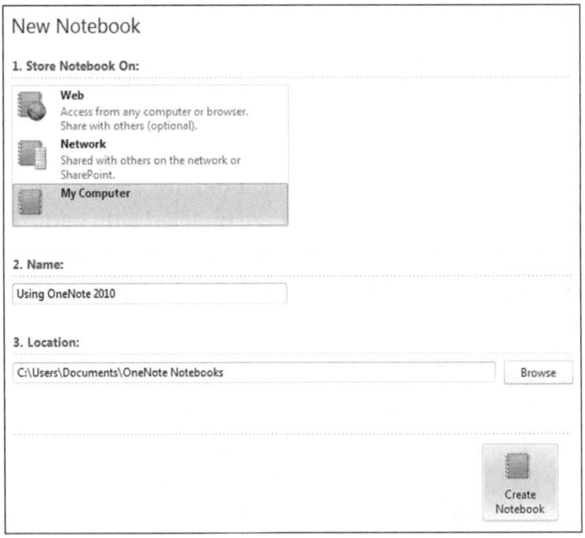

New Notebook

1. Store Notebook On:

Web
Access from any computer or browser.
Share with others (optional).

Network
Shared with others on the network or SharePoint.

My Computer

2. Name:

Using OneNote 2010

3. Location:

C:\Users\Documents\OneNote Notebooks   Browse

Create
Notebook

Figure 1.6   *The New Notebook interface on the File tab.*

4. In the box under Step 2 (Name), enter *Using OneNote 2010* as the notebook name.

5. Leave Step 3 (Location) as it is and then click the Create Notebook button near the bottom of the screen.

OneNote creates and opens a blank, new notebook, which consists of a single section that contains a single, untitled blank page.

I'll discuss the various elements of the OneNote workspace in Chapter 3, so don't worry about the terminology like pages, sections, and Backstage View right now.

Upgrading from a Previous Version

If you have never used OneNote before, you can skip this entire chapter for now. Although it does contain important information about the file format differences between the different versions of OneNote, this is important only when you are upgrading to OneNote 2010 from a previous version or when you have created shared notebooks in OneNote 2010 that you want to share with other people who might still be using an older version.

> You might want to return to the information in this chapter later, after reading Chapter 9, "Sharing Notes with Other People."

Upgrading from OneNote 2003

OneNote 2003 was the first-ever released version of OneNote. Although it was a noteworthy and capable debut in its time, it is now mostly incompatible with the majority of the features that have been introduced in both OneNote 2007 and OneNote 2010.

If you're upgrading to OneNote 2010 from OneNote 2003, you are prompted to update all of the files in your My Notebook folder (OneNote 2003 supported only a single notebook), so that you can use all of the features in OneNote 2010 with your old notes. This is highly recommended.

However, after your old notebook files have been updated, OneNote 2003 will no longer be able to read them. This is because the older program can't possibly understand a file format that was invented some seven years later. Before you choose to let OneNote 2010 update your old notes, first consider whether you will ever need to use them in the older OneNote 2003 program again (for example, if you have a second copy of OneNote 2003 on another computer that you won't be upgrading). If so, be sure to first create a complete backup of all of your old notebook files.

If you decline to update your OneNote 2003 notebook files as part of the OneNote 2010 upgrade, you can only view them in OneNote 2010 as read-only files, but you cannot edit them.

Upgrading from OneNote 2007

OneNote 2007 has several key features in common with the newer OneNote 2010 (among them, support for multiple notebooks and shared notebooks). Although OneNote 2007 naturally cannot read files in the newer OneNote 2010 format, OneNote 2010 fully supports opening, viewing, editing, and sharing notes in the older OneNote 2007 format. This means you can choose whether you want to keep using your existing notebook files in the older OneNote 2007 format, or whether you want to update them to the newer, more capable OneNote 2010 format.

If you choose to leave your notebook files in the older OneNote 2007 format, you will not be able to use the following OneNote 2010 features in your notebooks:

- Linked Notes
- Notebook Versioning
- Notebook Recycle Bin
- Multilevel Subpages
- Math Equations

To enable all of these features in OneNote 2010, updating your files to the newer format is required. Thankfully, however, you can change formats at any time, if needed, by using the built-in conversion utility in OneNote 2010. This utility lets you convert any notebook from the OneNote 2010 file format to the OneNote 2007 file format—and back again.

The ability to switch formats at will was included to maximize compatibility for shared notebooks in environments in which both OneNote 2007 and OneNote 2010 are in use at the same time. If you upgraded your older notes to the new OneNote 2010 file format and then realize you need to share those notes with people who are still using OneNote 2007, you can downgrade the files and then share the notebook among users of both versions.

The main caveat to downgrading your notes from the OneNote 2010 format to the older OneNote 2007 format is that your notes will lose or ignore the aforementioned newer features that only OneNote 2010 can understand, which means that you will also lose the information they created or provide. For example, if you used the Linked Notes feature and then downgrade those notes to the older OneNote

2007 format, the functionality is unavailable unless you update the file format again. However, simply upgrading to the new format once again will not automatically restore any information that was lost.

SHOW ME   Media 2.1—Viewing and Changing Notebook Formats

Access this video file through your registered Web Edition at
my.safaribooksonline.com/9780132182447/media.

LET ME TRY IT

Converting a Notebook to the OneNote 2007 Format

Use the blank, new notebook you created at the end of Chapter 1, "Introducing Microsoft OneNote," to see how easy it is to change the notebook file to the older OneNote 2007 file format.

1. Near the top-left corner of the OneNote program window, click the File tab. This opens the Backstage View, where you can manage your notebook files. (You'll learn more about the Backstage View later in Chapter 3, "A Tour of the OneNote Workspace.")

2. Under Notebook Information, find the practice notebook you created ("Using OneNote 2010") and then click the Settings button for that notebook.

3. On the menu that appears, click Properties (see Figure 2.1).

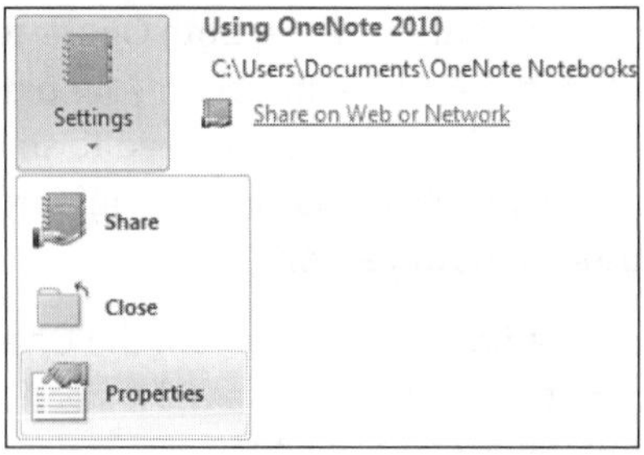

Using OneNote 2010
C:\Users\Documents\OneNote Notebooks

Settings

Share on Web or Network

Share

Close

Properties

Figure 2.1   *The Settings button lets you access the Notebook Properties dialog box.*

The Notebook Properties dialog box opens (see Figure 2.2). Here, you can rename the currently selected notebook, change the color of its icon, change its location, and convert its file format.

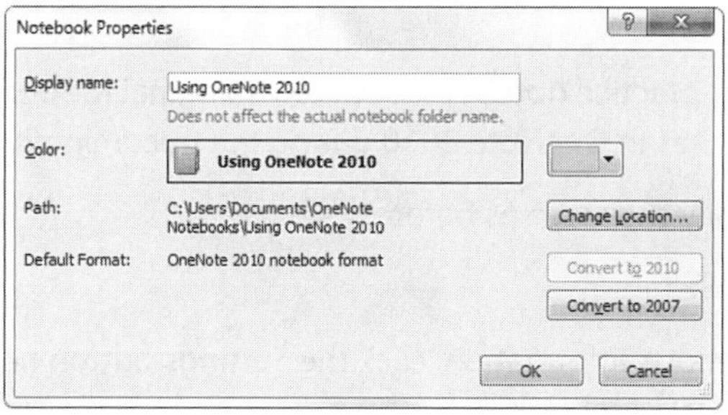

Notebook Properties

Display name: | Using OneNote 2010
Does not affect the actual notebook folder name.

Color: | Using OneNote 2010

Path: | C:\Users\Documents\OneNote Notebooks\Using OneNote 2010 | Change Location...

Default Format: | OneNote 2010 notebook format | Convert to 2010

Convert to 2007

OK   Cancel

Figure 2.2 *The Notebook Properties dialog box.*

If the current notebook is in OneNote 2010 format (which the Using OneNote 2010 notebook is), only the Convert to 2007 button is available. Similarly, if the notebook were in the older OneNote 2007 format, only the Convert to 2010 button would be available.

4. Click the Convert to 2007 button.

5. When the warning about the affected OneNote 2010 features appears, click OK to acknowledge the message.

When the dialog box closes, the notebook is converted to the older OneNote 2007 format.

You can verify that you're using a notebook in the OneNote 2007 format by looking at the title bar in the top center of the OneNote 2010 program window. If the words "Compatibility Mode" appear after the page title (see Figure 2.3), it means you're working in the older format.

Untitled page [Compatibility Mode] - Microsoft OneNote

Figure 2.3 *The Compatibility Mode warning in the OneNote 2010 title bar.*

 **LET ME TRY IT**

Converting a Notebook to the OneNote 2010 Format

Now convert your practice notebook back to its original (newer) format so you can use all of the features in OneNote 2010 during the upcoming practice sessions.

The steps are nearly the same as before:

1. Select the File tab.

2. Under Notebook Information, click the Settings button next to the Using OneNote 2010 notebook.

3. On the menu that appears, click Properties.

4. In the Notebook Properties dialog box, click the Convert to 2010 button.

5. When the warning about sharing the notebook with OneNote 2007 users appears, click OK to acknowledge the message.

When the dialog box closes, the notebook is converted to the newer OneNote 2010 format and the "Compatibility Mode" warning on the OneNote title bar will disappear.

Additional File Conversion Considerations

If you open a notebook that contains individual sections which are stored in the older OneNote 2007 format, an Information Bar appears at the top of every page in that section to warn you of the possible incompatibility. Click the Information Bar to convert that particular section (or the entire notebook the section is stored in) to the newer OneNote 2010 format.

If you should attempt to move any page or section from a notebook in one format to a different notebook in another format, OneNote 2010 will display a warning before attempting to convert your notes.

As with all important computer files, it's a good idea to create a complete set of backups that you'll store on a different hard drive for safekeeping before you experiment with notebook conversions (especially if you're upgrading from OneNote 2003).

⌾ *For more information about OneNote backups,* **see** *Chapter 8, "Security Features in OneNote."*

This chapter introduces you to the OneNote 2010
user interface and some of its terminology.

3

A Tour of the OneNote Workspace

Before you get started with some hands-on practice, first look at the most important components of the OneNote 2010 interface. Figure 3.1 shows the OneNote
program window as it appears in the sample notebook that you created in Chapter
1, "Introducing Microsoft OneNote."

The OneNote 2010 interface includes the following main components:

- The ribbon

- The Quick Access Toolbar

- The Backstage View

- The navigation bar

- Section tabs

- The Search box

- Page tabs

- The editing pane

 SHOW ME   Media 3.1—A Tour of the OneNote Workspace
Access this video file through your registered Web Edition at
my.safaribooksonline.com/9780132182447/media.

Let's take a closer look at each of these items and what you can do with them.

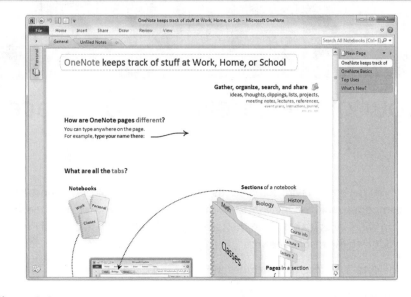

Figure 3.1   *The OneNote 2010 program window, the way it appears when you run OneNote for the first time.*

The Ribbon

If you're upgrading to OneNote 2010 from a previous version, the most prominent change to the interface is the inclusion of the "ribbon"—a bandlike interface that spans the top of the program window (see Figure 3.2). The ribbon replaces the menus and toolbars from previous versions and makes it easier to find and use the various commands and buttons that let you control the features in OneNote and the content you store in it.

Figure 3.2   *The ribbon in OneNote 2010, as it appears with only its tabs visible in the default view.*

The ribbon consists of several tabs (labeled File, Home, Insert, Share, Draw, Review, and View) that you can click to display contextual commands for each of these categories. When you click a ribbon tab, you'll see several labeled groups within it—each containing one or more commands. For example, on the Home tab, the groups are labeled Clipboard, Basic Text, Styles, Tags, and Mail. Within any of these groups, click any of the buttons representing the commands you want to use.

When you first launch OneNote 2010, the ribbon appears minimized, and only its tabs are visible (see Figure 3.2), allowing for more of your screen space to remain visible while taking or reading notes. This is especially useful if you're using OneNote on a laptop or netbook computer with a small screen. To use the ribbon in this minimized state, click any ribbon tab to temporarily reveal all of the commands available on that tab. As soon as you click a command, the ribbon hides itself again.

If you work on a desktop computer with a large monitor, or if your laptop computer has a decent sized screen, you can opt to keep the full ribbon visible at all times (see Figure 3.3). To do so, hold down the Ctrl key on your keyboard and then press the F1 key.

Figure 3.3   *The ribbon in OneNote 2010, expanded to full view.*

Keeping the ribbon always expanded is also a good idea if you're still new to OneNote and you want to explore and discover features more easily. You can always minimize the ribbon again later, when using the new interface has become second nature to you. To collapse the ribbon again at any time, just use the Ctrl+F1 keyboard shortcut.

Like in other Microsoft Office programs, the ribbon in OneNote 2010 can be fully customized to suit your needs and preferences. For example, you can easily modify and reorder any of the existing tabs, groups, and commands; turn off those that you don't need; and even create your own custom tabs that contain only the commands you want. You'll learn more about this in Chapter 12, "Customizing OneNote 2010."

The Quick Access Toolbar

Near the top-left corner of the OneNote program window is the Quick Access Toolbar (see Figure 3.4). It is a fully customizable area where you can keep shortcuts to the commands you use most frequently. Commands that you place on the Quick Access Toolbar are always visible while you use OneNote, no matter what ribbon tab is displayed.

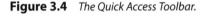

Figure 3.4   *The Quick Access Toolbar.*

When you first start OneNote, the Quick Access Toolbar contains shortcuts to the Back, Undo, Dock to Desktop, and Full Page View commands. You're not limited to these suggestions, however. Click the small arrow to the right of the toolbar's last icon to reveal some additional choices that you can toggle on or off—like Print or Print Preview (see Figure 3.5).

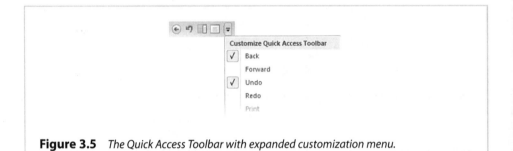

Figure 3.5   *The Quick Access Toolbar with expanded customization menu.*

If you don't like any of the available presets or you want to keep some commands handy that aren't listed, click More Commands on the menu to add virtually any command that's available in OneNote 2010. Remember, feel free to experiment. You can always turn off or reset commands you've added if you change your mind.

The Backstage View

OneNote's file and notebook management options—including opening, creating, sharing, and printing notebook files—are located in the Backstage View. You can access it by clicking the File tab on the ribbon (see Figure 3.6).

The Backstage View also provides an entry point for the OneNote Options dialog box, where you can specify many advanced OneNote settings. We'll cover some of these a bit later in this book.

To close the Backstage View, click the File tab again (or any other tab on the ribbon). You can also press the Esc key to close the Backstage View.

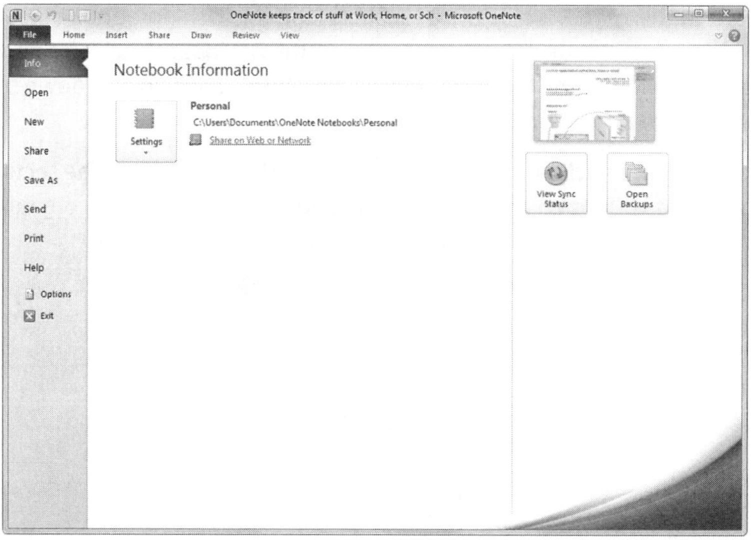

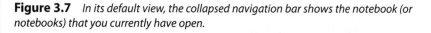

Figure 3.6   *The Backstage View, accessible by clicking the File tab.*

The Navigation Bar

Under the ribbon and docked to the far-left side of the OneNote program window is the navigation bar (see Figure 3.7). This area of the interface provides easy access to all of your notebooks, whether they are stored on your computer's hard drive, on your company's or school's network, or on the Internet.

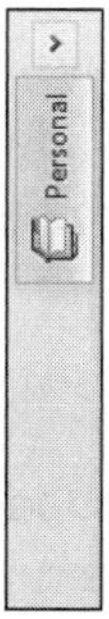

Figure 3.7   *In its default view, the collapsed navigation bar shows the notebook (or notebooks) that you currently have open.*

Like the ribbon, the navigation bar is shown in a collapsed view when you first start OneNote. In this mode, it displays a clickable icon for each notebook that you currently have open. Clicking a notebook icon on the navigation bar will switch to it so you can work with it. You can also drag the notebook icons up and down to rearrange them in your preferred order.

If you expand the navigation bar (see Figure 3.8), the hierarchy of the sections within each of your open notebooks is revealed, making it easier to organize and rearrange notes or to copy or move notes between notebooks.

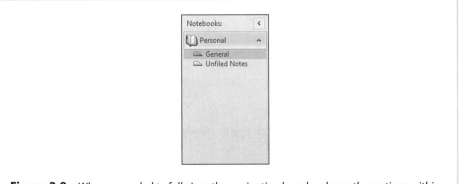

Figure 3.8   *When expanded to full view, the navigation bar also shows the sections within each notebook.*

When you first begin using OneNote, you'll probably work with a single notebook. Over time, you may create and use multiple notebooks or use shared notebooks at work or at school to collaborate with others. The first time you open any additional notebook, that notebook is added to the navigation bar so you can quickly switch between all of your open notebooks.

No matter if the navigation bar is expanded or collapsed, you can right-click any notebook icon on the navigation bar to see additional commands.

Section Tabs

The shark fin-like tabs just under the ribbon and near the top center of the OneNote program window are the notebook section tabs (see Figure 3.9). Like a paper-based, five-subject notebook with color tabs that you can label, OneNote notebooks can be divided into sections to keep notes organized based on subject matter, projects, locations, people, or anything else that makes sense to you. Unlike in paper-based notebooks, however, OneNote lets you add a virtually unlimited number of sections. You can just as easily remove or rename them, move or copy them, or change them to a different color whenever you feel like it.

Figure 3.9   *Horizontal tabs let you access and organize the sections in a notebook.*

Section tabs can be the target of links you create in your notes, which lets readers quickly jump to a specific section of the notebook, no matter where they are. This functionality lets you create wiki-style notebooks that you can use for training or reference at work, at school, or for your family.

Notebook sections in OneNote can be password protected to protect them from unauthorized access.

You'll learn more about working with notebook sections in Chapter 4, "Notebooks, Sections, and Pages."

The Search Box

Searching for information and finding it instantly is where OneNote 2010 really shines. Located just under the ribbon and near the right side of the program window, the Search box (see Figure 3.10) lets you enter a word or phrase for which to search, and OneNote will instantly show you where a result is found—on the current page, in the current section, anywhere in the current notebook, or even across multiple notebooks in different locations.

Figure 3.10   *The Search box gives instant access to any part of your notes.*

If you have tagged parts of your notes, you can also search by tag names and make instant lists of the search results. For example, you could search by the note tag that marks action items for you from your meetings at work. By searching on the appropriate note tag, OneNote can compile an instant to-do list for you to make sure that you don't forget important follow-up tasks.

The Search box also lets you find words or phrases within pictures and images that you've inserted into your notes. If you enable audio search, you can even find search results in audio clips that are part of your notebook.

You'll learn more about searching and tagging notes in Chapter 7, "Organizing and Searching Notes."

Page Tabs

Located just under the Search box and near the right side of the OneNote program window are the page tabs (see Figure 3.11). This column of tabs changes whenever you click a different section tab in the current notebook. Unlike a paper-based notebook that has a specific amount of pages in a section, each OneNote section can contain a virtually unlimited number of pages. Similarly, each page will never run out of "paper" because you can keep creating more space.

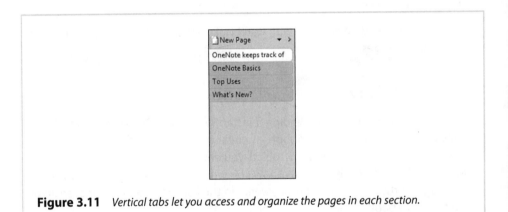

Figure 3.11   *Vertical tabs let you access and organize the pages in each section.*

To help organize groups of pages logically within the same notebook section, OneNote lets you indent page tabs to visually mark them as "subpages" of a parent page. For example, if you're using OneNote to plan a garden, your main pages could be labeled with the names of the flowers, plants, and trees you plan to have, and subpages underneath each main page could be your notes about their proper care from the research you've collected online.

Like section tabs, page tabs can be the target of links you create in your notes, which lets readers quickly jump to a specific page.

You can apply templates to new notebook pages, either to give them the appearance of a ruled notepad, to apply a decorative background that can function like stationery, or to add useful formlike functionality to pages in your notebook (for example, a to-do list, a calendar, or a message log).

You'll learn more about working with notebook pages, subpages, and templates in Chapter 4.

The Editing Pane

Smack in the middle of the OneNote program window is the editing pane (see Figure 3.12). It displays the page that is presently selected in the active section of the notebook that you have open, and it functions as a canvas where you can take notes, collect information, insert files or images, record audio and video, format and tag notes, and much more.

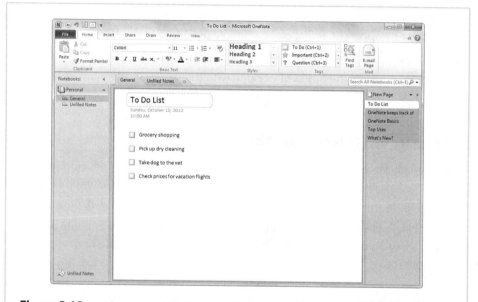

Figure 3.12   *In the center of the program window is the editing pane, where you can edit the pages in your notebooks.*

The top of each page can contain an optional page title and an optional date and time stamp that indicates when the page was first created. The page title is also shown as the title in the corresponding page tab on the right and in the title bar at the top center of the OneNote program window.

You'll learn more about working with notebook pages in Chapter 4 and more about taking and formatting notes in Chapter 5, "Taking and Formatting Notes."

This chapter teaches you how to work with the basic components that make up every electronic notebook in OneNote.

Notebooks, Sections, and Pages

If you've ever worked with a paper-based notebook or notes binder, you already know the purpose of pages and sections within a notebook: The pages hold your information and the sections let you organize it.

If you're new to electronic note-taking, however, there are many benefits that might not be apparent at first glance. Simply put, you can do a lot of things with OneNote notebooks that you can't do with a paper notebook.

This chapter covers the basics of working with the pages and sections in a notebook.

Working with Notebooks

You already learned how to create a notebook in Chapter 1, "Introducing Microsoft OneNote," which you called "Using OneNote 2010." You can keep using this practice notebook as you follow along with the procedures in this book.

If you'd like a refresher about notebook creation and to see how multiple notebooks show up on the navigation bar, follow these steps to create one more practice notebook.

 SHOW ME Media 4.1—Working with Notebooks
Access this video file through your registered Web Edition at
my.safaribooksonline.com/9780132182447/media.

LET ME TRY IT

Creating a New Notebook

To create a new, blank notebook, follow these steps:

1. In OneNote 2010, click the File tab and then click New.

2. Under Step 1 (Store Notebook On), click My Computer.

3. Under Step 2 (Name), type a name for the notebook. For example, you could call this notebook **Practice Notebook**.

4. Under Step 3, leave the suggested file path without making any changes.

5. Click the Create Notebook button near the bottom to finish creating the notebook.

Assuming you previously created the sample notebook in Chapter 1, you should now see three notebooks on the navigation bar. At the top is the sample notebook called "Personal." This is the notebook containing useful tips that OneNote created after you first installed it. Right underneath it is the "Using OneNote 2010" notebook that you created in Chapter 1. And below that is the new notebook called "Practice Notebook," which you created in the previous steps (see Figure 4.1).

You can change the order of notebook icons on the navigation bar. Although this doesn't change anything about the notebooks themselves, it can make it a bit easier to keep the notebook you use most often near the top. For example, to move the Practice Notebook to the top of the navigation bar, click its notebook icon and hold the left mouse button while you drag the icon upward, until it has switched positions with the Personal notebook icon.

Before you move on to working with the sections and pages in the notebook you just created, take a moment to learn a couple of additional notebook tasks— closing and deleting notebooks.

With OneNote 2010, manually closing and reopening notebooks between working sessions isn't necessary. As I mentioned in Chapter 1, there's no Save functionality in OneNote because it automatically and continually saves and remembers everything you do. This means that you can safely shut down OneNote at any time without first closing any notebooks that you have open. All of your information will be saved automatically—even across multiple notebooks that may be stored in different locations. Whenever you next start OneNote, all of the notebooks that appeared on your navigation bar will be automatically reopened.

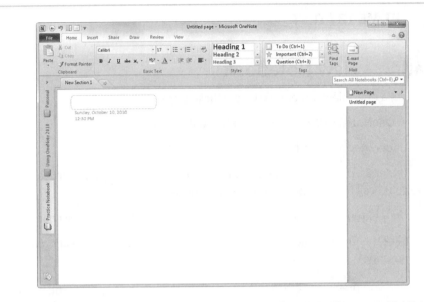

Figure 4.1   *OneNote 2010 lets you use multiple notebooks at once. The orange highlight on the left navigation bar indicates which notebook you're currently working in.*

 LET ME TRY IT

Closing a Notebook

Over time, you might be working with more and more notebooks, and the navigation bar might soon fill up with numerous notebook icons. If you prefer to keep things visually uncluttered, you can choose to temporarily close any notebooks that you're not actively working with (for example, notebooks for projects that you have completed and won't be working on in the future).

To close the Practice Notebook you created earlier in this chapter, follow these steps:

1. On the navigation bar, right-click the notebook that you want to close. In this example, right-click the notebook called "Practice Notebook" (see Figure 4.2).

2. On the menu that appears, click Close This Notebook. The notebook icon for the Practice Notebook disappears from the navigation bar.

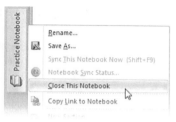

Figure 4.2   *When you right-click a notebook icon on the navigation bar and click the Close this Notebook command, OneNote removes the notebook from view without deleting it.*

When you close a notebook, it is not deleted. Like closing a book and putting it back on the shelf, the notebook still exists. OneNote simply closes the file and removes the notebook icon from the navigation bar to make room for other notebooks you might actively be working in. To put a notebook back on the navigation bar, simply reopen it.

 LET ME TRY IT

Opening a Notebook

To reopen the sample notebook again so that it appears on the navigation bar, follow these steps:

1. On the File tab, click Open.

2. Click the Open Notebook button.

3. In the Open Notebook dialog box, navigate to your OneNote Notebooks folder (which is typically located inside of your My Documents or Documents folder).

4. Double-click the folder called Practice Notebook and then click Open. OneNote immediately loads the sample notebook again and displays the last page you had open at the time when you closed the notebook.

There's a faster way to reopen notebooks that you have recently closed. On the File tab, click Open and then look for the notebook's name in the Recently Closed Notebooks list. Clicking a notebook's name in this list will instantly reopen the notebook and return you to the page you last had open.

 LET ME TRY IT

Deleting a Notebook

I'm including the following steps only for future reference, as people often wonder about the fact that OneNote does not have a built-in command for deleting notebooks.

When you decide you no longer need a specific notebook (including all of its sections, pages, content, and embedded files), you can delete it. Doing so destroys the notebook, so do this only if you've made a confirmed backup copy of the notebook or you're absolutely certain that the notebook and its contents are no longer needed.

To delete a notebook and its contents, follow these steps:

1. Open Windows Explorer and navigate to the OneNote Notebooks folder, which is typically located inside of your My Documents (or Documents) folder.

2. Right-click the folder matching the name of the notebook you want to delete and then click Delete. For example, you could delete the "Practice Notebook" that you created earlier in this chapter since you know it doesn't actually contain any notes. Once deleted, the notebook is sent to your Recycle Bin. To permanently destroy the notebook, right-click the Recycle Bin icon on your Windows desktop and then click Empty Recycle Bin.

Deleting a notebook from your hard drive, from a Web server, or from a remote or shared location like Windows Live SkyDrive permanently destroys the files. You cannot undo this, and no one will be able to recover these files for you, so be sure you only do this with notebooks you're certain you will never need again. To safeguard yourself from mistakes and accidental deletions, you can learn about backing up and restoring OneNote files in Chapter 8, "Security Features in OneNote 2010."

Now that you know the basics about notebooks, let's learn a bit more about what makes up the contents of every notebook.

About Sections and Pages

When you return to the "Using OneNote 2010" notebook that you created in Chapter 1 to follow along with the lessons in this book (if necessary, click its icon on the navigation bar to return to it), you may remember that the notebook was initially created with a single notebook section (called "New Section 1"), which contained a single, blank page (called "Untitled Page"). This is the basic structure of every notebook in OneNote when it is first created. Every notebook contains one or more sections, and every section within that notebook contains one or more pages.

One of the benefits of OneNote over a paper-based notebook is that your electronic notebooks have virtually no limit on the number of sections and pages that you can create and use. As a notebook grows in size over time, you never need to worry about transferring the information somewhere because you've outgrown your notebook. In OneNote, each notebook can grow with the size of the project or task it is associated with so you never run out of room.

Another nice thing about OneNote is the fact that it doesn't force you to be organized. There's no note-taking system to learn or adhere to, and you can literally let things fall as they may. OneNote won't nag you to clean up your notebooks.

Although you don't have to be terribly organized to use OneNote successfully, it makes sense to at least give meaningful names to your sections and pages, especially if you're going to be using a notebook for a specific project or goal. Section names and page titles are searchable, so the more meaningful or descriptive they are in relation to the notes they'll contain, the easier and faster it will be for you to find specific information within all of your notes.

Working with Notebook Sections

Let's begin by learning the basics about notebook sections. Whenever you create a new notebook, it will automatically contain one section tab, and that section tab will contain a single page. To begin using that first section, change its name.

 SHOW ME   Media 4.2—Working with Notebook Sections
Access this video file through your registered Web Edition at
my.safaribooksonline.com/9780132182447/media.

LET ME TRY IT

Naming and Renaming a Section

To name or rename a new notebook section, follow these steps:

1. On the navigation bar, click your "Using OneNote 2010" notebook, right-click the section tab called New Section 1 and then click Rename.

2. When the text in the section tab is highlighted, type a new name for the section. For this example, let's call this section **Trip Planning**.

3. Press Enter. The section is now called Trip Planning.

> If you change your mind, you can change the name of any section at any time. Just repeat the preceding steps and type a different name.

If you already know how you will want to organize a new notebook, you can easily create additional sections at any time.

 LET ME TRY IT

Creating a New Section

To create additional sections in your notebook, follow these steps:

1. Right-click any existing section tab in your notebook.

2. On the menu that appears, click New Section (see Figure 4.3).

3. While the new section's temporary name is highlighted, type a new name for the section and then press Enter. A new section containing a blank, untitled page is added to your notebook.

> An even faster way to create a new section is to click the small section tab with the little sparkle icon, located just to the right of the last section tab at the top of your notebook (see Figure 4.3).

Figure 4.3 *Creating new notebook sections is easily done by right-clicking any existing section tab and then clicking the New Section command.*

 **LET ME TRY IT**

Changing the Color of a Section Tab

OneNote randomly assigns a color to any new section you create. If you prefer, you can easily replace or remove a section color.

To replace a section color, follow these steps:

1. Right-click the tab of the section whose color you want to change.

2. On the menu that appears, click Section Color and then click the color you want to use for the selected tab.

> The color you choose for a section tab is also shown in the column where the page tabs appear. If you don't like a color you've chosen, simply repeat the previous steps and make another choice. If you don't like any of the available colors, select None near the bottom of the menu.

 **LET ME TRY IT**

Deleting a Section

If you no longer need a section, you can delete it. If you delete a section from your notebook, all of the pages and subpages in that section are also deleted.

To delete a section (and all of its pages and subpages), follow these steps:

1. Right-click the tab of the section you want to delete.

2. On the menu that appears, click Delete.

3. When prompted whether you're sure that you want to delete the section, click Yes.

 LET ME TRY IT

Moving a Section Tab to a Different Location

Section tabs in OneNote can be easily rearranged. This is useful when you want to reorganize or prioritize information within your notebook.

To move a section tab, follow these steps:

1. Click the section tab you want to move and hold the left mouse button while dragging the tab to the left or the right.

2. When the tab marker (a small, black, downward-facing arrow) appears in the location you want, release the mouse button (see Figure 4.4).

Figure 4.4   *When you click and drag a section tab to the left or the right, OneNote shows a small, black triangle icon between the section tabs where the moving tab will be placed when you release the mouse button.*

This covers the basics about sections, but there's a lot more you can do with them. You'll look at some of the more advanced features involving sections in upcoming chapters in this book.

Working with Notebook Pages

Let's continue by learning the basics about notebook pages. Whenever you create a new section in your notebook, it will automatically contain one blank page. You can click anywhere on the page and start typing notes. You don't need to worry about any constraints like those in other programs as the OneNote canvas is a completely flexible environment, much like a sheet of paper. With OneNote, nothing is set in stone, and you can freely change and move items on the page after you've created them.

As was the case with sections, it makes sense to first give the pages in your notebooks meaningful titles.

 SHOW ME   Media 4.3—Working with Notebook Pages and Subpages
Access this video file through your registered Web Edition at
my.safaribooksonline.com/9780132182447/media.

 LET ME TRY IT

Adding a Page Title

Whenever a new section is created, OneNote creates a blank, untitled page in that section. To begin using this page, first type a page title into the designated area at the top of the page.

Page titles are useful for labeling your pages with meaningful descriptions that will make your notes more easily identifiable when searching your notebooks and seeing your pages in a results list.

To add a page title, follow these steps:

1. If necessary, click the page tab of the page to which you want to add a page title.

2. At the top of the page, click inside of the dotted outline and then type a page title (see Figure 4.5).

Figure 4.5   *The area surrounded by a dotted line near the top of your pages is the page title. What you type here will also label the page in the page tabs column.*

The page title you enter is also shown in the corresponding page tab on the right and in the title bar at the top center of the OneNote program window.

 LET ME TRY IT

Changing a Page Title

If the content of a page changes over time and its page title is no longer accurate or descriptive enough, you can easily change it at any time.

To change a page title, follow these steps:

1. If necessary, navigate to the page you want to rename by clicking its page tab.

2. At the top of the page, click inside of the dotted outline, select the text that's there, and then overtype it with a new page title.

When a page title is changed in the page header area, it is also changed in the corresponding page tab on the right and in the title bar at the top center of the OneNote program window.

 LET ME TRY IT

Deleting a Page Title

If you don't care about page titles for some reason, you can easily turn them off. However, doing so removes both the title and the date and time stamp that indicates when the page was created. This information is typically very useful when searching your notes, so delete page titles only if you're sure you really won't ever need this information again.

To delete a page title, follow these steps:

1. If necessary, navigate to the page whose page title you want to remove.

2. On the ribbon, click the View tab and then click Hide Page Title.

Although the Hide Page Title button on the View tab works like an on/off switch that lets you hide or show the page title area at will, clicking the selected (orange-colored) button again to stop hiding a page title will restore only the dotted area where you can type a new page title. The original page title is permanently deleted when you hide it for the first time, and it cannot be recovered.

The one reprieve from accidentally clicking the Hide Page Title button is pressing the Ctrl+Z (Undo) keyboard shortcut immediately after you delete the page title.

When you've hidden (deleted) a page title, OneNote will use the first part of notes text on the page as the label for the page tab on the far right of the OneNote window. If you later unhide the page title area and type a new page title, that new title will serve as the new page tab label.

 LET ME TRY IT

Creating a New Page

There's virtually no limit to the number of pages a notebook section can hold.

To create additional pages in the current section of your notebook, follow these steps:

1. At the top of the page tabs on the right side of the OneNote program window, click New Page (see Figure 4.6). OneNote creates a new, blank, untitled page at the bottom of the other page tabs in the current section.

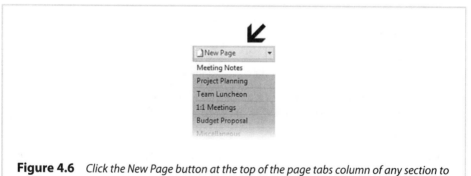

Figure 4.6   *Click the New Page button at the top of the page tabs column of any section to add a page to the current section.*

2. Add a page title by following the steps in the previous procedure.

If a notebook section already has a large number of pages and you don't want new pages that you create to appear at the very end of all of the other page tabs, you can use another method. Move the mouse pointer over the existing page tabs where you want the new page to appear and then click the floating New Page icon that appears just to the left of the page tabs. OneNote will insert a new page in between the two page tabs marked with a thick, black line.

 LET ME TRY IT

Changing the Appearance of a Page

To simulate sheets of paper, OneNote pages are typically white when you create them. However, you can freely customize the appearance of a notes page to simulate taking notes on a ruled notepad, on graph paper, or on sheets of colored paper. If you change your mind again later, you can easily replace or remove such visual page customizations.

To change the appearance of a page, follow these steps:

1. Go to the page whose appearance you want to customize.

2. On the ribbon, click the View tab.

3. In the Page Setup group, click Page Color, and then click the page color you want to use for the current page.

To change the selected color of the current page, repeat the previous steps and then make another selection. To remove the selected color, click No Color on the pop-up menu that appears when you click the Page Color button.

If you don't care to change the page color but would like the appearance of a ruled notepad or graph paper instead, follow these steps:

1. Go to the page whose appearance you want to customize.

2. On the ribbon, click the View tab.

3. In the Page Setup group, click the Rule Lines drop-down arrow, and then click the style of rule or grid lines you want to use for the current page.

To change the selected style of rule or grid lines for the current page, repeat the previous steps and then make another selection. To remove the selected style, click None on the pop-up menu that appears when you click the Rule Lines drop-down arrow. To have OneNote automatically create all future new pages with the same style of rule or grid lines applied, click Create new pages with rule lines at the bottom of the pop-up menu that appears when you click the Rule Lines drop-down arrow.

 LET ME TRY IT

Changing the Size of a Page

Aside from changing the appearance of your notebook pages, you can also specify the physical dimensions of the page.

To change the size of a page, follow these steps:

1. Go to the page whose dimensions you want to customize.

2. On the ribbon, click the View tab.

3. In the Page Setup group, click Paper Size.

4. In the Paper Size task pane that opens, change the Size setting to the paper size you want. After you've made a selection, you can then further customize the size and margins of the page.

Because OneNote is primarily designed to replace all of your paper-based notes, you can typically just accept the default settings that your notebook starts with. Still, it's nice to have these customization options available for when you might need them.

 **LET ME TRY IT**

Changing the Date or Time Stamp on a Page

You'll notice that OneNote stamps every new page with the date and time when the page was created. This is especially useful when searching your notes. For example, if you're looking for specific information a year from now, you'll have a record of when the information was added to your notes.

To modify the creation date and time stamp on a page, follow these steps:

1. To change the creation date of a page, click the date stamp under the page title, click the small calendar icon that appears next to it (see Figure 4.7), and then select the date you want.

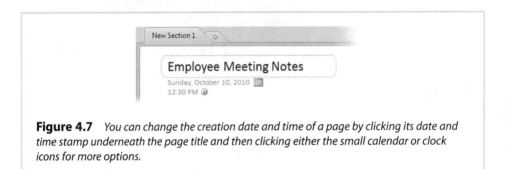

Figure 4.7   *You can change the creation date and time of a page by clicking its date and time stamp underneath the page title and then clicking either the small calendar or clock icons for more options.*

2. To change the creation time of a page, click the time stamp under the page creation date, click the small clock icon that appears next to it (see Figure 4.7), and then select the time you want.

If you prefer, you can remove the creation date or time of a particular page entirely. This can be useful when you're distributing a set of notes whose creation date and time is not important. To delete the date stamp of a page, click to select it, and then press the Del key on your keyboard. Likewise, to delete the time stamp of a page, click to select it, and then press the Del key. Again, you should only do this if you're really sure that you won't need this information. Deleting the date and time stamps from your notes pages prevents you from using this information in your notebook searches, which is the fastest and most effective way for OneNote to help you find information again.

There's another kind of date and time stamp available in OneNote, and that's the kind that lets you insert the current date and/or time as text in your notes. This is useful if you use OneNote for chronological call logs, time sheets, or to update to-do lists. To insert this kind of time stamp, click the Insert tab on the ribbon. In the Time Stamp group, click any of the three available buttons—Date, Time, or Date & Time—to insert that information into your notes.

 **LET ME TRY IT**

Moving a Page Tab to a Different Location

Like section tabs, page tabs in OneNote can be easily rearranged. This is useful when you want to reorganize or prioritize information within your notebook.

To move a page tab, follow these steps:

1. Click the page tab you want to move and hold the left mouse button while dragging the tab up or down.

2. When the tab marker (a thick, black line) appears in the location you want, release the mouse button (see Figure 4.8).

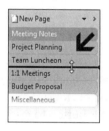

Figure 4.8   *When you click and drag a page tab up or down, OneNote shows a thick black line between the page tabs where the moving tab will be placed when you release the mouse button.*

 LET ME TRY IT

Quickly Minimizing or Maximizing Page Tabs

In Chapter 3, "A Tour of the OneNote Workspace," I mentioned how you can minimize both the ribbon and the navigation bar so you have more room on your screen for taking and reading notes. The same can be done with the page tabs on the far-right side of the OneNote program window.

When you minimize the page tabs, the titles on the tabs appear truncated, but the page titles are not actually shortened. You can freely minimize the page tabs and restore them again to their full size whenever you want.

To minimize and maximize page tabs, follow these steps:

1. At the top of the page tabs, locate the two small arrows to the right of the New Page button. The first is pointing downward, and the one next to it is pointing to the right.

2. Move the mouse pointer over the second arrow that's pointing toward the right. A ToolTip appears that reads Collapse Page Tabs. Click this button to shrink the page tabs (see Figure 4.9).

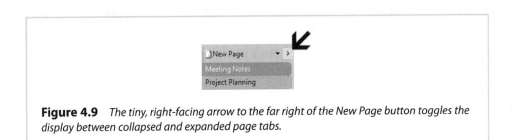

Figure 4.9   *The tiny, right-facing arrow to the far right of the New Page button toggles the display between collapsed and expanded page tabs.*

3. To restore the tabs to their original size, move the mouse pointer over the same arrow (which now points toward the left). A ToolTip appears that reads Expand Page Tabs. Click this button to restore the page tabs to their original size.

 LET ME TRY IT

Manually Changing the Size of Page Tabs

If the quick page tabs display toggle in the previous steps isn't to your liking, you can manually adjust the width of your page tabs. This is beneficial whenever many or all of your page titles begin with an identical word, phrase, or prefix and the pages can be told apart only by the end of their titles. For example, if your pages are each titled "Daily Call Log," followed by a series of dates, you may want to expand the width of the page tabs so you can see the full page titles at all times ("Daily Call Log 10/10/2010," "Daily Call Log 10/11/2010," and so on).

To manually change the size of page tabs, follow these steps:

1. Make sure that the page tabs are currently expanded. See the previous steps for instructions.

2. Slowly move the mouse pointer over the vertical line that separates the left side of the page tabs and the right side of the page canvas to the left of the page tabs.

3. When the mouse pointer changes to a horizontal line with a left and right arrow on its sides, click and hold the left mouse button, and slowly drag the line to the left.

4. When the page tabs are wide enough for you to read the page titles, release the mouse button.

After manually resizing page tabs, you can still use the quick method to minimize and maximize page tabs when needed. Click the Collapse Page Tabs arrow on the far right of the New Page button to minimize the page tabs. When you click the same arrow to expand the page tabs again, OneNote will remember the custom page tab size that you selected in the previous steps.

 LET ME TRY IT

Deleting a Page

If you no longer need a particular page in your notebook, you can delete it. When you delete a page, all the objects and inserted items on that page are also deleted.

To delete a page, follow these steps:

1. Right-click the tab of the page you want to delete.

2. On the menu that appears, click Delete.

Working with Subpages

Subpages in OneNote work exactly like regular pages, but their tab labels appear slightly indented. The main purpose of subpages is to let you visually structure a group of related pages to help you recognize which of them contain important notes or key subject areas and which of them contain supplementary information that supports the subject of the main pages. In terms of hierarchy, think of a normal page as a parent, whereas each subpage is a child of that parent.

You can create a new subpage under any normal page, or you can demote an existing page to a subpage and then drag it where you want it. Within a group of pages and subpages, you can have two levels of indentation for subpage tab labels, which can help you organize information more easily. Depending on their level, subpages may also appear lighter in color than normal pages.

 LET ME TRY IT

Creating a New Subpage

To create a new subpage in the current section, follow these steps:

1. On the right side of the OneNote program window, click the page under which you want to insert a new subpage.

2. At the top of the page tabs on the right side of the OneNote program window, click the small, downward-facing arrow right next to the New Page button.

3. On the menu that appears, click New Subpage (see Figure 4.10). OneNote creates a new page with a slightly indented tab label and a lighter tab color immediately below the page you were on.

New Page	▼ >
Meeting Notes	New Page (Ctrl+N)
Project Planning	New Subpage
Team Luncheon	Default
1:1 Meetings	Simple To Do List
Budget Proposal	Simple Meeting Notes 1
	Page Templates...

Figure 4.10 *Click the drop-down arrow to the right of the New Page button to display this menu, from which you can click the New Subpage command.*

4. Type a page title in the header of the subpage to distinguish it from the other pages.

If you want to create additional subpages that relate to the main page you had originally selected, repeat steps 2–4 for each additional subpage that you want to create.

 **LET ME TRY IT**

Demoting a Page to a Subpage

You can demote a page to a subpage with new, blank pages or with existing pages that already contain notes.

To demote an existing normal page to a subpage, follow these steps:

1. Click the page tab that you want to change to a subpage.

2. When selected, right-click the page tab.

3. On the menu that appears, click Make Subpage. OneNote slightly indents the tab label and lightens the tab's color to indicate that the selected page is now a subpage of the next normal page preceding it.

OneNote supports two levels of subpage indentation to help you organize groups of pages by their type of content. To demote an existing subpage to the lowest level and further indent its tab label, double-click to select the subpage, and then repeat steps 2–3 in the previous steps. Note that for the second level of subpage indentation, the tab color is even lighter than that of the first-level subpage and that of normal pages.

You can demote existing pages to subpages more quickly by using your mouse. Move the mouse pointer over the page tab you want to demote, and then click the left mouse button. Slowly move the page tab to the right, until you see a horizontal, two-sided arrow as the mouse pointer. Drag the tab label to the right, taking care to choose between the first (smaller) indentation level or the second (larger) one. When the tab label of the page is indented at the level you want, release the mouse button.

If the notes on a subpage gain in importance again later on, you can promote it in level. For example, you can promote a second-level subpage to a first-level subpage, or you can promote a first-level subpage to a normal page.

 LET ME TRY IT

Promoting a Subpage to a Page

You can promote a subpage to a page with new, blank subpages or with existing subpages that already contain notes.

To change an existing subpage back to a normal page, follow these steps:

1. Double-click the subpage tab that you want to change to a page.

2. When selected, right-click the page tab.

3. On the menu that appears, click Promote Subpage. OneNote removes the indent from the tab label and darkens the tab's color to indicate that the selected subpage is now a normal page.

To promote an existing subpage from the lowest level to the higher subpage level, double-click to select the subpage, and then repeat steps 2–3 in the previous steps. Note that going from the second level of subpage indentation to the first, the tab color is darkened slightly but still lighter than normal pages.

Here, too, you can use your mouse to promote existing pages to subpages more quickly. Move the mouse pointer over the subpage tab you want to promote, and then click the left mouse button. Slowly move the page tab to the left, until you see a horizontal, two-sided arrow as the mouse pointer. Drag the tab label to the left, taking care to choose between the first (smaller) indentation level (if the selected page is a level 2 subpage) or the nonindented normal page level. When the tab label is at the level you want, release the mouse button.

When you work with multiple groups of pages and subpages, it can become difficult to retain oversight of your main pages and how they should be organized. To help you keep your thoughts and ideas organized, OneNote lets you collapse subpage tabs so that they're hidden from view. This lets you more easily scan the titles of your main pages. Another benefit of collapsing subpages is that you can then drag the tab of the parent page to another location and its collapsed subpages are moved together with the group.

Collapsed subpages are still fully searchable—the same as normal pages.

 **LET ME TRY IT**

Collapsing a Group of Subpages

The following steps show you how to hide the subpage tabs below a parent page to reduce visual clutter or to keep the subpages together with their parent page while moving that page to a new location in the page tabs column.

To collapse a group of subpages, follow these steps:

1. Make sure that the page tabs are currently expanded. (See "Quickly Minimizing or Maximizing Page Tabs" earlier in this chapter for instructions.)

2. On the right side of the OneNote program window, move the mouse pointer over the page tab of any parent page containing one or more subpages.

3. Near the right side of the parent page tab, click the small, upward-facing arrow to collapse the subpages below. OneNote reminds you of the collapsed pages by showing a slightly cascaded border effect underneath the parent page tab and changing the direction of the small arrow to face downward (see Figure 4.11).

Figure 4.11   *A page tab that shows a cascaded border effect and a small downward-facing arrow at the far right of the page tab indicates that this parent page contains one or more subpages. Click the small arrow to expand these pages.*

While a parent page has its subpages collapsed, you can reorganize it by moving its tab up and down the page tabs column. The collapsed subpages will travel with it.

While dragging page groups up or down in the page tab column, take care not to move the mouse to the left, or you may inadvertently demote the parent page to a subpage of its own. If that happens, the collapsed subpages will be expanded and shown. You can use the Undo command on the Quick Access Toolbar (or press Ctrl+Z) to correct the mistake, collapse the subpages again, and then try moving the parent page again.

This covers the basics about pages and subpages, but there's a lot more you can do with them. You'll look at some of the more advanced features involving pages in upcoming chapters in this book.

Using Page Templates

In OneNote 2010, you can use page templates to dramatically change the appearance of pages. Templates can add decorative designs and photorealistic backgrounds to your notes pages or let you create useful and functional documents like simple forms, calendars, and interactive checklists.

Templates offer a convenient way to give all of the pages in your notebook a consistent look. You can choose to apply templates to only specific pages that you create, or you can have OneNote create all new pages with a particular template already applied. In addition, you can customize any existing template design or create your own from scratch.

 SHOW ME   Media 4.4—Working with Page Templates
Access this video file through your registered Web Edition at
my.safaribooksonline.com/9780132182447/media.

 LET ME TRY IT

Applying a Template to a New Page

The first thing to know about templates in OneNote is that you can apply templates only to new pages. This isn't some terrible oversight by the developers but a legitimate trade-off for the freedom that the unique OneNote canvas provides. Unlike other programs that constrain their pages with lines, grids, or cells of some kind, OneNote's canvas is as free-form as a sheet of paper. As a result, applying a template that potentially contains several objects in specific locations on the page is very likely to cause collisions with objects that are already present on that page. Computers can do many things, but their artificial intelligence isn't yet so advanced that they can effectively guess how you would prefer to untangle such a mess if it were to happen. But don't worry—I'll show you a simple workaround later that lets you bring your existing notes and your favorite page template together after all.

To browse through OneNote's built-in templates and apply a template to a new page, follow these steps:

1. Open the section in which you want to apply the template.

2. Located over the page tabs in the right margin, click the small drop-down arrow next to the New Page button, and then click Page Templates (see Figure 4.12).

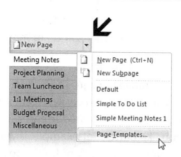

Figure 4.12 *The small, downward-facing arrow next to the New Page button over the page tabs provides the entry point to the Templates interface.*

3. In the Templates task pane that opens, click a category to view the templates it contains (see Figure 4.13).

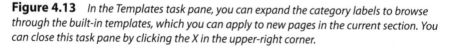

Figure 4.13 *In the Templates task pane, you can expand the category labels to browse through the built-in templates, which you can apply to new pages in the current section. You can close this task pane by clicking the X in the upper-right corner.*

4. To browse through the list of available templates, click any of their names in the expanded category list. As long as the current page is still free of notes, OneNote will reuse the same page to apply the template you select so you can see what it looks like.

5. When you've found a template that you like and it has been applied to the page, click the X in the upper-right corner of the Templates task pane to close it.

6. If the page wasn't created where you wanted it, click and drag its page tab to move it to the position that you want. In Chapter 7, "Organizing and Searching Notes," I'll cover notebook organization in more detail.

After a template is applied to a page, you can start to add notes to it. Templates that don't just provide a decorative background but also include some page content don't have to be used "as is;" you can easily delete any parts of the template placed on the page. You can also modify the formatting of any of the template content to something that you like better. For example, if you like the template that you've applied, but you prefer a different font for the text it uses, feel free to simply change it.

 LET ME TRY IT

Applying a Template to an Existing Page

As I mentioned in the previous section, it's technically not possible to apply a template to an existing page that already contains notes. However, in most situations, you can use the following simple workaround to achieve the same result.

To apply a template to an existing page, follow these steps:

1. Click the small drop-down arrow next to the New Page button over the page tabs and then click Page Templates.

2. In the Templates task pane, find the template you want and then apply it to a new page.

3. On the page, delete any template page content that you don't want to keep.

4. In your notebook, navigate to the page of notes that you want to use with the template you applied to the new page.

5. Click anywhere on the page and then press Ctrl+A three times in a row. Ctrl+A is the keyboard shortcut for the Select All command, which works incrementally in OneNote. Depending on the contents of your page and the location of your cursor, you might need to press Ctrl+A up to three times in a row to select everything on the page.

6. On the Home tab, in the Clipboard group, click Copy.

7. Navigate back to the new page to which you applied the template.

8. Click anywhere on the page and then press Ctrl+V. This is the keyboard shortcut for the Paste command.

The success of this workaround depends on the complexity of your existing notes page. You might need to clean up the new page a little after pasting your notes onto it to make sure that all of your note containers and objects are where you want them. You might also want to copy and paste the page title and date and time stamp of the original page.

If copying and pasting all of the page contents at once proves to be a bit too error-prone for your particular page, try selecting and copying individual note containers and then pasting them one by one instead.

Again, this is merely a suggested workaround to the technical limitation, so it's probably best to keep your expectations reasonably low. Remember that the Undo command (Ctrl+Z) on the Quick Access Toolbar can quickly put things back to the way they were.

 LET ME TRY IT

Automatically Applying a Template to All New Pages

If you're working on a notebook that will have lots of pages whose content is related, you might want to consider formatting those pages with a consistent template applied. Even just a subtle visual page background can give the pages you create within a section a common feel to them, reminding you where you are in your notebook. Later, when you learn to share notebooks with others, this can also be useful to signal people you work with that they're in the right place.

Going through the steps to apply a template can get tedious if you're working with a lot of pages. Thankfully, OneNote lets you specify a particular template to be used for all new pages that are created in the current section.

To automatically apply a template to all new pages, follow these steps:

1. If you closed the Templates task pane, you can open it again by clicking the small drop-down arrow next to the New Page button over the page tabs, and then clicking Page Templates.

2. In the Templates task pane, look for the heading Choose default template, which is located near the bottom of the task pane.

3. In the drop-down list, find and select the name of the template you want to be applied to all new pages in the current section.

4. Click the X in the upper-right corner of the Templates task pane to close it.

The default template that you choose in the Templates task pane is only applied to pages in the current section. If you switch to a different notebook section and create a new page there, it will use the default blank page unless you also take the time to specify a new default template for that particular notebook section.

 LET ME TRY IT

Customizing an Existing Page Template

If you don't want to take the time to design a brand-new page template from scratch, you can start with a template that you already have, modify its contents and appearance, and then save it as a new template that you can then apply to new pages.

To customize an existing page template, follow these steps:

1. Click the small drop-down arrow next to the New Page button over the page tabs and then click Page Templates.

2. In the Templates task pane, find the template you want and then apply it to a new page.

3. Change any of the page content that you want to modify. For example, you could change the character and color formatting of text, remove any objects you don't want to keep, insert objects you want to add, or move things around on the page where you want them.

4. When the templates page is to your liking, go back to the Templates task pane and look for the heading Create new template, which is located near the bottom of the task pane.

5. Click Save current page as a template.

6. In the Save As Template dialog box, give the template a new, unique name. If you want to automatically apply this template to new pages in this section, click the check box underneath the Template Name field, and then click Save.

7. OneNote creates a new category called My Templates, which appears at the top of the list of categories in the Templates task pane. This shortcut makes it easy to find and apply your custom templates again.

 **LET ME TRY IT**

Creating Your Own Page Template

This method is very similar to customizing an existing template, except that you start with a blank page and then add your own elements. You may want to wait to follow along with this example until you know OneNote a little better. Later in this book, I'll cover how to format pages and insert content on them. When you have these skills, you'll be better prepared to create more useful and compelling templates.

To create your own page template, follow these steps:

1. Click the small drop-down arrow next to the New Page button over the page tabs and then click Page Templates.

2. In the Templates task pane, expand the Blank category and then click Default. This creates a new, blank page in the current section that you can use as the basis of the new template you're creating.

3. On the blank page that OneNote created, create and arrange content that you want the template to contain. Take care to not include too much placeholder text or obtrusive sample content as you'll just have to remove or replace it again when the template is applied to new pages in the future. Simple templates are often best.

4. When the page is to your liking, go back to the Templates task pane and look for the heading Create new template, which is located near the bottom of the task pane.

5. Click Save current page as a template.

6. In the Save As Template dialog box, give the template a unique name. If you want to also automatically apply this template to new pages in this section, click the check box underneath the Template Name field and then click Save. OneNote creates a new category called My Templates, which appears at the top of the list of categories in the Templates task pane. This shortcut makes it easy to find and apply your custom templates again.

If you want to share your custom template with someone else, first apply the template to a new page. Switch to that new page, click the File tab on the ribbon, and then click Save As. Under Step 1, select Page. Under Step 2, select OneNote 2010 Section. Click Save As, type a filename, and then click Save. You can send the saved file in e-mail or copy it to a file share or USB thumb drive. Recipients can double-click this file on their computer to open it in OneNote, where they can add it to their own list of templates.

 LET ME TRY IT

Downloading Additional Page Templates

You're not limited to the built-in templates that OneNote 2010 provides. You can download hundreds of free templates from the Microsoft Office website.

To download additional page templates, follow these steps:

1. Click the small drop-down arrow next to the New Page button over the page tabs and then click Page Templates.

2. In the Templates task pane, immediately underneath the list of template categories, click the Templates on Office.com link.

3. On the web page that opens in your browser, look in the left column called All Templates and then scroll down and click the My Programs link.

4. In the Microsoft Office 2010 column, click OneNote 2010 and then click Save.

5. In the Search box at the top of the web page, enter a keyword (for example, **Calendar**) and then press Enter. The search results are now filtered for OneNote 2010, and you can download any of the templates you find.

Websites are frequently changed. If the previous steps don't exactly match what you're seeing on the live website, go to Office.com and then use the site navigation to go to the Templates site and then filter your results for OneNote 2010. In the search results, you may see many templates marked as "OneNote 2007" and "OneNote 2003." These are all safe to use with OneNote 2010, as this version specification indicates the lowest version of OneNote that the template can be used with. Because OneNote 2010 is the newest version of the program, you're not limited to which templates you can download from the site.

This chapter covers the many ways in which you can create and format notes on your notebook pages.

5

Taking and Formatting Notes

In this chapter, let's look at some of the ways in which you can type notes, bring information into OneNote, and format it in ways that make the content more useful to you and others. Later in this book, you'll learn ways to organize, share, and protect that information.

As in the previous chapters, I encourage you to follow along and try out these steps so you can see for yourself how easy using OneNote really is.

Taking Notes

In the world of OneNote, the phrase "taking notes" means a bit more than it says. Sure, you can use OneNote to take notes in meetings or in class, but after seeing more of its features and learning how to use them, it's unlikely that taking notes is all you'll want to do with this useful program.

Typing and formatting text in OneNote works much the same as you're probably already used to from other Office programs like Microsoft Word. However, unlike other programs that restrict your editing area by well-meaning lines, rows, columns, cells, or fields, the OneNote canvas is truly free-form and you can place content on a page wherever you want it.

 **LET ME TRY IT**

Typing Notes on a Page

To start taking notes on a page, follow these steps:

1. In the Practice Notebook you created in Chapter 4, "Notebooks, Sections, and Pages," create a new, blank page.

2. Type a title into the dotted page title area at the top of the page.

3. Click anywhere in the blank part of the page underneath the page title.

4. When you see a flashing cursor, begin typing your notes (see Figure 5.1).

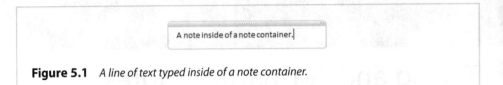

A note inside of a note container.

Figure 5.1   *A line of text typed inside of a note container.*

As you type in OneNote, a small gray frame appears around the text you type. These frames are called note containers. They are only visible while you type or format the text within them, or while you move the mouse over them. Think of note containers as little helpers that make it easier for you to line up text and objects on your page. They don't show up when you print a page or share a page with someone over e-mail.

You can resize a note container by clicking the tiny double arrows shown on the right side of the frame's top border and then dragging the mouse to the left or to the right to make the container smaller or larger. This lets you quickly adjust the wrapping of text, the way a text box would in a page layout program. For example, to make a long, continuous paragraph of text easier to read and format, you could make its note container narrower to mimic a column in a newspaper or magazine.

If a note container doesn't appear quite where you want it, you can freely move it around on the page by clicking its top border (marked with a short row of small rivets) and then dragging the container to the position on the page you want.

 SHOW ME   **Media 5.1—Taking Notes in OneNote**
Access this video file through your registered Web Edition at
my.safaribooksonline.com/9780132182447/media.

Note containers can be copied and pasted, deleted, or dragged and merged into other note containers on the page. This kind of flexibility makes OneNote ideal for brainstorming, ruminating over ideas that are still changing and taking shape, and planning projects that will change often over time (such as the outline for this book, for example, which I created entirely in OneNote).

You can type all of your notes into a single note container or click around the page and create several different note containers and then line them up the way you want. It's up to you.

If, for some reason, you don't want note containers to be displayed around your text, you can easily turn them off. Click the File tab, and then click Options. In the OneNote Options dialog box that opens, click the Display category, and then deselect the Show note containers on pages check box. Although you can't move entire boxes of text around on the page anymore when note containers are hidden, you can still move individual text paragraphs. To do this, mouse over any line of text and then click the four-headed arrow icon that appears to the left of that paragraph. Once selected, drag the icon to a different location on the page. You can also select multiple paragraphs and then move them all at once by dragging the selection to the location you want. If you make a mistake, click the Undo button on the Quick Access Toolbar (or press Ctrl+Z on your keyboard) to go back to the way it was and then try again.

 LET ME TRY IT

Copying and Pasting Text

Aside from typing, one of the easiest ways to bring information into OneNote is by copying text from any file, document, or web page and pasting it on your notes pages. You probably already know how to do this, but OneNote 2010 has a few new paste options that give you greater control over the ways that copied information can appear in your notebook.

To copy and paste text, follow these steps:

1. In OneNote, on any notes page, select a line of text.

2. On the Home tab, in the Clipboard group, click Copy (or press Ctrl+C on your keyboard) to copy your text selection. This keyboard shortcut is a standard Windows shortcut, so if you want to copy text from another document or program, select the text there and then press Ctrl+C before switching to OneNote.

3. In OneNote, click in a blank part of the notes page where you want to paste the copied selection of text.

4. On the Home tab, in the Clipboard group, click the small downward-facing arrow under the large Paste button to reveal additional choices.

At this point, OneNote presents you with a small menu of four icons that you can click (see Figure 5.2).

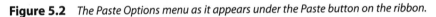

Figure 5.2 *The Paste Options menu as it appears under the Paste button on the ribbon.*

Moving the mouse over each icon displays a ToolTip that tells you what will happen to pasted text when you click that particular button:

- **Keep Source Formatting** will paste your copied text with its original format-ting intact. For example, if you copy red, bold text and paste it elsewhere on your page, the copied text will still appear red and bold. This option is the default paste option if you click the Paste button on the ribbon or whenever you press Ctrl+V to paste copied text.

- **Merge Formatting** will paste your copied text and match the style format-ting of the text paragraph you're pasting it into. For example, if you copy red, bold Calibri 11 text and you paste it into an existing paragraph of black, italic Arial 10 text, your pasted text will still appear red and bold, but the font will be changed to Arial 10 and it will turn italic.

- **Keep Text Only** will paste the copied text as standard text, stripped of any formatting. This is the easiest way to bring clean text from multiple sources into OneNote.

- **Picture** will create a small, digitized image of the copied source text. You might find this option useful when you want to preserve the exact appear-ance of the source text (for example, if it was rendered on a web page in a particular font that you don't have installed on your computer). Although this option creates a picture of the copied text that you cannot edit after pasting, OneNote can include such pictures in search results when you search your notebooks for keywords that are shown in pasted images.

For a faster way to paste copied text in the way that you want, right-click the page where you want the copied text to appear, and then, on the shortcut menu (see Figure 5.3), click the Paste Options button you want.

If you prefer to paste text without first choosing a paste option, that's okay. You won't miss out on the new paste options in OneNote 2010. That's because OneNote lets you adjust the formatting of text even after it has been pasted on the page.

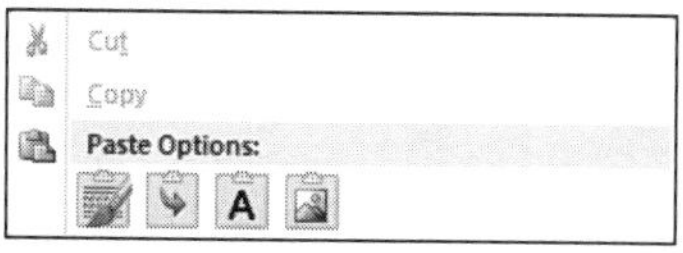

Figure 5.3 *Paste Options on the right-click shortcut menu.*

Near the bottom of pasted text, OneNote displays a small button with a clipboard icon. You can click this button—or press the Ctrl key as a simple shortcut—to open the Paste Options menu (see Figure 5.4). When you click the option you want, the formatting of the pasted selection is updated to your preference.

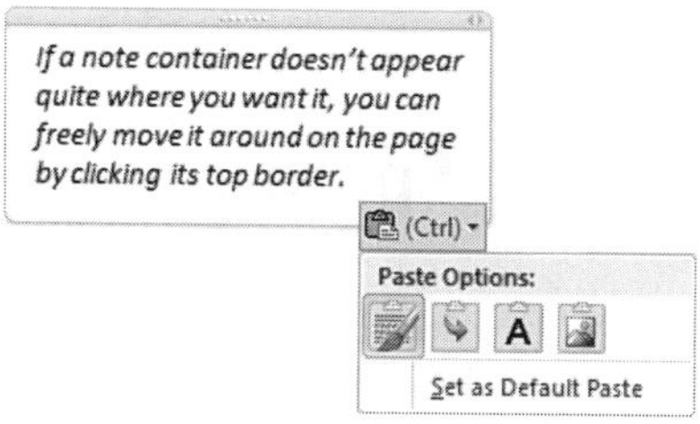

Figure 5.4 *The Paste Options button appears after you've pasted copied text.*

If you don't like the result, you can click the button again to reopen the menu and make a different choice.

 **LET ME TRY IT**

Changing the Default Paste Option

If you prefer a different default formatting option for text you'll paste into OneNote (for example, if you always want to paste plain, unformatted text), you don't have to override the default setting with the Paste Options menu each time. Instead, follow these steps to set a different default option:

1. On any notes page, copy and then paste a line of text.

2. At the bottom of the pasted text, click the Paste Options button that appears (or press Ctrl).

3. Click the icon of the paste option you want (for example, click the A icon for Keep Text Only if you prefer to always paste copied text without formatting).

4. Now click the Paste Options button again (or press Ctrl again) and then click Set as Default Paste.

Once you have set a new paste option, it is automatically applied whenever you paste text using the Paste button on the ribbon or whenever you press Ctrl+V on your keyboard. If you change your mind again later, you can set a different default paste option by repeating the previous steps and choosing a new paste option in step 3.

 **LET ME TRY IT**

Creating More Writing Space in the Middle of a Page

Ever take notes in a paper notebook during a class or a meeting, only to find the presenter jumping back to a previous topic, erasing part of the whiteboard, and writing down more important things? Now you have to scribble little subnotes on your paper pages to later remind you of the order in which the information was talked about.

With OneNote, you can not only move existing notes around, you can also create more writing space wherever you need it—even in the middle of a page that's already full of notes.

To create more writing space, follow these steps:

1. Open a notebook page that contains a bunch of notes, such as a long paragraph of text. (If you don't yet have a page with a lot of notes on it but you want to try this example, you can copy and paste some text from a web page.)

2. On the ribbon, click the Insert tab, and then click Insert Space. The button will turn orange to let you know that you're in the Insert Space mode.

3. Slowly move the mouse pointer back over your page containing the notes. You will see a thick horizontal line moving up and down with your mouse pointer (see Figure 5.5). Position the line where you want to create space and then click and drag the mouse downward in the direction of the arrow.

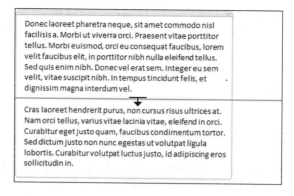

Figure 5.5   *Align the bar and arrow where you want to begin creating writing space.*

4. As you drag the arrow, OneNote shows you where displaced text and objects will move below the space you're creating (see Figure 5.6). Release the mouse when you have created as much space as you want or need.

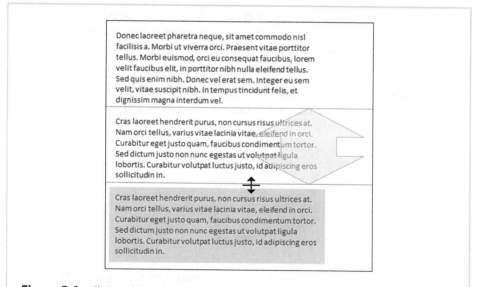

Figure 5.6   *Click and drag downward to create writing space between paragraphs.*

 SHOW ME   Media 5.2—**Creating More Space on a Page**
Access this video file through your registered Web Edition at
my.safaribooksonline.com/9780132182447/media.

If you have any trouble the first time and you create too much or too little space, remember to use the Undo command on the Quick Access Toolbar (or press Ctrl+Z) and then start over.

 LET ME TRY IT

Creating More Writing Space at the End of a Page

If you're taking or pasting a large amount of notes on a page and you don't want to keep writing near the bottom edge of the OneNote program window, you can quickly create about half a page of space at the end of your notes.

To create more writing space at the end of the page, follow these steps:

1. Open a notebook page that contains a bunch of notes, such as a long paragraph of text. (If you don't yet have a page with a lot of notes on it but you want to try this example, you can copy and paste some text from a web page.)

2. Look for the vertical scrollbar that appears near the right side of the OneNote program window and just to the left of the page tabs. If there is not enough text to fill the page, type or paste some more text to extend its note container past the current page display.

3. Under the vertical scrollbar, look for a small page icon just below the scrollbar arrow. This is the Scroll Down by Half Page button (see Figure 5.7).

Figure 5.7   *The Scroll Down by Half Page button appears under the vertical scrollbar.*

4. When you click this button, OneNote scrolls to the very end of the current page and then creates about half a page of blank space so you can continue typing in the middle of the screen.

You can click this button as often as you like to keep creating more space at the end of the current page. Using this button is a bit faster than repeatedly pressing the Enter key to create several blank lines of writing space at the end of a notes page.

 **LET ME TRY IT**

Checking the Spelling of Your Notes

Like the other programs in the Microsoft Office suite, OneNote lets you verify the spelling of words in your notes. This is most useful when you plan to share your notes with other people and grammatical accuracy is important.

To check the spelling of your notes, follow these steps:

1. Open the page for which you want to check the spelling.

2. If you want to only check the spelling of a particular paragraph of text, select the text you want to check. Otherwise, if you do not make a text selection, OneNote will check the entire page.

3. On the ribbon, click the Review tab, and then click Spelling.

4. If OneNote detects any words that are possibly misspelled, they will be displayed in the Spelling task pane near the right side of the screen. There, you can change a misspelled word to its correct form, ignore a suggested correction, or add any particular word to your custom dictionary, so that OneNote will not question it again in the future.

5. When OneNote tells you that the spell check is complete, click OK to dismiss the Spelling task pane.

By default, OneNote checks the spelling of text as you type. You might be used to this feature from other Microsoft Office applications, such as Microsoft Word. When OneNote senses a possibly misspelled word, a red squiggly line appears underneath it. You can right-click such words and then acknowledge (or ignore) the suggested correction for that word. If you find this to be too distracting, you can turn this feature off and later perform a manual spell check whenever your notes are finished. To disable automatic spelling, click the File tab, click Options, and then click Proofing. Under When Correcting Spelling in OneNote, clear the Check Spelling As You Type check box, and then click OK.

Saving Notes

Over the years, computer programs have taught us a fundamental lesson: If you care about it, make sure you save it. Indeed, clicking the Save button periodically has long been second nature to most of us.

Why am I mentioning this? Well, by now you might have noticed something rather curious: OneNote does not have a Save button anywhere. Rest assured that this isn't some terrible oversight but an intentional choice.

To make writing in your OneNote notebooks as natural and intuitive as scribbling in a paper notebook, OneNote saves your work continuously, without you having to remember it or think about it. Any changes that you make to your notes are saved instantly, as are any changes you make to your notebook's organization and structure. You can freely switch pages, sections, and notebooks at any time, without having to save anything first. You can even shut down OneNote immediately after typing something without ever worrying about losing that information. Don't believe me? You can try this for yourself; I promise that the last thing you typed before shutting down OneNote will appear in your notebook the very next time you start OneNote again.

Although a Save As command is provided in the Backstage View, it is intended to let you export specific pages or sections from your OneNote notebook to publish elsewhere or to share with others. Be sure not to use the Save As command as a Save replacement or you may inadvertently create duplicates of your notes in multiple locations. For day-to-day use of your notes, learn to fully trust OneNote to do all of the saving for you!

Taking Audio and Video Notes

Note-taking and capturing information in OneNote isn't just limited to typing or importing text. In certain situations where you're given more information than you can jot down quickly (for example, in a class lecture, in a group presentation, or in an interview), you can make use of OneNote's excellent audio and video recording features.

Audio and video clips that you record in OneNote are stored as part of your notes, so even though they are saved in their native Windows Media formats, you'll always have everything together in your notebook, even if you move it to a different location.

In OneNote 2010, audio recordings are particularly useful. That's because spoken words in audio clips can be included in a notebook search. If an audio clip (or the audio portion of a video clip) contains the words or phrase you're looking for, the clip will be included as a search result. Additionally, you can link audio recordings that you create with OneNote to notes you type during the recording. When you play back the audio clip afterward, OneNote automatically moves the cursor through your notes to indicate which paragraph of text goes with a particular part of the audio recording.

The usefulness of audio and video notes in OneNote 2010 should not be underestimated, especially by people in certain professions. Journalists, doctors, attorneys, teachers, students, corporate trainers, administrative assistants, and people in similar professions may consider these features to be indispensable.

 LET ME TRY IT

Creating an Audio Recording

Before you attempt to create an audio recording with OneNote, make sure you have a microphone connected to your computer. Many laptops have a built-in microphone, which can also be used.

To create an audio recording, follow these steps:

1. On the ribbon, click the Insert tab, and then, in the Recording group, click Record Audio.

2. OneNote displays the contextual Audio & Video ribbon tab at the top of the program window (see Figure 5.8). This tab contains the controls and commands for using audio and video recordings in OneNote.

Figure 5.8   *The Audio & Video tab appears when you create an audio or video clip.*

3. When you have finished recording an audio clip, click the Stop button in the Playback ribbon group.

When the recording begins, OneNote places a WMA (Windows Media Audio) file icon on the current page and marks it with a date and time stamp (see Figure 5.9).

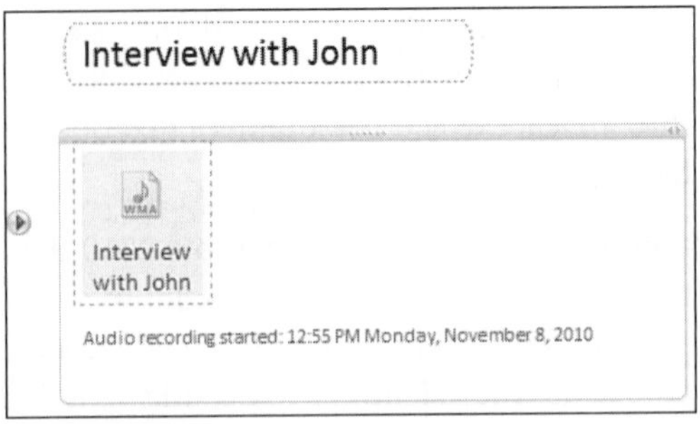

Interview with John

Interview
with John

Audio recording started: 12:55 PM Monday, November 8, 2010

Figure 5.9   *An audio recording file icon as it appears on the current page.*

While OneNote is recording the audio clip, you can type notes underneath the audio icon in the same way you would normally do on a notes page. Taking notes while recording audio establishes an automatic link between the recording's timeline and the position of your cursor within your notes. When you later play back the recording, you can choose to see the playback cursor move from line to line in your notes to show you which parts of your notes correspond to segments in your recording.

If you're unable to create an audio recording, verify that your microphone is properly configured. Open the Windows Control Panel, click Hardware and Sound, and then click Sound. In the dialog box that opens, click the Recording tab, select your recording device, and then click Properties. To fine-tune audio settings in OneNote, click the File tab on the ribbon, click Options, and then click Audio & Video. Under Audio Recording Settings, verify that the correct recording device, input method, codec, and sound format are selected.

LET ME TRY IT

Playing Back an Audio Recording

To play back an audio clip in OneNote, you can do any of the following:

- Click to select the WMA audio file icon on the page and then click the Play button in the Playback group on the ribbon.

- Click to select the WMA audio file icon on the page and then click the small, round Play icon that appears just to the left of the notes container.

- Double-click the WMA audio file icon on the page.

- Right-click the WMA audio file icon on the page and then click Play on the shortcut menu. (Alternately, click Open if you want to play back the audio file in Windows Media Player instead.)

While an audio recording is being played back, you can use additional command buttons in the Playback group on the ribbon—including Pause, Stop, Rewind 10 Minutes, Rewind 10 Seconds, Fast Forward 10 Seconds, and Fast Forward 10 Minutes.

 LET ME TRY IT

Exporting an Audio Recording

Any audio recordings that you create with OneNote will automatically be saved as part of the notebook they appear in. If you copy or move the notebook folder, the recordings travel with the notebook. However, there might be times when you want to export a particular audio recording to your file system so you can use it in other programs or send a copy to other people. To export any OneNote audio recording, follow these steps:

1. Right-click the WMA audio file icon of the recording you want to export, and then click Save As on the shortcut menu.

2. Navigate to the folder on your hard drive where you want to save the file, and then click Save.

 LET ME TRY IT

Creating a Video Recording

Before you attempt to create a video recording with OneNote, make sure you have a webcam connected to your computer. Many laptops have a built-in webcam, which can also be used.

To create a video recording, follow these steps:

1. On the ribbon, click the Insert tab, and then, in the Recording group, click Record Video.

2. OneNote opens a pop-up window that lets you monitor the current recording. Behind it, the contextual Audio & Video ribbon tab containing the audio and video controls appears at the top of the OneNote program window.

3. When you have finished recording a video clip, click the Stop button in the Playback ribbon group.

When the recording begins, OneNote places a WMV (Windows Media Video) file icon on the current page and marks it with a date and time stamp (see Figure 5.10).

Figure 5.10   *A video recording file icon as it appears on the current page.*

If you're unable to create a video recording, verify that your webcam is properly configured. Open the Windows Control Panel, click Hardware and Sound, and then click Devices and Printers. Find your webcam or camera device in the list, right-click its icon, and then click Properties. Alternately, you can right-click the device icon and click Troubleshoot to see tips for proper configuration. If the webcam or camera did not come with your computer, refer to the documentation and installation software from the manufacturer and check their website for updates and compatibility. To fine-tune video settings in OneNote, click the File tab on the ribbon, click Options, and then click Audio & Video. Under Video Recording Settings, verify that the correct video recording device and Windows Media profile are selected.

LET ME TRY IT

Playing Back a Video Recording

To play back a video clip in OneNote, you can do any of the following:

- Click to select the WMV video file icon on the page and then click the Play button in the Playback group on the ribbon.

- Click to select the WMV video file icon on the page and then click the small, round Play icon that appears just to the left of the notes container.

- Double-click the WMV video file icon on the page.

- Right-click the WMV video file icon on the page and then click Play on the shortcut menu. (Alternately, click Open if you want to play back the video file in Windows Media Player instead.)

While a video recording is being played back, you can use additional command buttons in the Playback group on the ribbon—including Pause, Stop, Rewind 10 Minutes, Rewind 10 Seconds, Fast Forward 10 Seconds, and Fast Forward 10 Minutes.

 LET ME TRY IT

Exporting a Video Recording

Like audio recordings, any video recordings that you create with OneNote will automatically be saved as part of the notebook they appear in. If you copy or move the notebook folder, the recordings travel with the notebook. However, there might be times when you want to export a particular video recording to your file system so you can use it in other programs or send a copy to other people. To export any OneNote video recording, follow these steps:

1. Right-click the WMV video file icon of the recording you want to export, and then click Save As on the shortcut menu.

2. Navigate to the folder on your hard drive where you want to save the file and then click Save.

LET ME TRY IT

Enabling Searching in Audio and Video Recordings

One of OneNote's most impressive features is the ability to instantly find any information again in your notes. You'll learn more about the search features in Chapter 7, "Organizing and Searching Notes." However, if you plan to frequently record audio or video notes instead of typing them, you can enable the ability to search for keywords and phrases within your OneNote recordings.

To enable searching in audio and video recordings, follow these steps:

1. Click the File tab and then click Options.

2. In the OneNote Options dialog box that appears, click the Audio & Video category in the left column.

3. On the right side, under Audio Search, select the Enable searching audio and video recordings for words check box.

The success rate of finding spoken words in audio recordings and in the audio portion of video recordings depends on the sound quality of each recording. This, in turn, depends on several factors, including the quality of the audio components in your computer, proper tuning and configuration of your microphone and webcam, the right distance between the speaker's mouth and the microphone, and the presence of ambient noise. Before you routinely make recordings with OneNote, spend some time fine-tuning your equipment to make sure the results match your expectations.

Taking Notes in Your Own Handwriting

If you have a Tablet PC running Windows XP Tablet Edition or any edition of Windows 7, or you have a Single Touch or Multi-Touch PC running any edition of Windows 7, you can use the handwriting capabilities that are built in to OneNote 2010. Instead of typing notes on your keyboard, you can handwrite them in your notebooks by writing directly on your computer's screen with a stylus or Tablet pen.

If you're running OneNote 2010 on Windows 7, you can easily determine if your PC has Touch capabilities by clicking the Start button on the Windows taskbar, and then right-clicking the word Computer (look for it near the right column on the Start menu). On the pop-up menu that appears, click Properties. In the System dialog box that opens, look for the Pen and Touch confirmation under the System heading. If you see "Pen and Single Touch Input Available" or "Pen and Multi-Touch Input Available," you can use OneNote's handwriting features. If you see "No Pen or Touch Input is available for this display," you'll have to stick to the keyboard for now.

Handwriting features can have a number of benefits in electronic note-taking. For starters, if you handwrite better and faster than you type, taking notes will obviously be easier for you in this mode. In meetings or in a classroom, typing notes on a noisy keyboard in front of others can be distracting and even considered poor etiquette, whereas handwriting your notes is virtually silent. Additionally, if you frequently draw or sketch as part of your work, you can do so right on the notes page you're writing on, without having to rely on predrawn shapes or imported images.

Another nice feature of digital handwriting is that your pen strokes can be formatted much like text (for example, you can change the thickness and color of your handwriting) and OneNote can even convert a selection of handwriting to text whenever you want to send a copy of your handwritten notes to colleagues or classmates in a more legible and reusable text format.

The following step-by-step procedures assume that you're using OneNote on a Tablet PC. If you don't yet have a device that lets you enjoy OneNote's handwriting features, feel free to skip this section for now.

 LET ME TRY IT

Handwriting and Drawing Notes

OneNote defaults to typed text input, but you can easily switch to Pen mode for handwriting and drawing on a page.

To use the handwriting and drawing notes features, follow these steps:

1. On the ribbon, click or tap the Draw tab. You'll notice that the Select & Type button appears orange, which means it's currently selected and you're using the keyboard and mouse for input (see Figure 5.11).

2. In the Tools ribbon group, move the mouse over any of the color pens until a ToolTip appears, informing you of the precise thickness and color of each available pen.

3. Click or tap the pen that you want to use. As soon as the pen is active, note that the Select & Type button is no longer selected, signaling you that you're now in Pen mode.

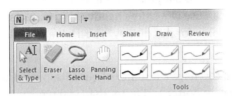

Figure 5.11 *The Select & Type tool on the Draw tab is highlighted whenever you're working in normal text-based input.*

4. Now pick up your Tablet PC pen or stylus and begin drawing or writing notes directly on your screen.

5. To end Pen mode, click or tap the Select & Type button on the Draw tab again.

SHOW ME   Media 5.3—Handwriting and Drawing Notes
Access this video file through your registered Web Edition at
my.safaribooksonline.com/9780132182447/media.

If you don't have a Tablet PC, you can use the built-in handwriting features in OneNote 2010 by purchasing an external drawing tablet or digital pen and connecting it to your computer. Although you can't draw directly on your computer screen with these devices, they do give you the same freedom from your keyboard—allowing you to easily handwrite, draw, and sketch notes. A quick Internet search for "PC drawing tablet" or "OneNote digital pen" should point you in the right direction. Just make sure you check the manufacturer's system requirements list to ensure OneNote 2010 and Windows compatibility before committing to a purchase.

 **LET ME TRY IT**

Displaying Additional Pens and Highlighters

At first glance, the Draw tab on the ribbon shows you only 10 pens of different colors and degrees of thickness and four highlighters in as many colors. By expanding the gallery to full view, you can reveal additional presets.

To display additional pens and highlighters, follow these steps:

1. On the Draw tab, in the Tools group, click the More drop-down arrow in the lower-right corner of the box showing the pens and highlighters (see Figure 5.12).

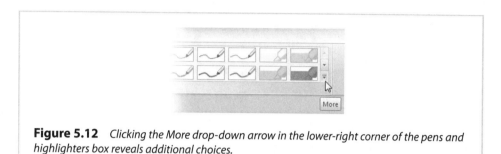

Figure 5.12 *Clicking the More drop-down arrow in the lower-right corner of the pens and highlighters box reveals additional choices.*

2. Click or tap any of the additional pens that are displayed in the Built-in Pens section of the gallery.

 LET ME TRY IT

Customizing a Pen or Highlighter

If the colors and line thickness of the pen and highlighter presets don't meet your needs, you can create your own custom pens by following these steps. Although it might seem tempting to click the big Color & Thickness button that's shown on the Draw tab of the ribbon, that command applies only to shapes and existing ink strokes.

To change the color and thickness of pens and highlighters, do the following:

1. On the Draw tab, in the Tools group, click the More drop-down arrow in the lower-right corner of the box showing the pens and highlighters (see Figure 5.12).

2. Click or tap the More Colors and Thickness Options command that appears near the bottom of the menu.

3. In the Pen Properties dialog box that opens (see Figure 5.13), click or tap a custom line thickness and color that you want your new pen or highlighter to have. You can rest the mouse pointer over the thickness and color swatches to display a ToolTip describing the line thickness and color properties.

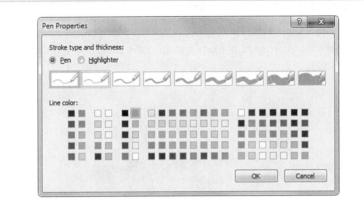

Figure 5.13   *In the Pen Properties dialog box, you can create custom pens and highlighters by choosing the line thickness and line color you want.*

4. Click OK to create the new pen or highlighter with the properties you selected. New pens and highlighters are automatically added to the Favorite Pens list on the ribbon. Click the More drop-down arrow (see Figure 5.12) whenever you want to see the full list of your pens and highlighters.

You can add a handful of your favorite pens and highlighters to the Quick Access Toolbar over the ribbon. First customize your favorite pens the way you want, and then click the drop-down arrow to the right of the Quick Access Toolbar (see Chapter 3, "A Tour of the OneNote Workspace"). Toggle any or all of the Favorite Pen or Favorite Highlighter commands on the Quick Access Toolbar menu to display the pens near the top of the OneNote program window. The benefit of pinning them to the toolbar is that they'll never disappear from view, even when you click away from the Draw tab. If you have more pens that you want to keep at your fingertips, consider creating a custom ribbon group with all your pens and highlighters and then place it on any ribbon tab you want. For more information about customizing the ribbon, see Chapter 12, "Customizing OneNote 2010."

 **LET ME TRY IT**

Choosing a Handwriting Mode

When you use the handwriting features in OneNote 2010, it allows for the creation of both handwriting and drawings at the same time. If necessary, you can override this default setting to a more specific selection. For example, on a particular page, you could restrict your handwriting to only create drawings so that OneNote will know not to attempt to convert these drawings to text later on.

To choose a handwriting mode, follow these steps:

1. On the Draw tab, in the Tools group, click the More drop-down arrow in the lower-right corner of the box showing the pens and highlighters (see Figure 5.12).

2. Click or tap the Pen Mode command and then click or tap any of the three options you want.

If you're not sure what mode to use, leave the default setting Create Both Handwriting and Drawings.

There's a fourth option available on the Pen Mode that can prove to be quite convenient: the Use Pen as Pointer option. Selecting this mode lets you use your selected pen like a mouse pointer so you can interact with certain elements on your screen by clicking or tapping them without constantly having to toggle Select & Type mode. For example, with a pen active, tapping the To Do note tag on a page would just draw around it. However, with the Use Pen as Pointer option selected, you're able to place a check mark in the To Do box, just like you would be able to do with your mouse pointer. When you're done using the pen as a pointer, click the Use Pen as Pointer command once more to toggle it off.

 LET ME TRY IT

Selecting Handwriting or a Drawing on a Page

Once you've handwritten or drawn something on a OneNote page, it appears as digital ink, which can appear free-form on the page canvas or within note containers.

You can select digital ink strokes in much the same way as you would select typed text on a page.

To select handwriting or a drawing on a page, follow these steps:

1. On the Draw tab, make sure that the Select & Type tool is selected (it will appear orange).

2. On the page, click any part of your handwritten text or drawing. OneNote will automatically include neighboring strokes that were created at the same time as the part of the handwriting you're clicking.

3. While selected, eight control handles will surround the handwriting object to let you know you can now interact with the ink selection (see Figure 5.14). You can click and drag any of the handles to enlarge, shrink, stretch, or squeeze the selection as many times as you like.

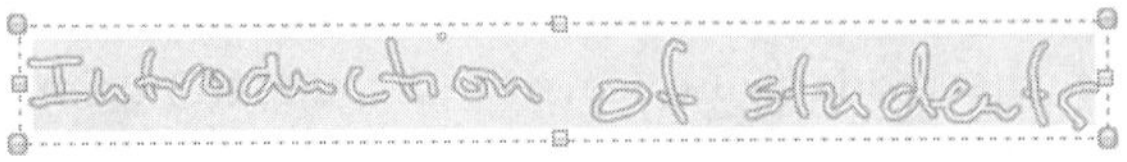

Figure 5.14   *You can click and drag the center of a selected handwriting object to move it to another location or click and drag the object handles surrounding the selection to change its appearance.*

To quickly select all objects on a page, including handwriting and drawings, use the Ctrl+A keyboard shortcut. This command works incrementally, so depending on where your cursor is located when you do this, you might need to press Ctrl+A up to three times in a row to include everything in your selection.

LET ME TRY IT

Creating a Custom Selection from Handwriting or from a Drawing

On occasion, OneNote's best guess about which ink strokes belong together to form a selection might not be to your liking. In these cases, you can easily create a custom selection by using the Lasso Select tool.

To create a custom selection from handwriting or from a drawing, follow these steps:

1. On the Draw tab, click the Lasso Select tool.

2. Click and drag a circle around only those ink strokes that you want to include in your selection (see Figure 5.15). For example, you might select only a single handwritten word or character in a line of text.

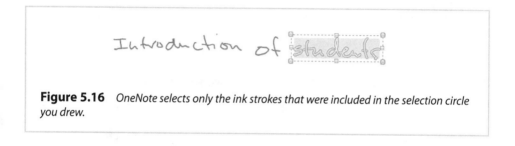

Figure 5.15   *Using the Lasso Select tool, click and draw a selection border around the ink strokes you want to select.*

3. When you release the mouse button, OneNote selects only the ink strokes that were included in the selection circle you drew (see Figure 5.16).

Introduction of students

Figure 5.16   *OneNote selects only the ink strokes that were included in the selection circle you drew.*

Once handwritten text or the ink strokes of a drawing are selected in the way you want, you can apply formatting to the selection or cut or copy and then paste the selection to another location. You can also have OneNote convert handwritten notes and handwritten mathematical expressions to text.

 LET ME TRY IT

Changing the Formatting of Handwriting or a Drawing

To change the color and thickness of your selected ink strokes, follow these steps:

1. Select the parts of your handwriting or drawing that you want to format.

2. On the Draw tab, in the Insert Shapes group, click the Color & Thickness button.

3. In the Color & Thickness dialog box that opens, change the thickness or color (or both) and then click OK to apply the changes to your selection.

For a quicker way to format a selection of handwriting, right-click the handwriting selection and then click the Color & Thickness button in the upper-right corner of the shortcut menu that appears.

 LET ME TRY IT

Converting Handwriting to Text

The built-in handwriting recognition in OneNote 2010 can convert a selection of handwriting to standard text. This is useful whenever you want to send a copy of your handwritten notes to colleagues or classmates in a more legible and reusable text format.

To convert handwriting to text, follow these steps:

1. Select the parts of your handwriting that you want to convert.

2. On the Draw tab, in the Convert group, click the Ink to Text button.

Text recognition depends on the quality and legibility of the selected handwritten text. If you repeatedly have trouble getting OneNote to recognize your handwriting, try again with larger and more legible writing.

For a quicker way to convert a handwriting selection to text, right-click the selection, and then click Ink to Text on the shortcut menu. To convert only a single word to text, first deselect all handwriting on the page and then right-click a single handwritten word. Near the top of the shortcut menu, click one of the conversion suggestions to change that particular word to the text you want.

If the Ink to Text command is not available on the ribbon or on the shortcut menu, you most likely selected Create Drawings Only mode. See "Choosing a Handwriting Mode" earlier in this chapter for instructions for how to create handwriting objects that can be converted.

If you write out mathematical expressions in your own handwriting, you can convert these just as easily by clicking the Ink to Math button on the ribbon or on the shortcut menu that appears when right-clicking a selected expression.

 **LET ME TRY IT**

Erasing Specific Parts of Handwriting or a Drawing

Although you can easily erase handwriting on most Tablet PCs by moving the back of your pen or stylus over your digital ink strokes, OneNote offers several built-in eraser options for greater control.

To erase specific parts of handwriting or a drawing, follow these steps:

1. On the Draw tab, click the small arrow under the Eraser button.

2. On the menu that appears, select the Small, Medium, or Large Eraser. The icon on the button will change to remind you of your selection, and moving the mouse pointer over the button will display the name of the eraser you have chosen.

3. Move the mouse pointer over the page containing handwriting or a drawing. Click and drag the eraser mouse pointer over the parts you want to erase.

If you make a mistake, remember to click the Undo command on the Quick Access Toolbar or press the Ctrl+Z keyboard shortcut.

For even more precision, choose the Stroke Eraser on the Eraser menu. In this mode, you can use the mouse, the pen, or even your finger to erase entire strokes at a time, including those in drawings and shapes. This is most useful when you want to replace a particular stroke without destroying the ink surrounding it.

In addition to the Eraser options, OneNote 2010 also recognizes the scratch-out gesture built in to Tablet PCs to delete unwanted handwriting or drawings. Using your Tablet PC pen or stylus, quickly scratch out existing handwriting on the page—the same way you would rapidly scribble lines of ink back and forth over text on a piece of paper. Using the scratch-out gesture will cause the crossed-out text on your page to disappear.

 **LET ME TRY IT**

Erasing an Entire Selection of Handwriting or a Drawing

To quickly erase a large amount of handwriting or a large drawing on your notes page, do the following:

1. Using the mouse or the Lasso Select tool on the Draw tab, select the parts of your handwriting or drawing that you want to erase.

2. On the Draw tab, in the Edit group, click Delete.

For a slightly faster way to delete a large selection of handwriting, right-click your selection and then click Delete on the shortcut menu.

 LET ME TRY IT

Scrolling Through Ink Selections on a Page

Normally, the horizontal and vertical scrollbars that appear in OneNote will suffice for getting around on a page. However, because handwriting and drawing objects are typically larger than typed text objects, scrolling can take more time and increase the chance of deselecting a complex selection of ink strokes that you want to bring into view.

To quickly scroll through the page without using the scrollbars, follow these steps:

1. On the Draw tab, in the Tools group, click the Panning Hand button (see Figure 5.17).

Figure 5.17   *Using the Panning Hand tool, you can bring other parts of the page into view without accidentally deselecting any handwriting objects on the current page.*

2. In this mode, the mouse pointer will change to the panning hand icon when you move it over the page.

3. Click and drag the panning hand in any direction to quickly bring other parts of the page into view.

4. When you release the mouse button, you're left on the position of the page that you were last looking at and all selected objects on the page will remain selected.

Formatting Text

Although OneNote is still a comparatively young program compared with flagship Microsoft Office applications like Word and Excel, it boasts an impressive arsenal of formatting tools. Although many of these are almost identical to the tools in other Office applications that you've learned to depend on over the years, there are some that are decidedly different because of OneNote's unique canvas.

In this section, let's take a closer look at some of the ways in which you can add formatting to your notes pages and the information you collect on them. Almost every single formatting feature serves as a reminder why a traditional paper notebook can't hold a candle to the things you can do with your OneNote notebooks.

 **LET ME TRY IT**

Setting the Default Font

Typed text in OneNote 2010 defaults to 11-point Calibri—a very legible font that's included with all Microsoft Office 2010 applications. If you have a different preference for how new text should appear in your notes, you can specify your preferred default font, font size, and font color.

To set the default font, follow these steps:

1. On the File tab, click Options.

2. In the OneNote Options dialog box that opens, look for the Default Font section.

3. Select your preferences from the Font, Font Size, and Font Color drop-down menus, and then click OK. Your preferences will be applied to all new text that you create in your notes.

If you have existing notes that were formatted in a different font and you want to quickly change all the text on your page to match the new default font you selected, press Ctrl+A on your keyboard to select all note containers on the page, and then change the Font, Font Size, and Font Color options on the Home tab to match those of your custom default font selection.

If your cursor is blinking in any note container on the page when you do this, you may need to press Ctrl+A three times in a row to make OneNote select all note containers, including the active one.

Changing Basic Text Formatting

If you've ever used text formatting tools in Microsoft Word, WordPad, or most other Windows programs, you likely already know most of the basic text formatting tools that are also available in OneNote.

 SHOW ME   Media 5.4—Applying Basic Formatting to Text
Access this video file through your registered Web Edition at
my.safaribooksonline.com/9780132182447/media.

Using the boxes and buttons in the Basic Text group (see Figure 5.18) on the Home tab of the ribbon, you can apply any of the following formatting choices to text that you have selected:

- Font
- Font size
- Bold
- Italic
- Underline
- Strikethrough
- Superscript or subscript
- Text highlight color
- Font color

Figure 5.18 *The Basic Text group on the ribbon contains the text formatting tools. If you rest the mouse pointer over any button, a ToolTip tells you what it does.*

If you want to change any formatting that you have already applied to selected text (for example, a specific font size), reselect the text, if necessary, and then simply make a different selection. If you applied formatting by using a button or command, for example, Bold or Italic, click the same button or command again to remove that effect. If you accidentally apply some text formatting that you don't want to keep, you can use the Undo command (Ctrl+Z) to restore text to the way it was before you applied the unwanted formatting.

If you do a lot of text formatting on a page and prefer not to repeatedly move the mouse back and forth between the ribbon and your page, you can use the Mini toolbar that appears when you're selecting text on a page (see Figure 5.19). As soon as you see the Mini toolbar appear over the text you're interacting with, move the mouse pointer directly over the toolbar, and then click the drop-down menus and buttons to make your formatting selections.

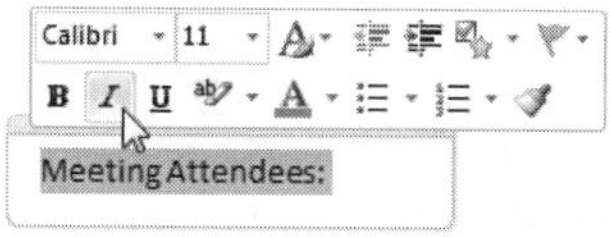

Figure 5.19 *The Mini toolbar appears when you select text on a page. Its formatting commands and buttons work the same as they do on the ribbon.*

LET ME TRY IT

Using the Styles Gallery

OneNote 2010 is the first version to support a basic gallery of styles that let you easily apply predefined text formatting. Using styles can give your notes a consistent look, improve their legibility, and speed up your note-taking and formatting.

To apply a style from the gallery, follow these steps:

1. On the page, select the text you want to format with a style.

2. On the Home tab, in the Styles group, click the name of the style you want to apply (see Figure 5.20). If the style you want is not visible, either scroll through the list or click the More button in the lower-right corner of the Styles gallery to display the entire list of styles.

> Heading 1
> Heading 2
> Heading 3
> Styles

Figure 5.20   *The Styles gallery lets you apply preset formatting combinations to selected text. On the right, click the two scroll buttons to move through the list, or click the More button in the lower-right corner to see all styles at once.*

SHOW ME   **Media 5.5—Using the Styles Gallery to Format Notes**
Access this video file through your registered Web Edition at
my.safaribooksonline.com/9780132182447/media.

Although it is not possible to modify or customize these styles like you can do in Microsoft Word 2010, you can easily use any of the 11 built-in styles as the basis for any further text formatting that you manually apply.

For example, you can apply the "Heading 3" style from the list, and then, while the text is still selected, click the Underline button in the Basic Text group to also add underline formatting to the heading. Using this method, you can apply as many combinations of style formatting and manual text formatting as you want.

Like the regular text formatting commands, styles are available for quick access on the Mini toolbar that appears over text when you select it (see Figure 5.19). On the Mini toolbar, immediately next to the Font Size box, click the Quick Styles button to display the full Styles list, and then click the text style you want.

If you plan to apply styles to your notes rather frequently, you might want to learn and use the keyboard shortcuts that are available for some of them (see Table 5.1).

Table 5.1   Keyboard Shortcuts

To Apply	Press
Heading 1	Ctrl+Alt+1
Heading 2	Ctrl+Alt+2
Heading 3	Ctrl+Alt+3
Heading 4	Ctrl+Alt+4
Heading 5	Ctrl+Alt+5
Heading 6	Ctrl+Alt+6
Normal	Ctrl+Shift+N

Note that the Page Title, Citation, Quote, and Code styles cannot be applied with keyboard shortcuts.

 LET ME TRY IT

Inserting Symbols and Special Characters

Aside from applying styles and changing the appearance of your notes text with different fonts and font sizes, you might need to generate any variety of foreign language characters, currency symbols, diacritical marks, and other special characters into your notes. OneNote 2010 has a full repository of these available at your fingertips.

To quickly apply a simple symbol (such as a trademark symbol or a Euro currency symbol) in your notes, do the following:

1. In your notes, place the insertion point where you want the symbol to appear.

2. On the Insert tab, in the Symbols group, click Symbol. A pop-up menu appears (see Figure 5.21).

3. Click the symbol you want to insert. If the symbol you want is not shown on the pop-up menu, click More Symbols to open the Symbol dialog box where you can choose from additional special characters.

When you click the More Symbols command on the pop-up menu that appears after clicking the Symbol button on the ribbon, OneNote displays the Symbol dialog box, where you have many additional choices for inserting special characters into your notes (see Figure 5.22).

Figure 5.21   *The Symbol button lets you pick from commonly used special characters that you can quickly insert into your notes. It also provides the entry point to a full repository that contains many more special symbols.*

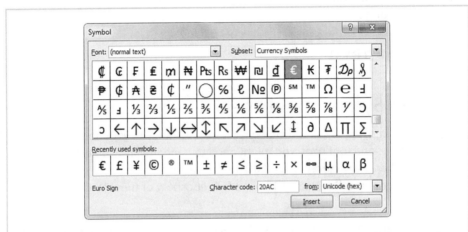

Figure 5.22   *The Symbol dialog box button lets you access a sophisticated repository of special characters. You can optionally select a specific font and symbol subset before making a choice.*

To insert a symbol from the dialog box, click the symbol you want, and then click Insert. Once you have used a symbol in this way, it will be added to the row of recently used symbols (see Figure 5.22) so you can easily find it again the next time you open this dialog box.

Aside from symbols and special characters, OneNote 2010 also fully supports the creation of mathematical equations as part of your notes. To access the hidden Equation Tools tab on the ribbon, click the Insert tab, and then click the top of the Equation button. If you're using OneNote on a Tablet PC or a Multi-Touch

PC that supports handwriting, you can click the Ink Equations button that appears to enter equations in your own handwriting into your notes. Because math equations are a bit outside of the realm of OneNote basics, I won't cover them here in greater detail, but I encourage you to search on the Web for more information about these powerful Microsoft Office 2010 features. To close the Equation Tools tab on the ribbon, press the Esc key.

 LET ME TRY IT

Copying and Applying Formatting with the Format Painter

The Format Painter (see Figure 5.23) is a useful and time-saving way in many Office programs that lets you copy the formatting of a selection of text and then apply ("paint") the exact same formatting to additional text on a page.

Figure 5.23 *The Format Painter tool on the Home tab lets you copy the formatting from one selection of text and paste it to another. If you click this button once, it will let you paste a copied formatting style once. If you double-click the button, you stay in Format Painter mode until you turn the tool off again, so you can paste a copied formatting style multiple times.*

This is most useful when you're supplementing existing notes (or notes you've received from someone else) with new information and you want the new notes to be formatted in the same way. Alternately, if you have a large amount of plain notes and you don't want to repeatedly go through multiple steps to apply a combination of formatting, the Format Painter lets you accomplish the same thing with just a couple of clicks.

 **SHOW ME** Media 5.6—Using the Format Painter
Access this video file through your registered Web Edition at
my.safaribooksonline.com/9780132182447/media.

To copy and paint a single occurrence of text formatting, do the following:

1. Go to a page that contains text whose formatting you want to copy and then select any part of that text. Your selection need not be precise because you are only copying the formatting style of the text you select, not the text itself.

2. On the Home tab, in the Clipboard group, click Format Painter.

3. The mouse pointer changes to an insertion point with a paintbrush symbol next to it (see Figure 5.24).

Figure 5.24   *When the mouse pointer changes to an insertion point with a paintbrush symbol next to it, OneNote is waiting for you to select the text to which you want to apply ("paint") the copied formatting.*

4. Without clicking anywhere else on the page, navigate to the text to which you want to apply the formatting you just copied, and then drag the insertion point over the text to apply the copied formatting.

While the paint cursor is displayed, take care not to click anywhere on the page except for the text that you want to format. If you make a mistake, simply press Ctrl+Z to undo your last action, and then try again. If you need to navigate to a different page than the current one, you can safely click the scrollbars, page tabs, and section tabs to bring the target text into view.

The Format Painter in OneNote can be used in an alternate way to help you save time when formatting multiple words or paragraphs of text.

By double-clicking the Format Painter button on the ribbon after you select the text from which you want to copy its formatting, OneNote will stay in Format Painter mode so you can apply the copied formatting to multiple selections of text until you turn off the tool. To do this, follow these steps:

1. Go to a page that contains text whose formatting you want to copy and then select any part of that text.

2. On the Home tab, in the Clipboard group, double-click Format Painter. Whereas single-clicking the button lets you paste a copied formatting style once, double-clicking the button causes OneNote to remain in Format Painter mode so you can paste a copied formatting style multiple times.

3. When the mouse pointer changes to the paint cursor (see Figure 5.24), navigate to the first occurrence of text to which you want to apply the formatting, and then drag the insertion point over the text.

4. After the text adopts the copied formatting, navigate to the next occurrence of text to which you want to apply the same formatting.

5. Repeat step 4 as many times as needed until the appearance of all of the target text on your pages has changed to the copied formatting.

6. When you're done applying the copied formatting, click the Format Painter button on the ribbon (or press the Esc key) to turn off Format Painter mode.

Although the steps in the preceding two procedures work well with quick little selections of words, phrases, or fairly short lines of text in your notes, there's an easier way to apply copied formatting to entire paragraphs of text with a single mouse click.

To do this, don't drag the paint cursor over a bunch of text when you see the paint cursor after clicking the Format Painter button. Instead, move the paint cursor over the note container of a paragraph that you want to format, and then click the four-headed arrow icon that appears just to the left of the note container (see Figure 5.25). All of the text will immediately adopt the copied formatting of the source selection. This method makes formatting large amounts of notes in a consistent way much less time-consuming.

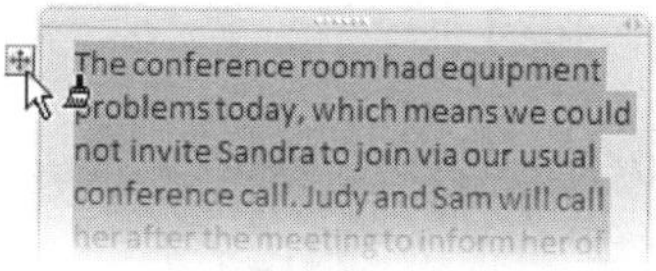

Figure 5.25   *While in Format Painter mode, clicking the four-headed arrow icon next to the note container whose text you want to format will apply the copied formatting to the entire paragraph of text without the need to manually drag over the entire text.*

An easily overlooked time-saver is the Format Painter's support for keyboard shortcuts. When using this mode, there is no visual feedback on the screen like there is when you use the Format Painter button. The result, however, is the same. First, select some of the text that contains the formatting you want to copy. On your keyboard, press Ctrl+Shift+C. You won't see the paint cursor appear, but don't worry—the formatting information has been placed on the Clipboard. Next, select the text to which you want to apply the formatting, and then press Ctrl+Shift+V to paint it. If you want, you can now keep using Ctrl+Shift+V to paint any additional target text with the copied formatting. Keep going for as long as you want.

 LET ME TRY IT

Clearing All Formatting from Text

Now that you know several different ways how to add formatting to the text in your notes, you're probably wondering if it's just as easy to get rid of text formatting. The answer is yes.

Removing all text formatting is especially useful when you're working with various notes that you've received from other people and you want a fresh start before applying your own formatting choices. Or, you simply might not need the emphasis of certain formatting anymore. No matter what the reason, the following steps let you change your text back to the basics:

1. Select the text whose formatting you want to clear.

2. On the Home tab, in the Basic Text group, click Clear Formatting (see Figure 5.26).

Figure 5.26   *The Clear Formatting button near the upper-right side of the Basic Text group on the Home tab instantly clears all of the formatting from a selection, leaving only the plain text on the page.*

The Clear Formatting button is also available in the Styles gallery, either when you expand the list of styles on the ribbon, or when you click the Quick Styles button on the Mini toolbar that appears when you select text on a page.

Formatting Paragraphs

Whereas text formatting changes the appearance of the typed characters in your notes, paragraph formatting lets you modify the alignment, spacing, and ordering of lines of text in your notes.

Like many other basic formatting tasks, these options are nearly the same in OneNote 2010 as they are in some of the other Office 2010 programs you might already be familiar with. Still, let's take a few moments to have a closer look at these features.

 LET ME TRY IT

Creating a Bulleted List

Bulleted lists are useful for arranging several pieces of written information on a page without the need to keep them in any particular order.

You can create a bulleted list in your notes by following these steps:

1. Place the insertion point on a new line where you want the bulleted list to start.

2. On the Home tab, in the Basic Text group, click the Bullets button (see Figure 5.27).

Figure 5.27 *Clicking the Bullets button on the Home tab starts or ends a bulleted list in your notes. The small arrow next to this button reveals the Bullets Library.*

3. When the first bullet appears, type the first item, and then press Enter. OneNote will keep creating bullets each time you press Enter.

4. To finish the bulleted list, press Enter twice in a row.

To change the symbol that OneNote should use for bulleted lists that you create, click the small arrow next to the Bullets button on the ribbon, and then click a different style of bullet from the Bullet Library that appears.

 LET ME TRY IT

Creating a Numbered List

Numbered lists are useful for arranging several pieces of written information on a page in a specific, numeric order—much like the numbered procedure steps you see in the "how to" sections in the chapters of this book.

You can create a numbered list in your notes by following these steps:

1. Place the insertion point on a new line where you want the numbered list to start.

2. On the Home tab, in the Basic Text group, click the Numbering button (see Figure 5.28).

Figure 5.28 *Clicking the Numbering button on the Home tab starts or ends a numbered list in your notes. The small arrow next to this button reveals the Numbering Library.*

3. When the first number appears, type the first item and then press Enter. OneNote will keep creating numbered items each time you press Enter.

4. To finish the numbered list, press Enter twice in a row.

To change the style of numbering that OneNote should use for numbered lists that you create, click the small arrow next to the Numbering button on the ribbon and then click a different style of numbering format from the Numbering Library that appears.

LET ME TRY IT

Aligning Text on a Page

Text alignment options in OneNote let you quickly move text to a specific location within its note container. You can choose to center text, flush it to the left, or flush it to the right.

To align text on a page, follow these steps:

1. Click anywhere within the line of text that you want to align.

2. On the Home tab, in the Basic Text group, click Paragraph Alignment (see Figure 5.29).

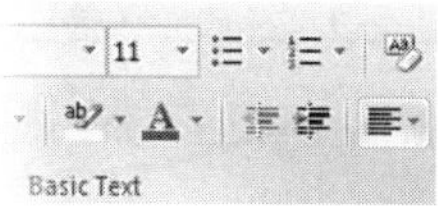

Figure 5.29   *Clicking the Paragraph Alignment button on the Home tab lets you control text alignment for a selected line of text.*

3. On the pop-up menu that appears, select the alignment you want—Align Left, Center, or Align Right.

Unlike a word processor, which typically uses the full dimensions of the current page, OneNote uses the dimensions of the note container containing the text that you want to align.

To change the alignment of text you have already aligned in a certain way, simply repeat the previous procedure and then make a different selection in step 3.

LET ME TRY IT

Changing Paragraph Spacing

By default, OneNote will use the default font or the font with which you formatted the text on a page to determine how much space to keep between the lines of text in a paragraph.

You can easily change the spacing of any paragraph by following these steps:

1. Click anywhere within the paragraph whose line spacing you want to change.

2. On the Home tab, in the Basic Text group, click Paragraph Alignment.

3. At the bottom of the pop-up menu that appears, click Paragraph Spacing Options (see Figure 5.30).

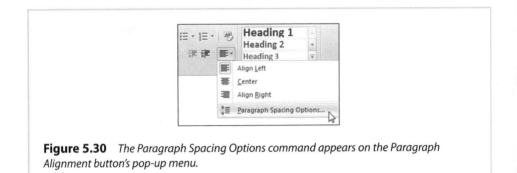

Figure 5.30   *The Paragraph Spacing Options command appears on the Paragraph Alignment button's pop-up menu.*

4. In the Paragraph Spacing Options dialog box that appears, enter the amount of space (in points) that you want OneNote to apply before or after a line of text. You can also set a minimum line spacing value in the last field (also in points).

5. Click OK to apply your preferences to the current paragraph.

If the values you enter in the Paragraph Spacing dialog box don't seem to change anything, try to significantly increase the values. You will start seeing a change in the line spacing as soon as you enter a value that's larger than the font size of the current line of text. For example, if the font size of the current text is 11, you could enter a 12 or a higher value for the Before or After values to see an increase in the spacing. OneNote thinks of the combined value (the font size and the increment you add) as the overall line height. For this reason, if you enter values that are equal or smaller to the current font size, the paragraph spacing will remain unaffected.

 **LET ME TRY IT**

Indenting Text on a Page

To help you format notes in a simple outline structure, you can increase or decrease the indent position of a line of text by following these steps:

1. Click anywhere within a line of text that you want to indent.

2. On the Home tab, in the Basic Text group, click Increase Indent Position (see Figure 5.31).

Figure 5.31 *The two Indent Position buttons on the Home tab let you decrease or increase the indent of a line of text. You can add multiple levels of indentation for quick and easy outline-style note-taking.*

3. If necessary, click the Increase Indent Position button any number of additional times to further increase the indent position.

Once you have increased the indent position of a line of text by at least one level, the Decrease Indent Position button on the ribbon becomes available so you can remove the indentation again later.

To quickly indent a normal line of text by one level, position the cursor to the left of the first character of text, and then press the Tab key. You can press the Tab key again for each additional indentation level you want to add. To decrease the indent position again by one level using your keyboard, position the cursor to the left of the first character of text, and then press the Backspace key. You can press the Backspace key again for each additional indentation level that you want to remove.

LET ME TRY IT

Creating a Hierarchical Outline in Your Notes

Outlines offer a condensed view of a particular subject. They're often created to plan and summarize a project (like this book, for example), and to account for its preparation and successful execution. Outlines are often created in the brainstorming or idea-gathering phase of a project or task, which means that the information is likely to change quite often. This is where paper notebooks have always failed us—once written down, you can never easily change the order of things again. OneNote, of course, offers all of the flexibility and benefits of electronic notetaking, never running out of paper and allowing its pages and content to be changed on a whim.

When you take notes in a hierarchical outline format, you can use the built-in level selection features in OneNote 2010 to quickly select text at certain levels of your outline. This type of selection makes formatting or rearranging of large outlines easier than ever before. Another benefit is the ability to collapse or expand any level of notes with the click of a mouse. This puts you in control of the information at all times—whether you want to see only the high-level headings of your outline or prefer to see all of the detail.

SHOW ME   Media 5.7—Structuring Notes as Outlines
Access this video file through your registered Web Edition at
my.safaribooksonline.com/9780132182447/media.

So, what does this look like? Let's imagine you have an outline with a main heading at the top and three levels of main points below—each of which with three lines of detail below that (see Figure 5.32).

To create this outline, I applied the Heading 1 style from the Styles gallery to the outline heading I typed. Next, I started a numbered list for the three outline levels. For each of the three lines of detail underneath each level, I pressed the Tab key to increase the indent position. OneNote detected that I was creating an outline and automatically changed the list formatting accordingly.

No matter how many levels or items you have in your outline, you can interact with it immediately. The first method is OneNote's excellent selection model, which lets you select specific text in your outline at common levels for the purpose of reordering or otherwise formatting that text.

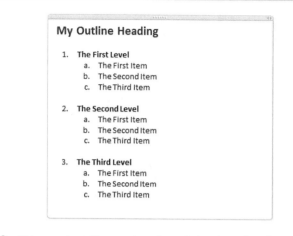

Figure 5.32   *This sample outline consists of a main heading, three levels, and three detail items underneath each level. The longer this outline gets, the more difficult it would be to format or view it. With OneNote, however, these tasks are easy.*

To select levels in an outline, follow these steps:

1. Move the mouse pointer over the main outline heading and watch for the four-headed arrow icon that appears next to it (see Figure 5.33).

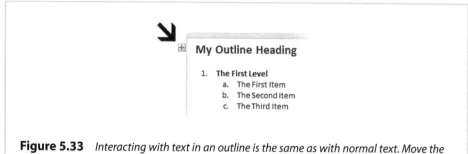

Figure 5.33   *Interacting with text in an outline is the same as with normal text. Move the mouse pointer over a line of text, such as the outline heading in this example, and then right-click the four-headed arrow icon for more options.*

2. Right-click the arrow icon and then, on the shortcut menu that appears, move the mouse over the Select command.

3. On the Select flyout menu, you can choose which level of the outline you want to select. For example, choose All at Level 2 to select all of the numbered headings in the list (see Figure 5.34).

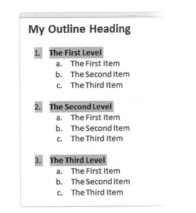

Figure 5.34 *In this outline, selecting All at Level 2 causes OneNote to select all of the numbered headings. While selected, you can format the headings or change their hierarchical level by using the indentation commands on the ribbon.*

While a level in your outline is selected, you can apply bulk formatting to it (for example, you can make all of the numbered headings bold or change them to red text) or you can use the Increase Indent Position and Decrease Indent Position buttons on the ribbon (Home tab, Basic Text group) to change the order of the selected items in the outline.

If you're working in a large and complex outline and you're not sure which level you're at, move the mouse pointer over one of the items at the level you want to select, and then choose Select All at same level from the Select command that appears on the right-click menu. Remember not to right-click text itself but the four-headed arrow icon that appears next to it.

As mentioned at the beginning of this section, there is another really great outlining feature in OneNote 2010, which lets you move entire blocks of your outline around and also allows you to control the amount of information that you see in your outline at any one time. With the click of a mouse, you can collapse (and later expand again) any level of notes.

Let's say that your outline has become quite lengthy and, to gain oversight, you want to see only the numbered level headings, not all of the detailed items below them. Hiding the details requires far less scrolling through the full outline and you can then more easily check to see whether the main points are still in the right order. If they're not, you can then move an entire level with all of its subitems to a new location in the outline. For written projects such as a book or a paper that you're outlining for school, this is especially useful.

In the sample outline, do the following:

1. Move the mouse pointer over the first numbered level heading (in the preceding example, "The First Level") and watch for the four-headed arrow icon that appears next to it (see Figure 5.35).

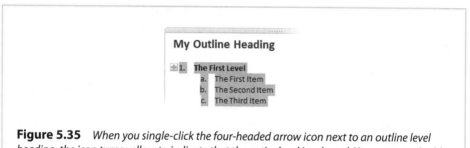

Figure 5.35   *When you single-click the four-headed arrow icon next to an outline level heading, the icon turns yellow to indicate that the entire level is selected. You can now double-click the arrow icon to collapse the detail items below the heading. Double-clicking the icon again restores the full view of the related items. To move the selected block to another location in the outline, click and drag the arrow icon and then drop the text where you want it.*

2. Click the arrow icon once. It will turn yellow to indicate selection, and all of the text at this level—including the subitems below it—will be selected.

3. To hide (collapse) the subitems below the numbered level heading, double-click the arrow icon next to the heading. Only the text of the level heading will remain shown, and the arrow icon will appear stacked to let you know that it has been collapsed (see Figure 5.36).

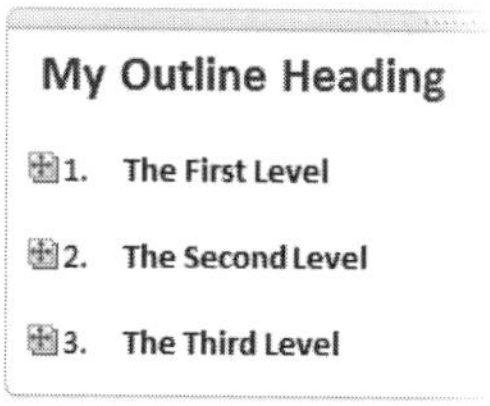

My Outline Heading

⊞1.   The First Level

⊞2.   The Second Level

⊞3.   The Third Level

Figure 5.36   *When you double-click the arrow icon next to an outline level, all subitems below that level will be hidden from view, and the arrow icon will appear stacked to indicate it can be expanded by double-clicking the icon again.*

4. If you want, you can click and drag a collapsed arrow icon to move the heading and the subitems it contains to another location in your outline. Once you've moved an item, you can double-click the collapsed arrow item again to unhide the subitems below it.

Aside from organizing an outline for yourself, the ability to show and hide detail in this way is helpful in other situations, too. For example, you could type a list of vocabulary words and then add their definitions in a level below them and then test your knowledge of these words using the show/hide functionality, much like paper-based flash cards. It's a great way to study for any question-and-answer-based subject.

Another situation where this feature comes in handy is when you're speaking during a presentation and you need to stay on script. You can keep only the level headings shown to keep you on track overall, but you can also easily double-click any of the headings to remind you of important details that you might not remember in the moment. This is an easier way to quickly locate information than staring at the wall of text of an entire outline.

By the way, the simple outline example in the screenshots isn't meant to suggest that you must use a numbered list. You can use any available style of bullets and numbering or choose not to use them at all and only rely on multilevel indentation for your own outlines.

However you decide to make use of OneNote's useful outlining features, they're sure to help you stay organized and save time.

Collecting and Researching Information

Although it's perfectly all right to use Microsoft OneNote strictly as a note-taking tool, you'll be missing out if you do. That's because OneNote offers some really great features that let you use your electronic notebook as a living repository for all kinds of information that you collect over time and from various sources (see Figure 6.1).

No matter if you use OneNote at home, work, or school, think of a OneNote notebook as a limitless scrapbook in which you can collect, paste, and save everything that interests you. If you're not into the idea of scrapbooking, think of your electronic notebook as your virtual junk drawer—or a never-ending bookshelf—that can hold everything you'll eventually need to find again, no matter if the contents relate to each other or not. You don't have to keep things organized if you don't want to, and your notebook will neither run out of space nor take up a lot of it.

OneNote is also great when you're collecting information for specific research, no matter if you're looking to make travel plans, pricing a new purchase, or gathering facts for a work project or a school paper.

In this chapter, we'll take a closer look at some of the features that make it easy for you to supplement your own typed or handwritten notes with information from other sources—be it from computer files and documents, images and multimedia files, information from the Web, or scans and digital printouts. We'll also take a quick look at the built-in research tools that Microsoft has included with OneNote 2010.

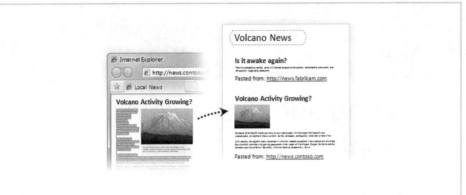

Figure 6.1   *It's easy to bring information into OneNote from other files and programs.*

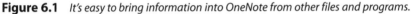

Meet the OneNote Screen Clipper and Launcher

Before getting started with examples of using OneNote 2010 for collecting information and doing research, I want to first take a moment to draw your attention to a small and often overlooked component of OneNote 2010—the OneNote Screen Clipper and Launcher, which unlocks additional functionality that can make using OneNote on your computer even more convenient.

The Screen Clipper and Launcher is a tiny program that loads itself when your computer starts up and stays in memory until you turn your computer off again. Keeping it enabled lets you:

- Launch the full OneNote 2010 program with a keyboard shortcut instead of hunting down and double-clicking its program icon.

- Create so-called "side notes," which are an electronic version of the yellow sticky notes that might be plastered all over your computer monitor right now.

- Use a hotkey to bypass the user interface for creating instant screen clippings.

- Record new audio clips in your notes without first having to start OneNote.

SHOW ME   Media 6.1—Using the OneNote Screen Clipper and Launcher
Access this video file through your registered Web Edition at my.safaribooksonline.com/9780132182447/media.

This small but useful program is often overlooked for two main reasons. For one, it's placed in the Windows Startup folder on your computer when OneNote 2010 is first installed (see Figure 6.2). Over the past few years, many computer users have gotten in the habit of clearing the contents of their Startup folder in an effort to save every last bit of available memory. I can understand this quite well. It seems that just about every other program that you install these days leaves a little icon near the clock display on the right side of the Windows taskbar. Most of these icons take up both space and memory without any real benefit. Up until the most recent versions of Windows, which hide these icons after a time, it wasn't uncommon for a typical computer user to see a cluttered row of some 10–20 icons on the Windows taskbar.

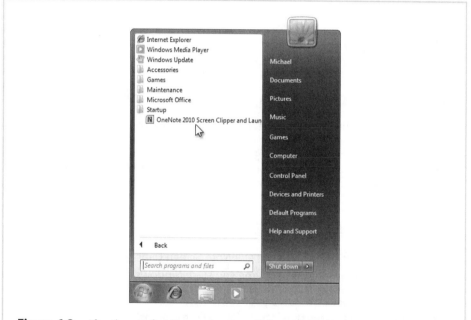

Figure 6.2   *After the very first time you've started Microsoft OneNote 2010 on your computer, the OneNote 2010 Screen Clipper and Launcher is placed into the Startup folder in Windows.*

Personally, I'm all for disabling any unnecessary apps and useless add-ins to help keep your computer running smoothly. However, I do recommend keeping the OneNote Screen Clipper and Launcher available, especially if you come to appreciate the functionality that it provides.

Another reason why the OneNote Screen Clipper and Launcher is often overlooked even when it's running is due to a design change in the way taskbar icons are displayed in the most recent versions of Windows, including Windows 7 and Windows Vista. To eliminate the clutter of icons that can accumulate over time as you install more and more programs, Windows eventually begins to hide the icons that install themselves in the notification area on the Windows taskbar.

Although I personally love this feature in Windows 7, it means that I must manually unhide any icons of the programs that actually offer some functionality by staying in the background, such as the OneNote Screen Clipper and Launcher.

Before you can enjoy the benefits of keeping the OneNote Screen Clipper and Launcher running in the background, take a moment to check whether it is loading properly on your computer and learn how to unhide its icon in the Windows taskbar notification area.

 LET ME TRY IT

Turning the Screen Clipper and Launcher On or Off

To check whether the OneNote Screen Clipper and Launcher is loading on startup, follow these steps:

1. Click the Windows Start button, click All Programs, and then click the Startup folder.

2. Look for a purple OneNote icon labeled OneNote 2010 Screen Clipper and Launcher (see Figure 6.2).

If the icon is there, it means that the OneNote Screen Clipper and Launcher program is loaded automatically each time you start Windows.

If you (or someone else who uses your computer) disabled the startup program for some reason, you can reenable it by following these steps:

1. In OneNote, click the File tab and then click Options.

2. In the Options dialog box that opens, click Display in the left column.

3. On the right side, select the check box that's labeled Place OneNote Icon in the Notification Area of the Taskbar.

4. Click OK to save changes.

On rare occasions, it's possible that the check box in the OneNote Options dialog box is properly shown as selected, but the OneNote Screen Clipper and Launcher isn't actually loading. This can happen if the program was manually terminated in the Windows Task Manager, either by you or someone else using your computer. In this case, you can easily restore the correct setting by following steps 1–4 in the previous procedure twice in a row—first deselecting the check box and clicking OK and then reselecting the check box and clicking OK.

If the Screen Clipper and Launcher icon was shown in your Startup folder and if the display check box in the OneNote Options dialog box is selected, but you can't see a small OneNote icon near the right side of your Windows taskbar, it means Windows has hidden it from view to avoid taskbar clutter.

Take a moment now to unhide the icon so you'll have easy access to the features that you'll learn about in the rest of this chapter.

 LET ME TRY IT

Keeping the Screen Clipper and Launcher Permanently Displayed

If you're running any edition of Windows 7, you can easily turn on and off the icons of any programs that are running in the background—including the OneNote Screen Clipper and Launcher.

Here's how:

1. On the Windows 7 taskbar, click the small, upward-facing arrow near the clock display in the lower-right corner of your screen. In the little pop-up menu that appears, you'll see a small version of the OneNote icon, plus any other icons of programs hidden from view.

2. Click Customize (see Figure 6.3).

3. In the Notification Area Icons dialog box that opens, scroll through the list and find the OneNote icon labeled as Microsoft OneNote Quick Launcher (merely an alternate, shorter name for the OneNote 2010 Screen Clipper and Launcher).

4. Click the drop-down menu next to the OneNote icon and then select Show icon and notifications (see Figure 6.4). The OneNote icon will now appear in the notification area. It is no longer hidden.

Figure 6.3 *Clicking the Customize link in the Show hidden icons menu opens the display options for your notification area icons.*

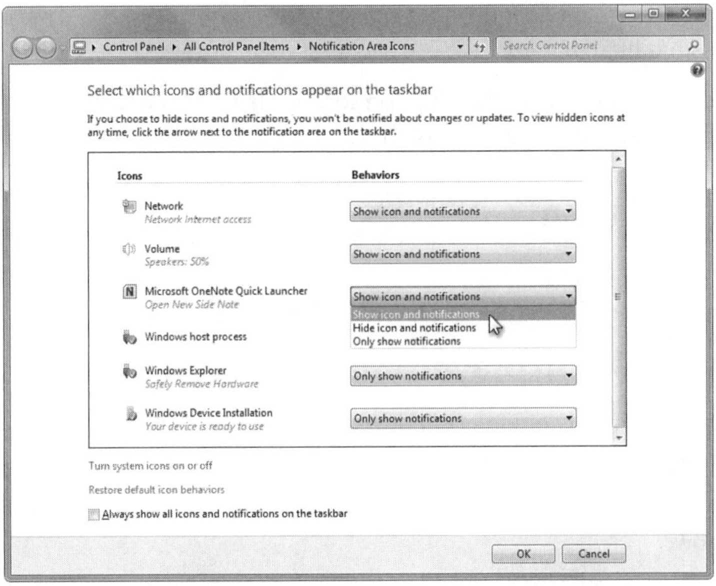

Figure 6.4 *Options in the Notification Area Icons window let you control which icons in the notification area on the Windows taskbar are shown or hidden from view.*

   5. Click OK to save your changes.

After you've followed these steps, the icon remains visible, and its functionality can be accessed by right-clicking it or by using the keyboard shortcuts shown on the right-click menu (see Figure 6.5).

If you're using Windows Vista, you can control the display of your notification icons in a similar way. Right-click the clock display in the lower-right corner of the taskbar and then click Customize Notification Icons. In the Customize

Notification Icons dialog box that opens, find the OneNote icon and then change its listed behavior from Hide to Show. Click OK to save your changes.

It's possible that Windows Vista may forget your display preferences for notification icons again after some time or after you install a new program on your computer. If that happens, set your display preference for the OneNote icon again. This issue is specific to Windows Vista only.

Happily, all editions of Windows 7 properly honor your icon display preferences after you've set them.

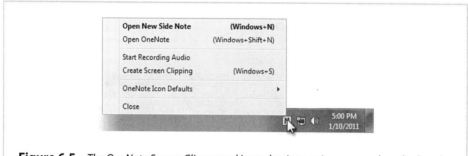

Figure 6.5   *The OneNote Screen Clipper and Launcher icon as it appears when displayed in the notification area of the Windows taskbar. When the icon is visible here, the keyboard shortcut combinations shown next to the commands provide instant access to those commands, even when OneNote 2010 isn't running.*

I'll talk more about the customization options for the OneNote Screen Clipper and Launcher in Chapter 12, "Customizing OneNote 2010." Now that you know how to run and display it, let's continue by learning how it helps you with your collection of information and research in OneNote.

Inserting Pictures and Screen Clippings

Admit it, one of the things that made your old paper notebook so appealing was the ability to gather a bunch of handouts, note scraps, scribbles, doodles, and printouts, toss them into your notebook, and then take it all with you. Sure, it was messy and unorganized, but at least you had that cozy feeling of having everything with you—even if it was going to be a time-consuming affair to leaf through it all and find anything again.

OneNote 2010 does it one better. It matches the ability of a paper binder to keep everything together and take it all with you, but it also lets you easily find everything again. With OneNote, you'll also never have to worry about one of the scraps of paper falling out of your notebook.

First things first, though: Take a closer look at the many ways in which you can collect and import all kinds of information into your OneNote notebook.

 **LET ME TRY IT**

Inserting a Picture from a File

Pictures can be placed inside of a notes container or as free-floating objects on any page in OneNote (see Figure 6.6).

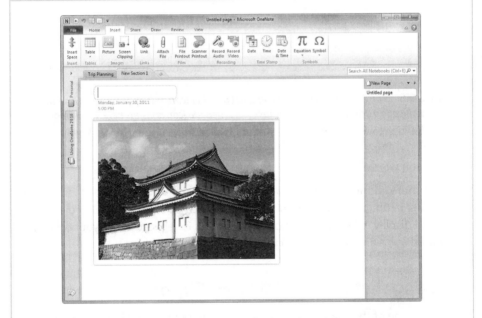

Figure 6.6   *A digital image file, as it appears after being inserted onto a notes page.*

A picture can be any image file that your computer supports, such as a photo that you've taken with your digital camera, a stock photograph that you've purchased on a website, a piece of clip art that you've downloaded, or a screenshot that you've captured with your computer.

SHOW ME   Media 6.2—Inserting Pictures into Notes
Access this video file through your registered Web Edition at
my.safaribooksonline.com/9780132182447/media.

LET ME TRY IT

Inserting Pictures into Notes

Although you can simply copy an image from somewhere on your computer and then paste it into OneNote, properly inserting the actual picture file may produce higher-quality results, especially with pictures that contain text or other kinds of information.

To insert a picture into your notes, follow these steps:

1. Open or create the page in your notebook where you want to insert a picture.

2. Click the place on the page where OneNote should place the imported picture. A blinking cursor will confirm where the picture will be placed.

3. On the Insert tab, in the Images group, click Picture.

4. In the Insert Picture dialog box that opens, navigate to the folder on your computer where the picture file is stored.

5. Click to select the picture you want to insert and then click Insert.

OneNote 2010 lets you import a large variety of image file types, including the following:

- Joint Photographic Expert Group (.jpg, .jpg, .jpe, .jfif)

- Portable Network Graphics (.png)

- Graphics Interchange Format (.gif)

- Tagged Image File Format (.tif, .tiff)

- Encapsulated PostScript (.eps)

- Windows Bitmap (.bmp, .dib, .rle)

- Windows Metafile (.wmf)

- Windows Enhanced Metafile (.emf)

- Compressed Windows Enhanced Metafile (.wmz)

- Macintosh PICT (.pct, .pict)

- Compressed Macintosh PICT (.pcz)

- Computer Graphics Metafile (.cgm)

- WordPerfect Graphics (.wpg)

To import a picture from a web page, use the same steps as given previously, except in step 4, type or paste the full URL of the image at its web location into the File name box and then click Open.

 LET ME TRY IT

Inserting a Picture from a Scanner

If you have a scanner, it's easy to import pictures that you don't already have in a digital format. This is not only a convenient way of importing old photographs, but for scanning business cards, receipts, sketches, napkin scribbles, and diagrams as well.

To import pictures that you don't already have in digital format, follow these steps:

1. Open or create the page in your notebook where you want to insert the scanned picture.

2. Click the place on the page where OneNote should place the imported picture. A blinking cursor will confirm where the picture will be placed.

3. On the Insert tab, in the Files group, click Scanner Printout (see Figure 6.7).

Figure 6.7 *If you have a scanner connected to your computer, you can use the Scanner Printout command on the OneNote ribbon to scan pictures and documents right into OneNote.*

4. In the Insert Picture from Scanner or Camera dialog box, make sure the make and model of the scanner you're using is selected as the active device (see Figure 6.8).

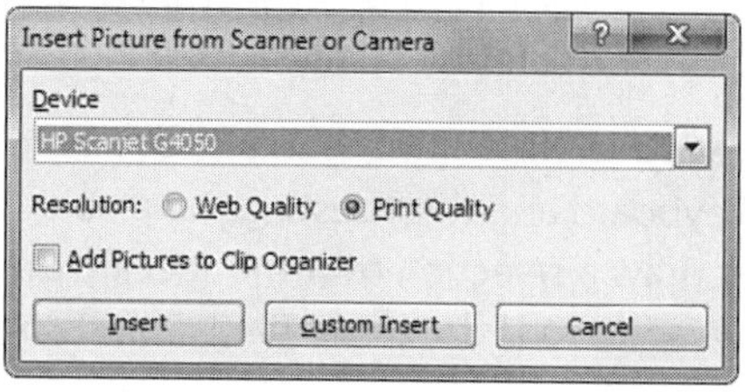

Figure 6.8   *After you click the Scanner Printout button in OneNote, options for the make and model of your scanner might appear, such as choosing a quality setting for the scan.*

5. Choose from the available resolution settings by clicking either Web Quality (if you're only going to be looking at the scanned image on your screen) or Print Quality (if you plan to print the notes containing the scanned image).

6. Click Insert.

Depending on the make and model of your own scanner, you might see a slightly different user interface after you click the Scanner Printout button, but the results should be the same. As long as your scanner is properly configured and you can successfully scan images with it in other Windows programs, it should work perfectly fine in OneNote, too.

If you're having trouble scanning, please refer to the documentation that came with your scanner and make sure you download the latest drivers for it from the manufacturer's website.

If you want to save an image that you've scanned into OneNote to your hard drive, either for archiving purposes or to use it in other programs, you can do so by right-clicking the scanned image in OneNote and then clicking the Save As command on the shortcut menu.

Note that this is not necessary if you want to keep all of your scans in OneNote. Inserted and scanned images that appear on your notes pages in OneNote have already been saved automatically as part of your notebook.

LET ME TRY IT

Inserting a Screen Clipping on the Current Page

OneNote includes a super-easy way to take a picture of anything on your computer screen and place it into your notes.

Although you can already do this for the whole screen by pressing the PrtScn (print screen) key on your keyboard and then pasting the result where you want it, OneNote lets you first draw a selection over the specific part of your screen that you want to capture. A so-called "screen clipping" then is placed into your notes.

 SHOW ME Media 6.3—Creating Screen Clippings
Access this video file through your registered Web Edition at
my.safaribooksonline.com/9780132182447/media.

To create a screen clipping, do the following:

1. On your computer screen, bring into view whatever it is that you want to capture. For example, open a particular page on a website in your browser.

2. In OneNote, navigate to the page where you want to insert the screen clipping and then click on the page where you want it to appear.

3. On the Insert tab, in the Images group, click Screen Clipping.

4. OneNote hides itself and brings back into view what you had on your screen before. The screen dims and the cursor changes to a crosshair symbol, prompting you to select the part of the screen you want to capture.

Move the mouse to the upper-left corner of the area you want to capture, click and hold the left mouse button, and then drag a rectangular selection over the screen until everything you want to include in the screen clipping is selected (see Figure 6.9).

5. When your selection is complete, release the mouse button. OneNote restores itself and places your screen clipping on the current page where you had activated the cursor.

Figure 6.9   *When you initiate a screen clipping, OneNote hides itself and dims the screen of what you were looking at before. You can click and drag a selection with your mouse to capture that portion of the screen as an image, which is then inserted into your notes.*

After a screen clipping is inserted into your notes, the image is still available on the Windows Clipboard, which means you can paste it anywhere else you might want to keep it—such as a Microsoft Word document or a Microsoft PowerPoint presentation. You don't need to paste it elsewhere, of course; you can always copy it from your OneNote page again later.

If you make a mistake and grab too much (or too little) of the screen, delete the screen clipping and simply take another. You can remove screen clippings that you no longer want by clicking the image and then pressing the Delete key to delete it.

Screen clippings are ideal for quickly capturing and importing all kinds of information that you just want to capture and don't need to edit again. For example, if you're doing research for a trip and you want to compare the cost of airfare between several airlines, you could take screen clippings of the fare tables and compare them side by side in OneNote. As such information is sure to change quickly at the source, your screen clippings can provide a lasting record of such information.

Screen clippings are also great for taking screenshots of software for which you're providing training materials. If you're a blogger, you can use screen clippings to create illustrations for your blog posts. If you use OneNote to maintain information related to your hobbies, such as gardening or keeping an inventory of a recipe or movie collection, you can clip photos of your flowers, recipes, or DVDs and import them into your notes to make them more visually interesting. In school, you can quickly grab your class schedules, lab info, study group agendas, and just about anything else that appears on your school's website or digital handouts.

LET ME TRY IT

Inserting a Screen Clipping with Quick Filing

If you plan to import a whole bunch of information as screen clippings and you don't want to always first go to the place in your notes where the images should be placed, you can use an alternate way of inserting them.

Instead of placing each screen clipping image at the location of your cursor on the page, OneNote will prompt you with its quick filing dialog box, in which you can select the specific page to which the current screen clipping will be sent.

To insert a screen clipping using the quick filing dialog box, follow these steps:

1. On your computer screen, bring into view whatever it is that you want to capture. For example, open a particular page on a website in your browser.

2. At the far right of the Windows taskbar, right-click the small OneNote icon in the notification area—the Screen Clipper and Launcher that you learned about earlier in this chapter—and then click Create Screen Clipping (see Figure 6.10). For the same result, you can also hold down the Windows key on your keyboard and then press S.

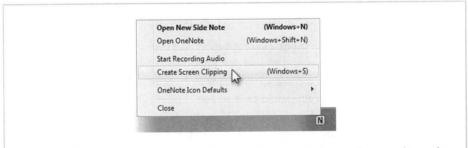

Figure 6.10 *By initiating a screen clipping from the OneNote Screen Clipper and Launcher icon on the Windows taskbar, you can decide where the screen clipping should be placed after it has been created. Using the icon also means you don't always first have to switch to OneNote to initiate a new screen clipping.*

3. The screen dims and the cursor changes to a crosshair symbol, prompting you to select the part of the screen you want to capture. Move the mouse

to the upper-left corner of the area you want to capture, click and hold the left mouse button, and then drag a rectangular selection over the screen until everything you want to include in the screen clipping is selected.

4. When your selection is complete, release the mouse button. Unlike what happened with the Insert Screen Clipping command in the previous procedure, OneNote now displays the Select Location in OneNote dialog box, which is also known as the quick filing feature.

5. In the list, click the notebook section where you want the screen clipping to appear, and then click Send to Selected Location (see Figure 6.11).

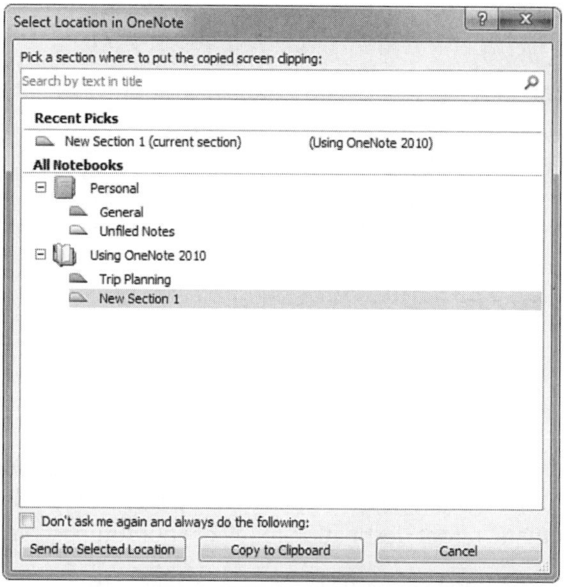

Figure 6.11   *This quick filing dialog box appears after you initiate a screen clipping from the OneNote Screen Clipper and Launcher icon. It lets you choose a destination for the screen clipping you've just taken.*

This method is easier for collecting multiple screen clippings because you don't have to first decide where on a specific page in a specific notebook you want each screen clipping to go. Another benefit of using this method is that you can do it anytime you see something on your screen that you want to capture, without first switching over to OneNote.

Using the quick filing method, OneNote will automatically create a fresh, new page for each screen clipping you take and place it in the section that you've selected. You can later consolidate or discard specific screen clippings, after you've had time to review them all and move the ones you want to keep to specific sections in your notebooks. You'll learn more about moving pages and sections in your notebooks in Chapter 7, "Organizing and Searching Notes."

If you don't want to use the quick filing feature for screen clippings, you can copy a screen clipping to the Windows Clipboard. In step 5 of the previous procedure, try using the Copy to Clipboard button at the bottom of the Select Location in OneNote dialog box after you've taken a screen clipping. After you've clicked this button, press the Ctrl+V (Paste) keyboard shortcut to manually paste the screen clipping wherever you want it—on a page in OneNote, into a Word document or an e-mail message, or wherever else you want it.

Whether you quick file your screen clippings or copy and paste them, either of these methods makes collecting information with multiple screenshots much faster than clicking the Screen Clipping command on the Insert tab of the ribbon each and every time.

 LET ME TRY IT

Collecting All Future Screen Clippings in One Place

If you want to make the process of collecting multiple screen clippings a complete no-brainer, consider creating a special section in your main notebook that you'll use as the automatic target destination for all of your future screen clippings.

To collect multiple screen clippings in one place, follow these steps:

1. In your notebook, create a new section and name it "**My Screen Clippings**" (or a similarly meaningful description).

2. Bring into view what you want to capture, right-click the small OneNote icon in the notification area (or hold down the Windows key and press S), and then click Create Screen Clipping.

3. When the screen dims, drag a selection with the mouse to create your screen clipping.

4. In the Select Location in OneNote dialog box, find the "My Screen Clipping" section you created in step 1 and click it once to select it.

5. Just underneath the list of notebooks and sections, select the check box labeled Don't Ask Me Again and Always Do the Following (see Figure 6.12).

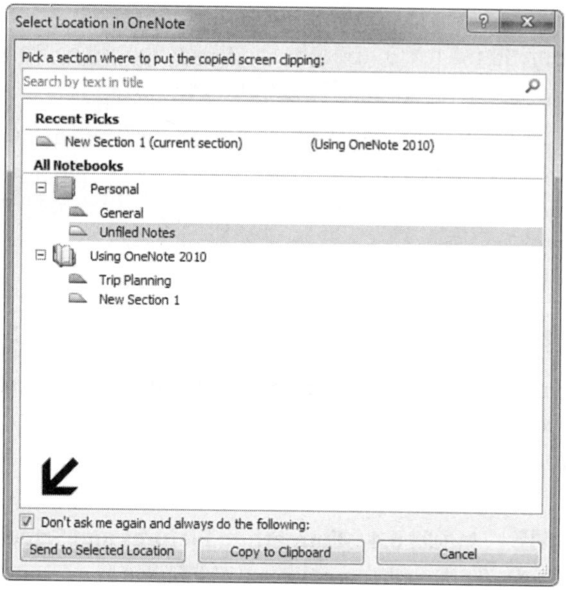

Figure 6.12   *Selecting the check box at the bottom of the quick filing dialog box will send all future screen clippings that you'll capture to the notebook section that you select here. It's a convenient way to have OneNote automatically gather all screen clippings in one place.*

6. Click Send to Selected Location.

OneNote creates a new page for your screen clipping in this section. In addition, because you checked the box that told it to stop asking for a destination the next time, all of your future screen clippings that you initiate from the OneNote icon in the Windows taskbar notification area or with the Windows key + S keyboard shortcut will be sent to this location automatically without you having to make a decision or selection each time you take a screen clipping.

This is the fastest way to take a bunch of screen clippings for collecting information and research and then review the "My Screen Clippings" section in your notebook later, where you can consolidate, delete, or move screen clippings to where you ultimately want them.

If you later decide you want the quick filing feature to prompt you again about where you want each screen clipping to be saved, you can restore the appearance of the Select Location in OneNote dialog box. Click the File tab and then click Options. In the OneNote Options dialog box that opens, click the Send to OneNote category in the list on the left, and then change the Screen clippings option to Always ask where to send. Click OK to save your preference.

This procedure will restore the quick filing dialog box after each screen clipping that you initiate with the OneNote icon in the Windows taskbar notification area or with the Windows key + S keyboard shortcut.

Formatting Pictures and Screen Clippings

Now that you've learned all about importing pictures, scanned images, and screen clippings into your notes, it's time to learn how to make them appear in your notes the way that you want.

 SHOW ME   Media 6.4—Formatting Pictures and Screen Clippings
Access this video file through your registered Web Edition at
my.safaribooksonline.com/9780132182447/media.

 LET ME TRY IT

Resizing or Scaling a Picture

Whether you insert a picture from an image file, by using your scanner, or by creating a screen clipping, you can modify its dimensions by resizing or scaling the picture.

Resizing lets you shrink or enlarge the appearance of pictures that contain text or small details that you want to preserve even at a smaller size in your notes.

Scaling can be used for making pictures appear taller or wider so they fit into your notes. Scaling usually distorts the original image, so it works best with pictures containing sketches or drawings, instead of photographs or screen clippings.

To resize a picture on a page without abnormally stretching or squeezing its appearance, do the following:

1. Click the picture you want to resize. Eight dots (called "handles") appear around the picture selection (see Figure 6.13).

Figure 6.13 *The eight dots that appear around a picture when you click to select it are selection handles. You can click and drag some of them to manipulate the selected image in different ways.*

2. Click the round, dot-shaped handle in the lower-right corner of the selected picture and then drag the handle to the left or to the right to make the picture smaller or larger. Release the mouse button when the picture is the size you want.

To scale an image horizontally or vertically, do the following:

1. Click the picture you want to scale. Eight dots appear around the picture selection.

2. To scale the image horizontally, click the small, square-shaped handle in the middle of the picture's right border and then drag the handle to the left or right.

3. To scale the image vertically, click the small, square-shaped handle in the middle of the picture's bottom border and then drag the handle up or down.

If you make a mistake, especially when scaling a picture's dimensions (which can cause the image to appear distorted), remember that you can use the Undo command on the Quick Access Toolbar (or by pressing the Ctrl+Z keyboard shortcut) at any time to undo the damage and then try again.

If a picture is pasted outside of a notes container, you can resize or scale the picture with more precision by using the arrow keys on your keyboard instead of dragging with the mouse.

To resize or scale a picture with more precision, follow these steps:

1. Make sure the inserted picture is not inside of a notes container. If it is, click to select the picture, press Ctrl+X to cut it, click the page anywhere outside of the notes container, and then press Ctrl+V. When you reselect the picture now, you should only see the eight selection handles around its border, not the gray notes container.

2. Click to select the picture, right-click it, and then click Resize on the short-cut menu. (If the Resize command is not available on the menu, the pic-ture is still inside of a notes container.)

3. When the handles around the image have disappeared, look for a white, four-headed arrow to appear over the middle of the selected picture. Use any of the four directional arrow keys on your keyboard to make the pic-ture as small or as large as you want. If you want to resize the picture pro-portionally without scaling it, you'll need to press the up or down arrow keys the same number of times as the right or left arrow keys.

4. If you distort the image too much, press the Esc key and try again. When the picture appears the way you want, press the Enter key to accept the new dimensions.

 LET ME TRY IT

Restoring a Modified Picture to Its Original Size

Changing the appearance of pictures in OneNote by resizing or scaling them does not actually modify the size of the picture file itself.

For example, if you size down an inserted photo to a very small size on your notes page, the original, underlying image file is still saved in its original file size and dimensions. This lets you restore any picture that you've modified in OneNote to its full, original glory at any time.

To restore a modified picture, follow these steps:

1. Right-click a modified (resized or scaled) picture on your notes page.

2. On the shortcut menu that appears, click Restore to Original Size.

If you don't want to restore an image on your notes page but want to save the original picture file to your hard drive, you can right-click the picture and then click Save As on the shortcut menu. When you open the saved picture file in Windows Photo Viewer or any other image viewer or editor, it will appear in its original size and appearance, not in the way it may have appeared in OneNote.

Preserving the original dimensions of picture files that you insert into your notes is just another way in which OneNote keeps all of your source information together in one place, while still giving you full control over how such items show up in your notes.

 LET ME TRY IT

Moving a Picture to Another Place on a Page

After you've inserted a picture into your notes, it's not stuck there. You can freely move it around on the page to the location you want.

To move a picture around on the page, follow these steps:

1. Click the picture you want to move.

2. Move the mouse pointer over the middle of the selected picture until the pointer changes to a white, four-headed arrow (see Figure 6.14).

Figure 6.14 *The white, four-headed arrow in the middle of a picture prompts you to move the picture in any direction on the page, either by clicking and dragging the mouse or by using the directional arrow keys on your keyboard.*

3. Click the left mouse button and then drag the image to its new location on the page.

4. Release the mouse button when the picture appears where you want it.

If a picture is pasted outside of a notes container, you can move it with more precision by using the directional arrow keys on your keyboard instead of dragging with the mouse.

To move a picture with more precision, follow these steps:

1. Make sure the inserted picture is not inside of a notes container. (If it is, see "Resizing or Scaling a Picture" earlier in this chapter.)

2. Click to select the picture, right-click it, and then click Move on the short-cut menu. (If the Move command is not available on the menu, the picture is still inside of a notes container.)

3. When the handles around the image have disappeared, look for a white, four-headed arrow to appear over the middle of the selected picture. Use any of the four directional arrow keys on your keyboard to move the picture to its new location on the page.

4. If your finger slips and you move the image too far off the page, press the Esc key and try again. When the picture appears where you want it, press the Enter key to accept the new location.

When moving objects such as pictures or screen clippings around on a page, you'll notice a slight hesitation every 12 pixels or so, as OneNote snaps the selected object to an invisible grid. This is a feature often found in page layout and web design programs to help a page author align multiple objects more easily. In the case of OneNote, it can be helpful to more precisely align multiple images with each other or to your notes' text. However, if you prefer not to use the Snap to Grid feature, you can override it by holding the Alt key on your keyboard whenever you drag an object around on the page with your mouse.

Note that this trick also works with notes containers, giving you full control over alignment of everything on your pages. If you don't like the Snap to Grid feature, you can add its command button to the ribbon for an easier way to turn it off. See Chapter 12 to learn how to do this.

 **LET ME TRY IT**

Rotating Pictures on a Page

Continuing in the vein of features borrowed from page layout programs like Microsoft Publisher and Adobe InDesign, OneNote also offers the ability to quickly rotate imported pictures and screen clippings.

This is most useful when importing scanned images or cell phone camera pictures that may appear sideways or upside down when first imported. A simple click of a button or two and you'll have it the way you want it.

To rotate a picture on the current page, do the following:

1. Click the picture you want to rotate.

2. On the ribbon, click the Draw tab and then, in the Edit group, click Rotate.

3. On the pop-up menu that appears, choose the rotation you want:

   - Click Rotate Right 90° to rotate the selected image clockwise by 90 degrees. Click this command up to three times to achieve the correct amount of rotation you want.

   - Click Rotate Left 90° to rotate the selected image counterclockwise by 90 degrees. Click this command up to three times to achieve the correct amount of rotation you want.

   - Click Flip Horizontal to create a horizontal mirror image of the selected picture.

   - Click Flip Vertical to create a vertical mirror image of the selected picture.

Each of the four rotation commands can be used in any combination with any of the other commands to achieve the result you want. For example, if an imported picture on your page is upside down and backward, you can click the Flip Vertical command and then the Flip Horizontal command to make the picture appear correctly. As always, you can press the Crtl+Z command once to undo the last action or multiple times to undo several of the last actions.

I should point out that OneNote 2010 does not offer the ability to freely rotate a selected image or object by any degree. If you need that kind of precision, it's best to import the original picture into an image-editing program like Adobe Photoshop and rotate it there. You can then save and import the result back into OneNote.

 **LET ME TRY IT**

Overlapping Multiple Images on a Page

Another useful page layout feature available in OneNote is the ability to control the layering of objects such as pictures and screen clippings.

This is most useful when you want to overlap multiple pictures to create a design on the page. You can also use this method to maximize page space by overlapping multiple images in such a way that only the parts you care about are shown.

The fancy term for the ordering of two-dimensional objects is "Z-order," which refers to the order of objects along the z-axis in coordinate geometry, where *x* typically refers to the horizontal axis and *y* to the vertical axis. When two or more objects overlap, their Z-order determines which object or layer appears on top of the other. For bitmap-type images, this means that the topmost layer covers up the ones below it. For image formats that can have a transparent background (such as GIF and PNG files), you can control the Z-order more creatively to create a composite picture or design from the layers of multiple, stacked pictures.

In OneNote, you can control the Z-order of page objects with the Arrange command, which works the same as in many popular page layout and web design programs. You can use this command to arrange multiple pictures that are different from each other or to arrange multiple copies of the same picture.

Ultimately, the usefulness and result of manipulating the Z-order in OneNote really depends on the specific objects (pictures, scanned images, screen clippings, or notes containers) that you will use on your own pages.

The following steps should give you an idea about how this works:

1. On the current page, insert two to three different pictures, scanned images, or screen clippings.

2. Click and drag the pictures you have just inserted and drag them together so they all slightly overlap (see Figure 6.15).

3. Click to select the picture that's farthest underneath the other two.

4. On the ribbon, on the Draw tab, in the Edit group, click Arrange.

5. On the pop-up menu that appears, rest the mouse pointer over the available commands to read the ToolTip descriptions that appear. You can choose from four commands:

    - Clicking the Bring Forward command promotes the selected picture or notes container to one layer higher than the current one. You can click this command multiple times, if necessary.

    - Clicking the Bring to Front command promotes the selected picture or notes container to the highest possible layer, covering up all other layers beneath it.

    - Clicking the Send Backward command demotes the selected picture or notes container to one layer lower than the current one. You can click this command multiple times, if necessary.

    - Clicking the Send to Back command demotes the selected picture or notes container to the lowest possible layer, hiding it behind all other layers that appear in front of it.

Figure 6.15   *When you combine several pictures so that they partially overlap on the page, you can select a particular picture and then change its Z-order to make the selected picture appear in front of or behind the other pictures.*

To conclude this procedure, you could click the Bring to Front command to make the picture you selected in step 3 appear in front of the other two.

It might take some practice for you to learn how to control the Z-order of multiple objects on a page, so practice this on your own for a bit using different types of pictures (for example, some that have a transparent background) and using a mix of notes containers and pictures.

One trick to mastering the arrangement of overlapping objects on a page is to be mindful of both the order in which to select items as well as for which items to change the ordering. If you're creating a design with overlapping objects and images, think of the layers you're controlling the same way as you might think of setting up multiple backdrops on a theater stage. By having the order of objects clearly in your mind, you can better differentiate between using the two extreme commands—Bring to Front and Send to Back—as well as the more incremental commands—Bring Forward and Send Backward—which nudge the ordering of the selected item forward and backward by just one layer.

Practice makes perfect and, as you've learned, the beauty of OneNote is that you won't waste any paper while attempting to master your techniques.

Before moving on, I want to mention a feature that many OneNote users have asked about because they can't seem to find it when they work with pictures in OneNote. It's the Crop command, which lets you cut off the edges of an inserted picture to strip away the parts of an image that you don't care about. Although cropping is available in most image-editing programs and some of the other Microsoft Office 2010 products, such as Word, PowerPoint, and Publisher, it's not available in OneNote 2010.

If you want to crop your images in OneNote, there's a workaround that I use that gets the same result. After inserting a picture on your page, hold the Windows key and then press S to start a new screen clipping. When the screen dims, drag with the mouse over the inserted image to select only the part of the image that you want to keep. When the Select Location in OneNote dialog box appears, click Copy to Clipboard and then use Ctrl+V to paste the screen clipping on your page. You can then delete the original picture you inserted. It's a quick-and-dirty workaround, but I find that it does the trick on most occasions.

 LET ME TRY IT

Copying Text from Pictures

After you begin to routinely insert screen clippings from web pages and your documents into your notes pages in OneNote, there will undoubtedly be times when you'll wish that you could occasionally edit the text in a screen clipping. Well, there's good news.

OneNote 2010 includes a fantastic feature called Optical Character Recognition (OCR). This is a fancy technical name for your computer's ability to electronically recognize and translate words in images and convert those words to editable text. OCR software is most commonly included with scanners, so that you can create text files from the documents you scan. Although you can certainly make your scanner do the work, the built-in OCR feature in OneNote lets you quickly extract text from your inserted images whenever you want to use the text within them.

To copy text from a picture, follow these steps:

1. Insert a picture, scanned image, or screen clipping that contains the text you want to copy. For example, you could insert a picture of a scanned business card or a screen clipping of a paragraph of text on a web page.

2. Right-click the picture and then click Copy Text from Picture (see Figure 6.16).

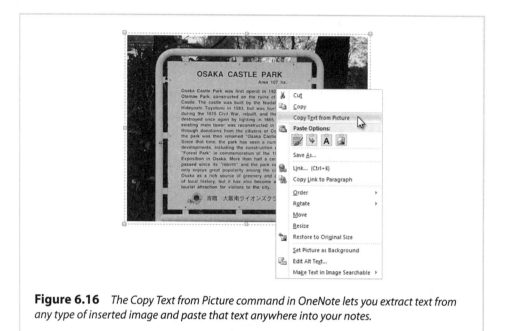

Figure 6.16 *The Copy Text from Picture command in OneNote lets you extract text from any type of inserted image and paste that text anywhere into your notes.*

3. Click anywhere else on the page where you want to paste the copied text, and then press Ctrl+V.

The quality of text recognition depends greatly on the quality and legibility of the picture containing the text. In most cases, handwriting or highly stylized or script-like fonts won't yield very good results.

If the text recognition produces just a few errors, you can quickly type the necessary corrections in place. This is infinitely faster and easier than retyping the entire original text yourself. Either way, the OCR feature in OneNote is sure to save you at least a little time.

 **LET ME TRY IT**

Entering Alternative Text for an Image

If you plan to publish any of your notes containing pictures as a web page, you can improve the reading experience for the visually impaired by describing each picture with a short sentence or phrase. In web browsers, this is called alternative text (or "alt text" for short).

To enter or change the alternative text for any picture in OneNote, do the following:

1. Right-click the picture you want to describe with alternative text.

2. On the shortcut menu that appears, click Edit Alt Text.

3. In the Picture Alternative Text dialog box that opens, enter a short, descriptive phrase for the selected image, and then click OK.

If you now save the current page as a web page (click File, Save As, Page, Single File Web Page, and then click OK), and you open the file in a web browser, the alternative text that you entered for the picture will appear as a ToolTip when you move the mouse pointer over that picture (see Figure 6.17).

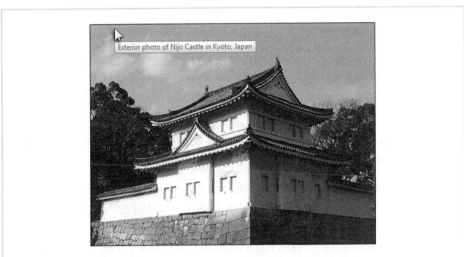

Figure 6.17   *When you specify alternative text for an inserted picture in OneNote and you then save the notes page as a web page, the alt text will appear in a ToolTip whenever the mouse pointer is moved over the image.*

Keep in mind that this feature is intended for visually impaired or blind people, so choosing meaningful alt text is very important. The user's computer will read standard text to them out loud with the speech capabilities built in to Microsoft Windows, but pictures can only be described by having the computer read the alt text out loud. The more specific you are when creating this descriptive text, the more helpful it will be.

For example, if your page contains a picture of a company logo that shows a red rose, you might describe the image as "the Rose Company logo" instead of

"Company logo" (What company?) or "This is a flower" (Why is it there? What does it have to do with the notes here?). Give your picture descriptions as much context as possible for people who'll depend on those descriptions.

In OneNote, entering alt text for pictures is optional. That's because most people won't publish their notes as HMTL web pages. Unless you decide to share your notes in this way, you probably don't need to bother with alt text.

 **LET ME TRY IT**

Setting a Picture as the Page Background

After a picture appears on your page the way you want it to, you have the option of leaving it in place on your notes page or merging it with the background of the page. This is slightly different than the Z-ordering that you learned about earlier in this chapter. When you set a selected picture as the background image, it becomes part of the page on which your notes appear.

Setting a picture as your page background has several uses. For one, you can use a decorative photo or piece of clip art to function much like a stationery design does for writing paper. This is how many OneNote templates are given a decorative background—you place a picture of a nice, subtle design into the upper-left corner of your page and then set that image as the background so that any typed and handwritten notes appear over it (see Figure 6.18).

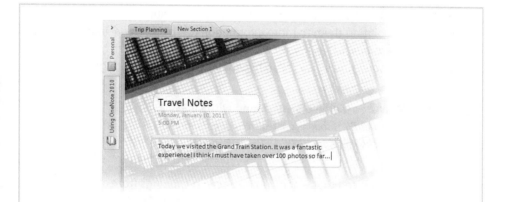

Figure 6.18 *A typical decorative stationery design in a OneNote template. Because the picture is set as the background, the person using this template can't accidentally mess it up. They can freely type their notes over the picture.*

Another benefit of setting a picture as the page background is to protect it from accidentally being selected, moved, resized, or scaled. A background picture can't be selected again until you right-click it and then turn off the Set Picture as Background option.

To set a picture as your page background, do the following:

1. On your notes page, position the picture that you want to set as your background image where you want it to appear.

2. Right-click the picture and then click Set Picture as Background.

When a picture is set as the background, you can no longer interact with it as you can with regular pictures on your page. If you need to select a background picture again, either to modify, reposition, or delete it, right-click the background image where it isn't covered with a notes container or another object and then click the selected Set Picture as Background option. When the picture has been removed from the background, its eight selection handles reappear to indicate that you can interact with the picture.

Working with Links

If you're using OneNote to take notes just for yourself, an important part of collecting information and doing research is to keep track of where important information came from, in case you later want or need to return to its source.

If you're using OneNote to also share your notes, information, and research with other people, pointing them to more information (or to additional information that relates to it) becomes just as important. In this section, you'll learn how to create and use links—sometimes also called hyperlinks—to achieve both goals.

 SHOW ME   Media 6.5—Working with Links
Access this video file through your registered Web Edition at
my.safaribooksonline.com/9780132182447/media.

You might have noticed that when you take screen clippings from a web page by using the Insert Screen Clipping command on the ribbon, OneNote automatically inserts into your notes a link back to the source page where the screen clipping was taken (see Figure 6.19).

Automatic source links make it easy for you to revisit the origins of an imported selection of text, a picture, or a screen clipping again in the future—for example,

> In publishing and graphic design, **lorem ipsum**[p][1][2] is placeholder text
> (filler text) commonly used to demonstrate the graphic elements of a
> document or visual presentation, such as font, typography, and layout. The
> lorem ipsum text is typically a section of a Latin text by Cicero with words
> altered, added and removed that make it nonsensical in meaning and not
> proper Latin.[1][2] A close English translation of the words *lorem ipsum* might
> be "pain itself" (**dolorem** = pain, grief, misery, suffering; **ipsum** = itself).
>
> Lorem ipsum - Wikipedia, the free encyclopedia
> http://en.wikipedia.org/wiki/Lorem_ipsum
> Screen clipping taken: 1/10/2011

Figure 6.19 *When you paste or import something from another source, such as a website, OneNote automatically includes a hyperlink back to that source so you can go back to it at a later time. If you don't want to keep the link, you can delete it.*

when you want to check whether the original information has been updated or supplemented since you captured it.

Such automatically created links are easy enough to deal with: You can keep and click them when you want or need to, you can ignore them, or you can delete them when they're no longer needed.

Now it's time to learn how you can create and modify your own links from the text and pictures that make up your notes.

 LET ME TRY IT

Creating a Link from Typed Text

While typing notes on a page in your notebook, you can quickly and easily have OneNote create a hyperlink by including certain parts of a link URL (short for uniform resource locator, better known as a web address that you type into a web browser).

To create a link from typed text, follow these steps:

1. Click anywhere on the page and begin typing the following sentence, followed by a space: **For more information, visit**

2. After the space, type **www.office.com**. As soon as you typed the prefix for World Wide Web, OneNote converted the text to an underlined blue style, which is a universal indicator for clickable text (also called hypertext, which is where the official term hyperlink got its name).

3. When you now move the mouse pointer over the blue underlined text of the web address, the pointer changes to a hand icon, indicating you're hovering over a clickable link (see Figure 6.20). If you click the text, OneNote will launch your web browser and open the web page that the link points to.

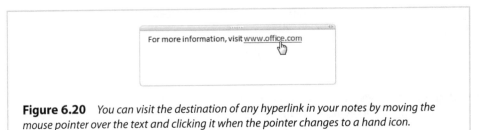

For more information, visit www.office.com

Figure 6.20   *You can visit the destination of any hyperlink in your notes by moving the mouse pointer over the text and clicking it when the pointer changes to a hand icon.*

The link prefix "www" (for World Wide Web) is a now widely accepted short form for a full hyperlink URL, which OneNote also recognizes. For example, you could have typed out the long form of the web address (in this case, http://www. office.com) and OneNote would create the same clickable link to the Microsoft Office home page on the Internet.

OneNote recognizes other prefixes as well, such as the "mailto:" prefix for creating clickable links that open an e-mail form (for example, mailto: someone@microsoft.com) and the "ftp." prefix for pointing to an FTP file exchange server (for example, ftp.microsoft.com).

For links that you want to create which OneNote does not automatically recognize, you can create links from typed text that you select. Proceed to the next procedure to learn how.

 **LET ME TRY IT**

Creating a Link from Selected Text

To manually create links from text in your notes, you can use OneNote's Link command. Follow these steps:

1. In your notes, select the text from which you want to create a link. If the link will be from a single word, double-click the word to select it. To select multiple words (for example, "Microsoft Office"), click and drag a selection with the mouse over the words you want to format as a link.

2. When the text you want is selected, click the Insert tab on the ribbon.

3. In the Links group, click Link.

4. In the Link dialog box, type the full website URL (for example, **http://www.office.com**) into the Address box and then click OK.

Unlike an automatic hyperlink, which exposes the web address right in the text, links manually created from actual notes text won't reveal their destination unless you move the mouse pointer over the link to reveal its URL in a ToolTip that appears (see Figure 6.21).

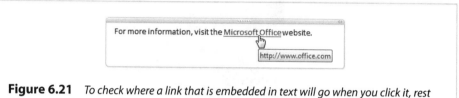

Figure 6.21   *To check where a link that is embedded in text will go when you click it, rest the mouse pointer over the text until a ToolTip with the web address appears.*

In most cases, links embedded in actual notes text are more useful because such links have immediate context and make your notes more readable than if a bunch of geeky URLs appear littered throughout your notes. This might not be an issue for you personally, but it's something to consider when you share your notes with other people.

 LET ME TRY IT

Creating a Link from a Picture

Quite similar to making text clickable, you can also format a picture, a scanned image, or a screen clipping to contain a link that points to a website.

To create a link from a picture, follow these steps:

1. In your notes, click an inserted picture from which you want to create a link.

2. On the ribbon, click the Insert tab.

3. In the Links group, click Link.

4. In the Link dialog box, type the full website URL (for example, **http://www.onenote.com**) into the Address box and then click OK.

Although linked text will tip you off about its clickability by changing to a blue and underlined type style, linked pictures do not show any obvious sign of containing a link.

However, when you move the mouse pointer over a picture that contains a link, a ToolTip appears, showing you the destination of the link (see Figure 6.22).

Figure 6.22   *To check where a link that is embedded in a picture will go when you click it, rest the mouse pointer over the picture until a ToolTip with the web address appears.*

Just below the web address in the ToolTip, you'll also see the instruction to hold the Ctrl button if you want to click and follow the link from the picture. This intentional link activation isn't meant to make life more difficult for you. It makes clicking a link from a picture a more deliberate action and it preserves the ability to easily select, format, and work with pictures that contain a link. Without this Ctrl key click confirmation, you could never again click to select a picture to format, move, or delete it without constantly opening its link in a web browser.

 **LET ME TRY IT**

Modifying a Link in Your Notes

If you want to update the web address that a link in your notes points to, you can easily edit it.

To modify a link in your notes, follow these steps:

   1. On the page, right-click the text or the picture that contains the link you want to modify.

2. On the shortcut menu that appears, click Edit Link.

3. In the Link dialog box that opens, the URL of the link is already selected for you in the Address box. Type over this address with the new or corrected link and then click OK.

For manually created links from a word or phrase of text that describes the link, or for links from pictures, you needn't do anything else to modify a link. However, if you used the previous steps to modify a text link that OneNote automatically created from a web address or URL that you typed, modifying the link in the dialog box will not change the clickable text you see in your notes.

For example, if the link you edited originally appeared in your notes as *www. microsoft.com* in a blue, underlined style, and you then change the Address field in the Link dialog box to *www.adobe.com*, the link will now point to the Adobe website but the displayed text will continue to appear as *www.microsoft.com*, as before. To avoid this, make sure that you also change the Text to display field in the Link dialog box right above the Address field whenever you're changing the existing URL of a link.

As a general rule, you should always manually test every link that you create, especially if you eventually plan to electronically share any part of your notes with other people.

 LET ME TRY IT

Removing a Link from Your Notes

If you want to delete a link from notes text or from a picture in your notes, follow these steps:

1. Right-click the text or the picture that contains the link that you want to delete.

2. On the shortcut menu that appears, click Remove Link.

If you accidentally remove a link that you wanted to keep, remember the Undo command on the Quick Access Toolbar (or press Ctrl+Z).

This covers the basics of creating and modifying links in OneNote 2010. Rest assured that OneNote has a few more tricks up its sleeve when it comes to intelligent linking. If you looked closely at the Link dialog box, some of that functionality was already foreshadowed. However, those advanced features fall more under the subject of notebook organization, which you'll learn about in Chapter 7.

For now, let's get back to the main topic of this chapter and learn how you can import existing content from your other files into your notes.

Inserting Documents and Files

As I often say, one of my favorite features in OneNote 2010 is the ability to drop virtually any content into my notebook and keep it there, along with everything else that relates to a particular project or subject. I don't have to worry about file names, file versions, accidentally overwriting newer information with old, or any of the usual housekeeping issues that come with manually managing files and folders on my hard drive. You've already seen how easy it is to collect information from text and pictures on websites, but what about information that exists in the files and documents that you use every day?

With its tight integration with Microsoft Office and Windows, OneNote 2010 can intelligently work with all of your computer files in a variety of ways. You can attach documents, spreadsheets, presentations, and other files much in the same way you would attach them to an e-mail message. You can also virtually "print out" your files in such a way that they appear visually in your notes—much like printouts appear on paper—allowing you to annotate their content by typing, writing, or drawing over it.

The combination of OneNote's sophisticated file import and management features gives you a whole new level of paperless reviewing and editing possibilities that doesn't quite exist in any of the other Office applications.

 SHOW ME   Media 6.6—Inserting Documents and Files into Notes
Access this video file through your registered Web Edition at
my.safaribooksonline.com/9780132182447/media.

 LET ME TRY IT

Inserting a Copy of a File on a Page

The easiest way to keep existing content from a computer file together with your notes is to insert a copy of the file on a page in your notebook.

To insert a copy of a file on a page, follow these steps:

1. If necessary, navigate to the page where you want to insert a copy of one of your computer files, such as a Word document, an Excel spreadsheet, a PowerPoint presentation, and so on.

2. On the ribbon, click the Insert tab.

3. In the Files group, click Attach File.

4. In the dialog box that opens, navigate to the folder where the file you want is located and then select one or more files that you want to insert into your notes. To select a single file, click it once. To select multiple files in a list, hold the Ctrl key while single-clicking one file after another.

5. Click Insert to import the selected file or files.

OneNote can insert any file that Windows understands. When you insert a file from your computer or a file server into OneNote, the original file still exists in its original location. OneNote merely makes a copy of the file and then stores that copy as part of your OneNote notebook.

It's important to understand that there is no magical link between any file on your computer that you then import into OneNote. Attaching a file in OneNote makes a copy of the original file, leaving you with two independent copies of the same file.

If you update the original file on your computer, the copy that you imported into OneNote is never automatically updated. Likewise, if you open and edit the copy of the file in OneNote, the original version of the file on your computer remains as it was before.

Importing copies of documents to keep them handy for reading and referring to is probably the easiest use for imported files, and one that doesn't require much thought. However, for any files you're still actively working on, or files that you actively share and revise together with others, you'll need to decide which version of the file is considered your master document. For example, you could consider the original file on your hard drive or network server to be the master file and the copy you insert into OneNote as your backup of that file.

In Chapter 9, "Sharing Notes with Other People," you'll learn about sharing your notes with others, so you can collaborate and edit notes together with other people in real time. In such circumstances, it might make more sense for you to keep all of your "living documents" right in OneNote. Until such time, however, be sure that you have it clear in your mind where various versions of your documents are located and where you consider their originals to be.

When you attach a document or file to a page in your notebook, its icon appears where you placed the copy of the file. These document and file icons work much the same way as they do in Windows. To open an attached file from within OneNote, double-click its icon and the content of the file will be opened in the program with which that file is associated (see Figure 6.23).

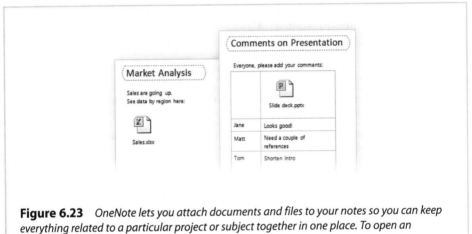

Figure 6.23 *OneNote lets you attach documents and files to your notes so you can keep everything related to a particular project or subject together in one place. To open an attached file from within OneNote, double-click its icon.*

For example, if you installed OneNote 2010 on your computer as part of a Microsoft Office 2010 suite, documents and rich text files will typically open in Microsoft Word, spreadsheets and workbooks will open in Microsoft Excel, slide decks and presentations will open in Microsoft PowerPoint, and so on.

Other, non-Office file types will work similarly. For example, Portable Document Format (PDF) files will open in Adobe Acrobat Reader, if you have it installed. In some cases, such as with image files, the result of double-clicking a file icon depends on which program is registered to handle such files on your computer.

For example, on a normal Windows installation, double-clicking a JPEG file will open in Windows Photo Viewer. However, if you have an image-editing program like Adobe Photoshop installed, it will open the file instead. If need be, you can edit these file associations in Windows to select certain programs to handle certain file types. OneNote will use whatever default file associations that Windows has registered.

When you double-click a file icon in OneNote to view the information it contains, you have the option of editing that version of the document or file. For example, if you double-click a text file you've inserted and it opens in Windows Notepad, you can modify the text while the file is open by typing new text or changing and deleting existing text. When you click Save, the copy of the file attached to your page in OneNote is modified. Because you work outside of OneNote whenever you do this, you cannot undo such changes.

Until you're sure you understand how the content of imported files is managed, be sure to keep backups of the original versions of your imported files or be sure to only open and view imported files without changing them.

 LET ME TRY IT

Inserting a File Printout on a Page

An alternate way to import content from a file on your computer into OneNote is to make it appear on your notes page like a printout on paper. This ensures that there's no confusion between an imported copy of a file and its original version on your hard drive, because the imported copy appears as a static image that cannot be edited.

Although this might seem limiting compared with importing an actual copy of a file, this option has two benefits. First, the layout and appearance of the original file is preserved perfectly, much like a PDF document would appear on your screen. Second, the images of the printout can be annotated with typed or handwritten text or with drawings, offering a much more flexible way to review and annotate content, especially when reviewing it together with other people.

To insert a file as a printout, follow these steps:

1. On your notes page, click to activate the cursor where you want the file printout to begin.

2. On the ribbon, click the Insert tab.

3. In the Files group, click File Printout.

4. In the Choose Document to Insert dialog box that opens, navigate to the folder containing the file you want to print to OneNote.

5. Click to select the file and then click OK. Depending on the size of the file and the processing speed of your computer, a progress indicator might briefly appear. When it reaches 100%, one or more static images resembling the

page (or pages) of your "printed" file appears on your notes page (see Figure 6.24).

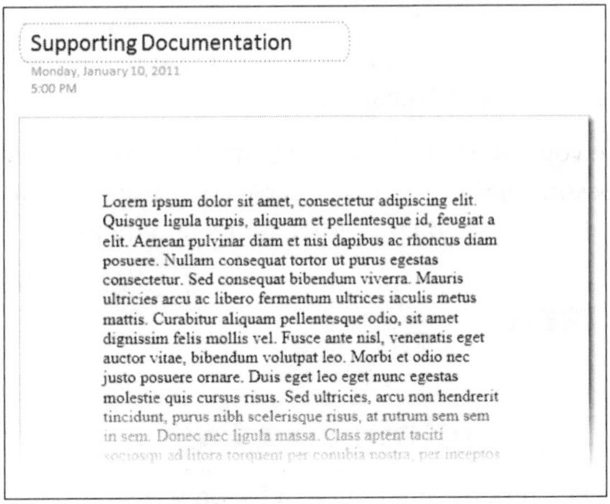

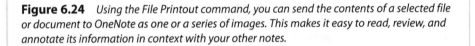

Figure 6.24   *Using the File Printout command, you can send the contents of a selected file or document to OneNote as one or a series of images. This makes it easy to read, review, and annotate its information in context with your other notes.*

If the terminology here is confusing you, let me be absolutely clear: A so-called "printout" of a file that you've inserted into your notes in OneNote never actually uses your printer in any way. It's just a figure of speech to explain how a computer file is sent to OneNote, where it appears as an inserted image, looking much the same way as the file would look had you actually printed it out on paper.

Because file printouts are very much like normal images on your page, you can apply to them all that you've learned in this chapter about controlling pictures. Each image in a file printout can be resized, scaled, moved, rotated, and ordered in layers—just like any other inserted pictures.

File printouts can be easily annotated by setting their images as the page background and then clicking over the image to create a notes container that holds your text annotations and other notes about the file's content. This is especially useful when reviewing visual content, such as the slides in a PowerPoint presentation deck.

When annotating file printouts with typed text, you can use the font formatting features that you've learned about earlier in this book to change your text to a different color whenever you want to provide more context for yourself or other reviewers (for example, you could use red text to annotate proposed changes that are still under review, and you could use green text for changes that have already been reviewed and agreed upon).

Another convenient imaging feature to remember for file printouts is the Copy Text from Picture command that's available whenever you right-click an inserted picture. In the case of file printouts, the images offer two slightly different commands on the right-click menu—one for copying text from just the selected image (or page) of the printout, and another for copying all text from all of the images (pages) in a file printout. Just like with regular images, this lets you copy the file's text and paste it into an editable annotation where you can then revise it with your proposed changes.

 **LET ME TRY IT**

Inserting a Scanner Printout on a Page

An alternate way to import existing content is to use your scanner. The same steps that you previously learned in this chapter for scanning pictures can be used to scan content from files that you've already printed out or to import information that exists only on paper.

Scanning paper-based documents into OneNote is also an effective way to preserve sole-surviving copies of important documents, such as purchase receipts, signed legal forms, or contracts. By scanning such documents into OneNote, you'll have an easier way of finding them again when you need them most, plus you'll never have to worry again about spilling a cup of coffee on them.

To insert a scanner printout on a page, follow these steps:

1. In OneNote, open or create the page in your notebook where you want to insert the scanned picture. For archiving scanned documents, you might want to create a separate page for each scan and then change its date stamp to match that of the scanned document.

2. On the page, click the location where OneNote should place the imported picture. A blinking cursor will confirm where the scanner printout will be placed.

3. On the Insert tab, in the Files group, click Scanner Printout.

4. In the Insert Picture from Scanner or Camera dialog box, make sure your scanner is selected as the active device.

5. For the Resolution, choose Print Quality. This yields a higher-quality scan for printed documents.

6. Click Insert.

Depending on the make and model of your own scanner, you might see a slightly different user interface after you click the Scanner Printout button in step 3, but the results should be the same. As long as your scanner is properly configured and you can successfully scan with it in other Windows programs, it should work perfectly fine in OneNote, too.

If you're having trouble scanning, please refer to the documentation that came with your scanner and make sure that you download the latest drivers for it from the manufacturer's website.

After you've scanned a document into OneNote, its image can be resized, scaled, moved, rotated, and ordered in layers—just like regular images.

You can also copy the text from a scanned document by right-clicking the scanned image and then clicking the Copy Text from Picture command. Just like with regular images, this lets you copy the original text of a file printout and paste it elsewhere into your notes as editable text.

> If you want to save a document that you've scanned into OneNote to your hard drive, either for archiving purposes or to use it in other programs, you can do so by right-clicking the scanned document in OneNote and then clicking the Save As command on the shortcut menu. Note that this is not necessary if you want to keep your scans in OneNote. The scans that appear on your page are already saved as part of your notebook.

In Chapter 10, "Using OneNote with Other Programs," you'll learn some additional ways of bringing content into OneNote, including how to control the way that file printouts from other programs appear in OneNote.

Doing Research with Side Notes

After having just learned about some of the many excellent ways in which you can collect information and bring content from anywhere into OneNote, seeing a separate section in this chapter about doing research with OneNote might seem a bit superfluous. Indeed, it might be, but I wanted to point out a few additional features that, depending on your work habits and needs, could come in really handy in your research work.

Let's start with side notes—the electronic equivalent of little yellow sticky notes that you can create with OneNote and position all over your monitor (see Figure 6.25).

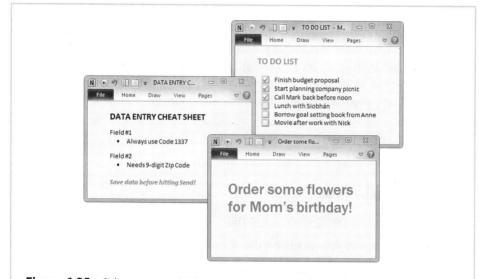

Figure 6.25   *Side notes are mini OneNote windows that strip away the user interface, leaving you just enough space to jot down brief, important notes to keep in view during the day. These pages instantly become part of your notebook and can be used and searched like regular pages in OneNote.*

What's the point of side notes? Quite simply, they are marvelous for keeping important lists, reminders, and reference information visible at all times while you work in other programs. You can keep less-important side notes in the background and pin the most important ones on top so they stay visible even over other windows.

 SHOW ME   Media 6.7—Creating and Managing Side Notes
Access this video file through your registered Web Edition at
my.safaribooksonline.com/9780132182447/media.

Unlike paper-based sticky notes, side notes come with all the benefits of a regular notes page in OneNote. You can format text, make lists, add pictures and screen clippings, add links, insert audio and video recordings, and tag important notes. Like all regular notes, side notes are automatically saved as part of your notebook, so that any information you jot onto them can be recalled again later and, if you like, be moved to the appropriate places in your actual notes. Have you ever tried consolidating all of your paper-based sticky notes in this way? Other than manually retyping everything, it just doesn't work. Only OneNote makes managing sticky notes easy by taking all of the work out of them.

Using side notes is as simple as pressing a keyboard shortcut to create them. The canvas of a side note may appear smaller, but it works the same as a normal page in OneNote. Type some text, either for important reminders, daily to-do lists, or stuff you want to have on your screen at all times, and you're set to go. The uses for side notes are as unlimited as those yellow sticky notes. In OneNote, however, they're not only more convenient, but also much more environmentally friendly.

 LET ME TRY IT

Creating Side Notes

To create a new side note, follow these steps:

1. On any page in your notes, on the ribbon, click View.

2. In the Window group, click New Side Note. A small window with a yellow background appears. Like any notes page in OneNote, you can click this note and begin typing (see Figure 6.26). To quickly format its text, select it, and then make your choices from the Mini toolbar that appears.

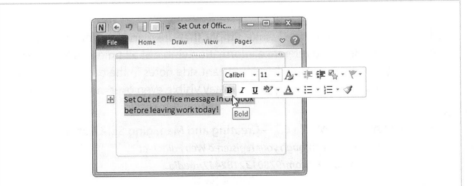

Figure 6.26 *They may be small, but the pages behind side notes can be fully formatted— the same as regular pages in your notebook. For really important reminders, you can make the text large and stand out with color.*

If you have the OneNote Screen Clipper and Launcher running in your Windows taskbar (you learned about this little helper app at the beginning of this chapter), you can create a new side note more quickly by using its keyboard shortcut. Hold down the Windows key and then press N to create a new side note at any time, even if OneNote 2010 isn't running. You can create an unlimited amount of additional side notes at any time—even while you're in another program or another side note.

To keep a side note visible at all times, do the following:

1. Switch to the side note that you want to keep on top of all other windows.

2. Click the View tab at the top of the small side note window. When the ribbon appears, click Keep on Top. The side note will now stay pinned on top of any other windows displayed on your monitor. To turn this option off again, click the View tab once more and then click Keep on Top again to turn the option off.

Because side notes work like regular notes in OneNote, you don't have to save them. They're automatically saved for you the very instant they're created. Side notes stay saved even if you click the red X in the upper-right corner to close a side note.

To quickly browse through all of your side notes, do the following:

1. Switch to any side note you currently have open.

2. Click the Pages tab and then click either Previous Page or Next Page.

3. Repeat step 2 until you find the side note you want. Alternately, you can press the Ctrl+PgUp (Page Up) keyboard shortcut to skip to the previous side note, or you can press the Ctrl+PgDn (Page Down) keyboard shortcut to skip to the next side note.

To make things easier, all side notes are sent to a special section called Unfiled Notes, which is stored in the default notebook you created when you first installed OneNote 2010. Think of the Unfiled Notes section as your virtual OneNote junk drawer, where you can temporarily toss all of the random things you collect until you later have time to discard what you no longer need and organize what you want to put where it really belongs.

As you use OneNote over time, you'll likely create multiple notebooks in which to work and to keep a variety of information. If you want to change the default location of your Unfiled Notes section at any time, you can easily do so. Click File and then click Options. In the OneNote Options dialog box that opens, click

Save & Backup and then click the Unfiled Notes Section path in the list. Click the Modify button to navigate to and then designate a different section as your Unfiled Notes section at the location you want. Until you're more familiar with this special section and its uses, however, it's probably best to leave things as they are for now.

As with all organizational features that are available in OneNote, cleaning out your Unfiled Notes collection is entirely optional. Even if you never organize it, you'll still be able to find everything stored there—including any and all side notes that you've created. This is because side notes and the Unfiled Notes section are automatically included in OneNote's search feature, which you'll learn more about in Chapter 7.

As we're on the topic of side notes, though, let me quickly teach you how you can access the Unfiled Notes section to view and review any side notes that you create.

 **LET ME TRY IT**

Reviewing Side Notes

To view all of the side notes you've created and collected, do the following:

1. In OneNote, near the lower-left corner of the program window, click the Unfiled Notes icon under the navigation bar (see Figure 6.27).

2. When the Unfiled Notes section is displayed, click its page tabs to quickly view all of the random and unfiled notes that you have collected here.

While looking at all of your side notes pages in the Unfiled Notes section, you can copy and paste any of the information from your side notes to your regular notes pages.

You can move more detailed or lengthy side notes to other sections in your notebook and even to other notebooks. Because this works the same as moving and organizing regular pages in your notebooks, I'll cover this in more detail in Chapter 7.

To exit the Unfiled Notes section and return to the place in OneNote where you were before, click the Back button on the Quick Access Toolbar (see Figure 6.28).

If you opened OneNote to the Unfiled Notes section, the Back button won't be available. In that case, click the icon of the notebook you want on the navigation bar and then click a section within that notebook.

Figure 6.27 *The special Unfiled Notes section can be opened by clicking the icon located at the bottom of the navigation bar.*

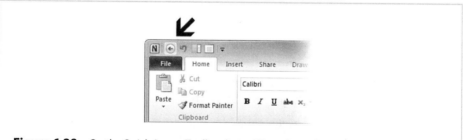

Figure 6.28 *On the Quick Access Toolbar, located just above the File tab in the OneNote program window, the Back button lets you navigate through recently visited notebooks, sections, and pages. It can be clicked multiple times to go backward through the parts of your notebooks that you visited in any single OneNote session.*

For now, let's learn how you can use the quick filing feature in OneNote to easily file away important side notes that you want to keep in your notes for a while.

LET ME TRY IT

Moving Side Notes to Your Existing Notes

Imagine you pasted a couple of charts or tables comparing current airfare rates into a side note while doing research online about the best routes and rates for an upcoming trip. After you have the information you want, you won't want to flip back and forth between your trip planning notes and that obscure little side note in the Unfiled Notes section. It would be like trying to find a random yellow sticky note when you need it most.

OneNote makes it easy to quickly file away your side notes. Because they work just like regular notes pages, you can quickly place them in the exact section of your notebook where you think they belong.

To try this out, you can use one of the side notes you created in this chapter and move it to another place in your notebook, such as the Trip Planning section in your Using OneNote 2010 notebook that you created in Chapter 4, "Notebooks, Sections, and Pages."

To move side notes to your existing notes, follow these steps:

1. Open or create a new side note. If you currently have any side notes open, press the Alt+Tab keyboard shortcut repeatedly until the side note you want comes into view. If you have no side notes open, hold the Windows key and press N, click the Pages tab in the new side note, and then click Previous Page (or press Ctrl+PgUp) repeatedly to go to a previous side note that you created.

2. When the side note you want to file away is in view, click the Pages tab, and then click Move Page.

3. In the Move or Copy Pages dialog box that opens, expand the Using OneNote 2010 notebook (if necessary) by clicking the + symbol next to it to reveal the Trip Planning section in that notebook (see Figure 6.29). If you're already working in the Using OneNote 2010 notebook and its sections are already shown here, you can skip this step.

4. In the list, click the section tab labeled Trip Planning as the destination and then click Move.

When you move a side notes page in this way, it is removed from the Unfiled Notes section (your "junk drawer") and placed into a real section in your notebook. You can keep it there on its own page or cut and paste its content to any of your existing notes pages in that section. However organized you choose to be is entirely up to you.

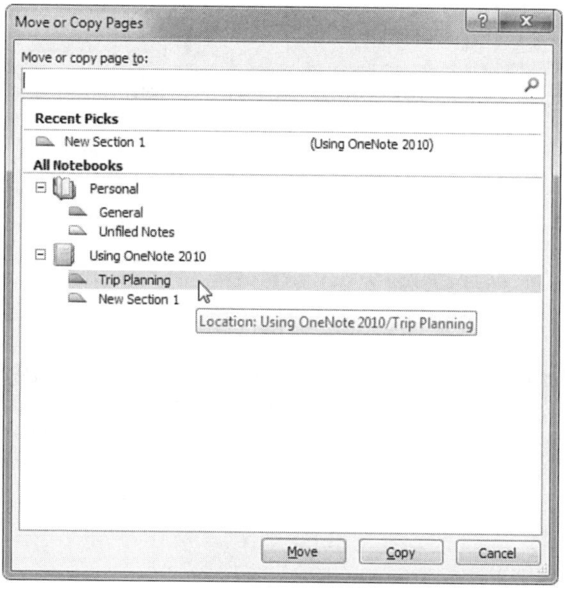

Figure 6.29 *The Move or Copy Pages dialog box is one of several so-called quick filing dialog boxes that allow you to quickly organize parts of your notebook. In this case, you can click a destination to which to send a side notes page.*

In Chapter 7, you'll learn how easy it is to organize and find everything again in OneNote, so don't worry too much about the housekeeping and organization of your notes for now.

Doing Research with Linked Notes

Linked notes are a convenient new feature in OneNote 2010 that allows you to dock the OneNote 2010 program window to the side of your desktop so that you can take notes on anything that you're reading and researching in other programs or in your Web browser. When you take notes in this side-by-side fashion, they are automatically linked to their source material in the programs in which they originated (see Figure 6.30).

Whenever you're in a linked notes session and you take notes on things you're looking at in Internet Explorer, in Word, or in PowerPoint, each paragraph in those notes will display a link icon when you hover your mouse pointer over any paragraph of the notes text. You can click these link icons to quickly return to the source material and the associated program that the notes relate to.

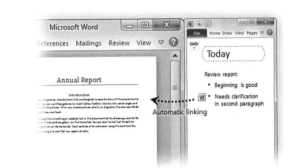

Figure 6.30   *In linked note-taking mode, you can take notes side by side with Internet Explorer web pages, Word documents, PowerPoint presentations, or other OneNote pages. Each paragraph of your linked notes remembers the program and file you were looking at when you took the notes in question, allowing you to easily revisit source and research material.*

Linked notes in OneNote are a revolutionary way for your computerized notes to retain the full context of your thought process by capturing and saving the relationship between your thoughts and ideas that originated at the time when you looked at the source materials that sparked those thoughts and ideas.

In addition to the automatic, clickable link icons that appear next to linked notes text, OneNote also indicates the program that the source material is linked with (for example, Internet Explorer), and it stores a small thumbnail image and a text excerpt of the page, so you can easily recognize the correct web page, document, or presentation slide again later on.

 SHOW ME   Media 6.8—Taking Linked Notes
Access this video file through your registered Web Edition at
my.safaribooksonline.com/9780132182447/media.

Because the linked notes feature is new to OneNote 2010, it can be used only while working in a notebook that's been created or saved in the OneNote 2010 format. If you're working in older, shared OneNote 2007 notebooks that have not yet been upgraded, you won't be able to use the linked notes feature. For more information, see Chapter 9.

LET ME TRY IT

Beginning a Linked Notes Session

The linked notes feature in OneNote is available when viewing a web page in Internet Explorer 8 or later, a Word 2010 document, a PowerPoint 2010 presentation, or any OneNote 2010 notes pages.

To start a linked notes session, do the following:

1. If you want to take linked notes on web pages that you'll be viewing in Internet Explorer, click the Tools button on the Internet Explorer toolbar, and then click OneNote Linked Notes (see Figure 6.31).

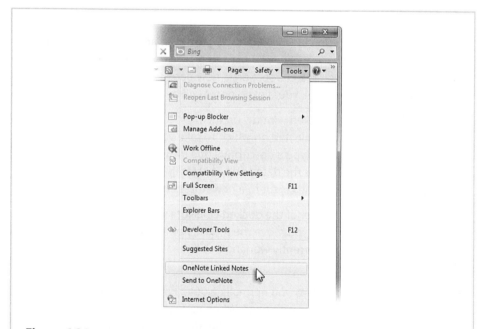

Figure 6.31 *To start a linked note-taking session with Internet Explorer, click the Tools button near the upper-right corner of the browser window and then click the OneNote Linked Notes command on the menu that appears.*

2. If you want to take linked notes on files you'll be viewing in Word 2010, PowerPoint 2010, or OneNote 2010, go to the ribbon in the program you want, click the Review tab, and then, in the Notes group, click Linked Notes (see Figure 6.32).

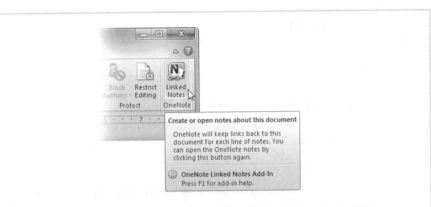

Figure 6.32 *To start a linked note-taking session in Word 2010, PowerPoint 2010, or OneNote 2010, click the Review tab on the ribbon and then click the Linked Notes button. Shown here is the entry point for Word 2010.*

3. In the Select Location in OneNote dialog box that appears, select the note-book section or page where you want to create your linked notes, and then click OK. If you select a section, a new page will be created in it. If you select an existing page, your linked notes will be added to that page.

4. OneNote opens a docked window on the right side of your screen and opens the page you selected on which to take your linked notes. If you selected a new page, type a descriptive title into the Page Title field at the top of the page, above the date and time stamp for the page, and then press Enter to move the cursor to a new notes container.

5. In the upper-left corner of the docked OneNote window, look for the chain-link icon. When you move the mouse pointer over it, a ToolTip will confirm that you're currently working in a linked notes session (see Figure 6.33).

6. Now, take notes the way you normally would. For example, switch to Internet Explorer and bring up a web page. When you return to the docked OneNote window and start typing notes, each paragraph of notes that you create while Internet Explorer is active in docked mode will be linked to the current web page that it displays. If you switch to another page and take more notes, those paragraphs will then be linked to the new page, and so on. Similarly, if you bring up any Word documents or PowerPoint presentations during your linked notes session, they will also be linked to any notes you take in the docked OneNote window.

Figure 6.33   *The small chain-link icon in the upper-left corner of the docked OneNote window indicates whether you're in a linked note-taking session or not. Move the mouse pointer over the icon to see a status ToolTip or click the link icon for more options.*

Regarding the choice you have in step 3, I recommend that you create each linked notes session on a fresh page in one of your notebook sections, at least until you become a bit more familiar with linked note-taking. After you've had a chance to really try out this feature with your real notes and it makes sense to you, you can mix and match future linked notes with your existing notes.

 LET ME TRY IT

Ending a Linked Notes Session

If you want OneNote to stop keeping links between the things you type in OneNote and the programs you're looking at, you can end a linked notes session that you've started.

To turn off linked notes, do either one of the following:

- In the upper-left corner of the docked OneNote window, click the link icon and then click Stop Taking Linked Notes.

- In the docked OneNote window, on the View tab, click the Normal View button.

When a linked notes session has been ended, the chain-link icon in the upper-left corner of the page will show a red circle with a slash through it (see Figure 6.34) to indicate that no further links will be created. Any notes that were linked to other programs up until that point are retained.

Figure 6.34   *A small red circle with a slash through it appears over the chain-link icon in the upper-left corner of the docked OneNote window to indicate that a linked note-taking session has ended.*

You can also end a linked notes session by clicking the selected Dock to Desktop button on the Quick Access Toolbar, which undocks the OneNote window and turns off your linked notes session. The same thing can be achieved by pressing the Ctrl+Alt+D keyboard shortcut.

 LET ME TRY IT

Viewing Linked Notes

You can return to the notes you took and the information you looked at during a linked notes session by doing any of the following:

- To view the notes you took during a linked notes session, simply open that notes page again in OneNote.

- To view the pages and documents on which your linked notes were based, move the mouse pointer over the paragraphs of notes that you took in a linked notes session. Just to the left of each paragraph, you should see a small icon representing the program that your notes are linked to (see Figure 6.35). When you move the mouse pointer over any of these program icons, you'll see a ToolTip with details about the linked document or page, including a visual preview to help you recognize the page again (see Figure 6.36).

- To return to any of the original information that you looked at during a linked notes session, click any of the small program icons to the left of your linked notes paragraphs to open the source pages or documents on which your linked notes were based.

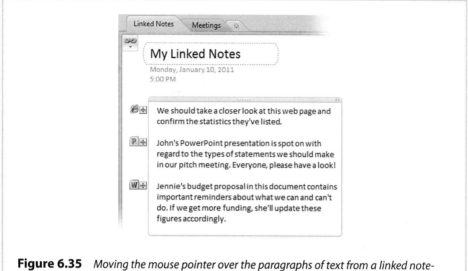

Figure 6.35 *Moving the mouse pointer over the paragraphs of text from a linked note-taking session reveals the icons of the applications with which the notes are associated. (Unlike in this screenshot, the icons are shown one by one, not all together.)*

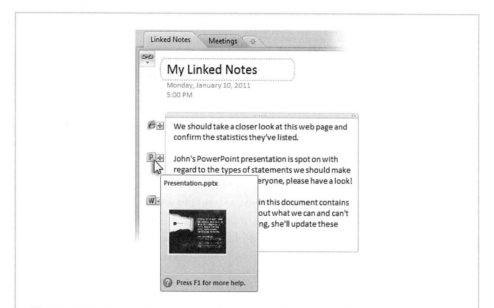

Figure 6.36 *Resting the mouse pointer over any of the program icons that appear to the left of the notes paragraphs from a linked note-taking session displays a thumbnail image of the page or file with which the notes are associated.*

LET ME TRY IT

Disabling or Reenabling Linked Notes

If you want to occasionally use the Dock to Desktop feature in OneNote but you don't want to begin a linked notes session, you can turn it off by doing the following:

1. In OneNote, press Ctrl+Alt+D to dock the program window to the side of your desktop.

2. In the upper-left corner of the page, click the link icon, and then click Stop Taking Linked Notes.

If you later want to reenable linked note-taking, do the following:

1. In a docked OneNote window, click the link icon in the upper-left corner.

2. On the pop-up menu that appears, click Start Taking Linked Notes.

If, for some reason, you don't like this feature, you can disable linked notes for good. In a docked OneNote window, click the link icon in the upper-left corner, and then click Linked Notes Options. On the right side of the Options dialog box that appears, look for the Linked Notes heading, deselect the Allow Creation of New Linked Notes check box, and then click OK. You'll now be able to dock and undock the OneNote window without worrying about starting any linked notes sessions. If you should decide at a later time that you want to work with linked notes again, simply re-select the Allow Creation of New Linked Notes check box in the OneNote Options dialog box.

Linked notes might take a little practice at first, but if you're using OneNote to frequently do a lot of research online, or you're working with other people to pore over and annotate lengthy documents or presentations, you might just find the linked notes feature to be an invaluable help to you.

Using the Research and Translate Tools

Before concluding this chapter, I want to quickly point to a couple of other, built-in resources that you might find useful when collecting information in OneNote or doing research online.

Like some of the other programs in the Microsoft Office 2010 suite, OneNote 2010 includes a Research task pane that provides web search integration and basic translation services. This tool can be helpful whenever you want to quickly look up information while typing your notes or if you want to translate a selection of text in another language.

OneNote 2010 also includes the Mini Translator, which provides a more interactive way to translate text in a foreign language in your notes.

 **LET ME TRY IT**

Setting Options for the Research Task Pane

To display the Research task pane in OneNote 2010 and set options for it, do the following:

1. On the ribbon in OneNote 2010, click the Review tab, and then, in the Spelling group, click Research.

2. In the Research task pane that opens, click the Research Options link at the very bottom of the task pane (see Figure 6.37).

Figure 6.37   *The Research task pane makes it easy to look up information without leaving the OneNote program window.*

3. In the Research Options dialog box, select any of the available reference books and sites that you want to use with this feature and deselect any that you do not want to consult. For example, if you're traveling on business to the United Kingdom, you might want to temporarily change your Thesaurus selection from the U.S. to the U.K. version.

4. Click OK when you've set the options that you want.

 **LET ME TRY IT**

Searching with the Research Task Pane

If, while taking notes, you suddenly need clarification about something, you can use the Research task pane to look it up without having to switch to your web browser.

To search with the Research task pane, follow these steps:

1. If you dismissed the Research task pane after the previous steps, you can return to it by clicking the Review tab on the ribbon and then clicking Research in the Spelling group.

2. In the Research task pane that opens, type a word or phrase into the Search for box. From the drop-down menu just below it, select the reference book or research site you want to use for your search, and then click the green Start Searching arrow.

For example, entering the word *constitution* in the Search for box and choosing Bing as the search engine will define the term you've searched for, yield a Wikipedia article about the U.S. constitution, and much more. You can click the blue link below each search result to fetch and display the full text of web articles in your browser. For results in books and dictionaries, you can click and select and then copy any of the text to paste it in your notes.

> For a faster way to look up a word or phrase, select it in your notes, right-click it, and then click Lookup on the shortcut menu that appears.

To modify a search (for example, to change from a Bing search on the Web to an Encarta Dictionary search), click the green Back button just above the search results list and then modify where OneNote should look for the word or phrase you previously entered (see Figure 6.38).

Figure 6.38 *To start a search, click the green, square-shaped arrow pointing to the right. To navigate between search results, click the green, circular-shaped arrows pointing left or right.*

For best results when searching with the Research tools, start with a broad search of a single or simple term and then slowly narrow the search with additional keywords, if need be. If you start by being too specific in your search (for example, "white fuzzy bunnies in the snow"), you might not find what you're looking for. Beginning with a much simpler search ("bunnies") is a better starting point from which to narrow your results.

When you're done using the Research task pane, you can dismiss it by either clicking the small X in its upper-right corner, or by clicking its command on the ribbon once more (Review tab, Research button).

 LET ME TRY IT

Adding Research Services

If you find the Research pane to be a valuable addition to your work in OneNote, or if you have need of a profession-specific resource for your research work, you might want to check out what else is available for it in the Office marketplace.

Please note that I cannot personally endorse any of these third-party companies or services, but I wanted to at least point out to you the availability of these services.

To add research services, do the following:

1. Near the bottom of the Research task pane, click Get services on Office Marketplace.

2. In the Available Research Services overview that opens, have a look at some of the additional services that you can add to your Research pane functionality in OneNote.

Finally, let's look at the built-in translation features in OneNote 2010.

 LET ME TRY IT

Translating a Word or Phrase with the Research Pane

Whether you're reviewing documents and notes from your company's foreign subsidiaries, or you work with an exchange student at your school, there might be times when you want a quick text translation when working in OneNote.

To translate a single word or short phrase in your notes, do the following:

1. Select the foreign word or phrase in your notes, right-click the selection, and then click Translate. The Research pane opens, this time with Translation set as the default search engine.

2. If necessary, select the appropriate languages in the From and To boxes under Translation. For example, if you've selected the word *étudiant* in your notes, you could select French in the From box and English in the To box (see Figure 6.39).

3. Click the green Start Searching arrow at the top of the task pane and then look for the translated result in the results list.

> If you frequently translate text in your notes in this way, you might want to set specific translation options to exclude languages that you'll never use. To do this, click the blue Translation Options link that appears under the Translation heading in the Research task pane, and then select your choices there.

If using the Research task pane for on-the-fly translations isn't quick enough for you, you can opt to use OneNote's built-in Mini Translator instead. This built-in translation engine lets you rest the mouse pointer over foreign words in your notes and translate on the fly. Using the Mini Translator, you can also play back certain text to hear its pronunciation.

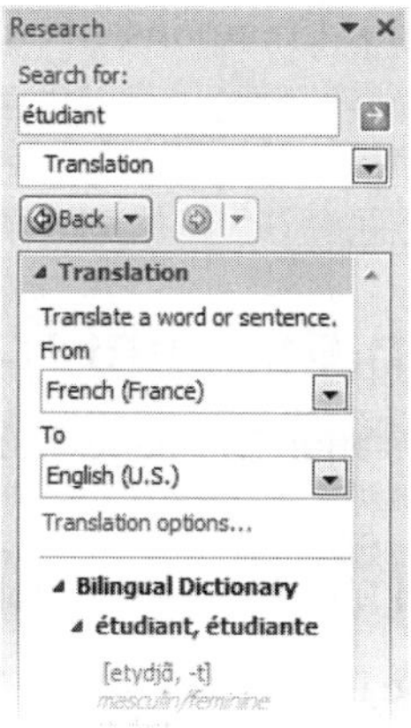

Research   ▾ ✕

Search for:

étudiant

Translation   ▾

⊙ Back | ▾   ⊙ | ▾

◢ **Translation**

Translate a word or sentence.

From

French (France)   ▾

To

English (U.S.)   ▾

Translation options...

◢ **Bilingual Dictionary**
   ◢ **étudiant, étudiante**

[etydjã, -t]
masculin/feminine

Figure 6.39 *When using the Research task pane for language translation, you can choose the language from which to translate and the language into which to translate the selected text.*

 LET ME TRY IT

Setting Your Preferred Mini Translator Language

Before you can use the Mini Translator, you must first set the language into which you want to translate selected text in OneNote.

To set your preferred Mini Translator language, do the following:

1. On the OneNote ribbon, click Review, and then, in the Language group, click the small downward-facing arrow at the bottom of the Translate button.

2. On the pop-up menu that appears, click Choose Translation Language.

3. In the Translation Language Options dialog box that appears, click the Translate to drop-down list and then select French (France) or any other language that you prefer.

4. Click OK.

Once your preferred translation language is set, you can start using the Mini Translator.

 **LET ME TRY IT**

Translating Text with the Mini Translator

Now that you've set your translation language, you're ready to translate any part of the text on your notes page.

To translate text with the Mini Translator, do the following:

1. If the Research task pane is still displayed near the right side of the OneNote program window from the previous procedures, go ahead and close it. Click the small X in the upper-right corner of the task pane to dismiss it.

2. On your notes page, type some text that you want OneNote to translate. For example, you could type **The world is watching!**

3. On the OneNote ribbon, click the Review tab, and then, in the Language group, click the Translate button.

4. On the pop-up menu that appears, click the second option, which appears as Mini Translator [French (France)].

5. Now that you're in translation mode, you can simply move the mouse pointer over one of the words in your text and then wait a moment until the Mini Translator appears in a slightly dimmed state. When it appears, move the mouse pointer over it to make it fully visible and read the translation of the word. For example, if you hovered over the word *world*, OneNote would correctly translate it into French as *monde*.

At the bottom of the Mini Translator pop-up window are several icons that provide additional functionality (see Figure 6.40):

- **Expand**—Click the leftmost icon to open the selected word in the Research task pane.

- **Copy**—Click the second icon from the left to copy the translation text to your Clipboard. You can use the Ctrl+V keyboard shortcut to paste the text anywhere into your notes.

- **Play**—Click the third icon from the left to hear the pronunciation of the selected word.

Figure 6.40 *The icons at the bottom of the Mini Translator window provide additional options.*

- **Stop**—Click the fourth icon from the left to stop playback of a word pronunciation. This button is usually only necessary if you have a long phrase of text selected whose pronunciation you're currently playing back and want to interrupt.

- **Help**—Click the last icon at the bottom of the Mini Translator to read tips for using the Mini Translator in OneNote.

You remain in Mini Translator mode until you turn it off. To do so, click the Review tab on the ribbon. In the Languages group, click the Translate button. You'll see that the Mini Translator [English (U.S.)] option appears selected. Click it once again to turn it off.

It's easy to see why OneNote is a great companion for information gathering and research, no matter if you're doing it for work, for school, or for personal projects at home. Though the tips in this chapter represent only the proverbial tip of the iceberg, I hope that they have helped to illustrate just how rich in features OneNote is under the hood.

If you use OneNote every day as part of your work or home life and you apply the functionality of its features to your specific professions or projects, you'll soon discover additional techniques that can save you time and help you master the oceans of information and details that we all have to deal with in our lives every day. When that time comes, I hope you'll share some of your own tips and techniques with other OneNote users—be it your friends, your family, your colleagues, your schoolmates, or people online with whom you share common interests and pursuits. You can find and interact with other OneNote users on Facebook (visit facebook.com/microsoftonenote) and on the Office Blog (visit blogs.office.com).

Organizing and Searching Notes

The previous chapter taught you how to bring all kinds of information into your electronic notebook and keep everything together in one place; this chapter demonstrates why making OneNote 2010 your primary information repository really pays off in the long run.

If you made a sour face when you saw the word *organizing* in the title of this chapter, don't be discouraged. You don't need to learn a specific filing system to stay organized in OneNote. OneNote won't pass judgment about your note-taking habits, and it won't nag you about any lack of personal organization on your part. No matter how organized—or disorganized—you are, OneNote will help you to instantly recall anything that you've put into it, no matter where you purposely or accidentally might have put it (see Figure 7.1).

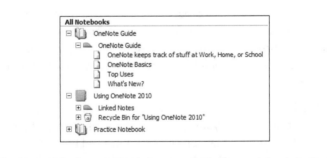

Figure 7.1 *Many of the features that help you organize your notebooks in OneNote also help to enable its sophisticated search capabilities—providing instant recall of information for all personality types, no matter how organized (or disorganized) you are.*

Organizing Items on a Page

Before we look at how you can keep all elements of your electronic notebooks organized, let's first examine how you can organize content that you've created or imported on your notes pages.

SHOW ME   Media 7.1—Organizing Items on a Page
Access this video file through your registered Web Edition at
my.safaribooksonline.com/9780132182447/media.

OneNote 2010 is great tool for capturing thoughts and ideas that you're just starting to ruminate in your head. But it's just as great at taking early ideas, writing
drafts, and half-baked plans to the next level by streamlining your notes about
them into a more cohesive plan or narrative.

Whether you're organizing your notes only for yourself to keep things straight, or
you'll eventually put together a proposal or presentation to persuade someone
why the time is right for your ideas, OneNote can help you.

 LET ME TRY IT

Merging Note Containers on a Page

If you're reading the chapters in this book in order, you've already learned about
moving and resizing note containers and organizing their content as outlines.
Those features are immensely helpful when you're still in the process of taking
notes, collecting information, or capturing ideas.

When you're ready to clean up some of your early drafts and begin to put those
thoughts and ideas in order, you'll see that note containers offer a couple of additional tricks to help you organize and consolidate the notes they contain.

For example, note containers provide the capability to merge text from one note
container with the text in another. This lets you move important items into your
main notes, leaving the things that don't make the cut on the side, where you can
review them once more before deleting them. This is especially useful if you're
tasked with organizing ideas that come out of a brainstorming meeting, for example, where you might have several note containers created by people who contributed their suggestions and ideas.

By merging multiple note containers into one, you can simplify tasks such as formatting and sharing when the main flow of text has been combined.

To see how this works, follow these steps:

1. Click anywhere on a blank page and type a line of text.

2. Click outside of the note container that holds the text you just typed and
    then type a second line of text so that you're left with two separate note
    containers (see Figure 7.2).

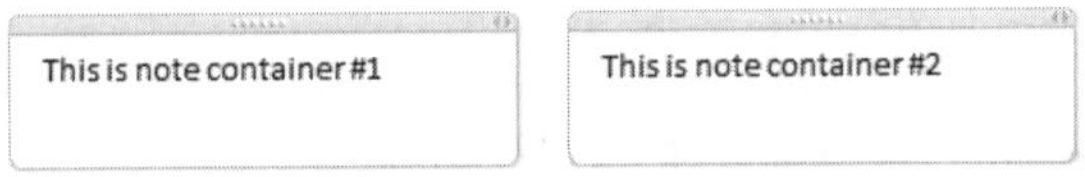

This is note container #1   This is note container #2

Figure 7.2   *You can arrange notes on the page by creating separate note containers for certain blocks of text. When you're ready to consolidate notes from various note containers into your main body of notes, dragging text from one note container into another will merge their contents.*

3. Move the mouse pointer over the line of text in the second note container until you see the four-headed arrow icon next to it.

4. Using the left mouse button, click the arrow icon and then drag the text over the first note container until the text pops into place. You'll notice that OneNote offers to snap the text to certain indentation choices near the margin by hesitating at points while you drag (see Figure 7.3).

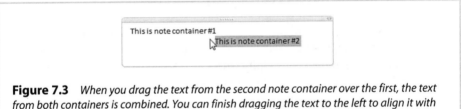

This is note container #1
This is note container #2

Figure 7.3   *When you drag the text from the second note container over the first, the text from both containers is combined. You can finish dragging the text to the left to align it with the other text in the combined note container.*

5. Align the text you're dragging to the first note container with the text that was already there, and then release the mouse button.

The reason I like this approach better than, say, cutting and pasting text from one note container to another is because I get immediate visual confirmation of where text comes from and where I want it to end up. Additionally, I can always change my mind and organize consolidated text again in its new location, as you'll see in the next procedure.

For best results, snap text out of its original note container by dragging with the mouse in a diagonal or vertical motion. If you drag horizontally, OneNote will assume you want to change the indentation of the text you've selected and extend the width of the note container. Remember that you can always use the Undo command (Ctrl+Z) while practicing if you need to correct a mistake before trying again.

 **LET ME TRY IT**

Organizing Notes Chronologically

Although the date and time stamp that appears near the top of each notes page tells you when that page was first created, the actual notes on the page aren't always created on the same day. You might want or need to know when a specific line or paragraph of text was added or updated.

For example, if you're consolidating notes from multiple notes pages or note containers, and you want to organize the seemingly random paragraphs in chronological order (for example, a transcription of events that happened at a seminar), you can look up a hidden date and time stamp that OneNote automatically applies to each paragraph of text when it is created or edited. When merging note containers and consolidating notes, you can use this information to put your text into the right order.

To check the hidden date and time stamp of a paragraph of text, follow these steps:

1. Move the mouse pointer over the line of text in the second note container until you see the four-headed arrow icon next to it.

2. Right-click the arrow icon.

3. At the bottom of the shortcut menu that appears, make note of the author of the selected text and the date and time when it was created or last edited (see Figure 7.4).

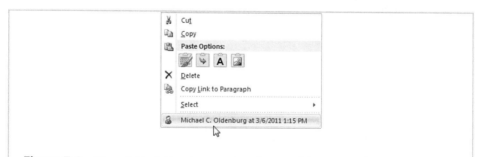

Figure 7.4 *When right-clicking the arrow icon for any of the paragraphs in a note container, this menu appears. The last line item displays the text's author and the date and time when the text was created or last updated.*

This information is hidden because it's actually metadata—a fancy word for "data about data" (or "information about information"). This kind of additional information exists in most other computer files, too. For example, in Microsoft Word 2010, you can display the properties of a document, which tell you all kinds of interesting information, such as how long the document was edited, how often it was saved, and so on.

Similarly, when you import a photo from your digital camera, its metadata tells you what camera you used to create the picture, what exposure (or ISO) setting you used, and other items of interest. Metadata is typically hidden from normal view because it is not always needed. You can consider it as a sort of "on-demand" feature. If you need to know this information, you can easily look it up.

In Chapter 9, "Sharing Notes with Other People," you'll learn where this feature can be even more useful, such as when multiple authors contribute to the same notebook in real time and you need to keep track of changes to content in a shared notebook.

The hidden date and time stamp of text assumes that the computer used to originally create or update this text was correctly set to the current, local time. The author's name shown in front of the date and time stamp is taken from the optional personalization you can apply to all of the programs in Microsoft Office 2010. If you didn't enter your name during installation or you want to update the name on a specific computer, click the File tab in OneNote and then click Options. In the OneNote Options dialog box that opens, in the General category, look under the Personalize Your Copy of Microsoft Office heading and then enter the name and initials of the person using that particular copy of OneNote. If two or more people use OneNote on the same computer, different names can be used for OneNote personalization with each Windows user account that you've created.

 **LET ME TRY IT**

Using Rule Lines and Gridlines to Organize Objects on a Page

Another way to organize information on the current page is to use the optional rule lines or gridlines that can change a blank notes page to resemble a paper notepad or college-ruled notebook. This can be useful if you're trying to better align paragraphs of handwritten notes or when you want to visually organize other objects on your page, such as multiple screen clippings you've captured or pictures you've inserted on the page.

To apply rule lines or gridlines to the current page, follow these steps:

1. On the ribbon, click the View tab.

2. In the Page Setup group, click Rule Lines.

3. On the pop-up menu that appears, click a style under either the Rule Lines or Grid Lines heading (see Figure 7.5). If you don't like the result, simply repeat the previous steps and choose another style, or click None to remove the last style you applied.

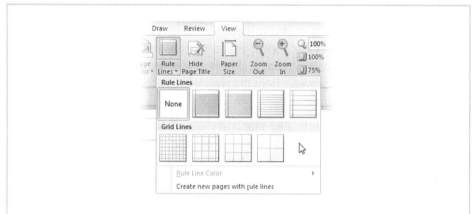

Figure 7.5 *To more precisely align text and objects on the page, you can apply rule lines or gridlines to appear on your page background—either temporarily or permanently.*

You don't have to keep rule lines or gridlines displayed if you only want to use them temporarily to line up the notes and objects on your pages. When you're done organizing the layout of your page the way you want, follow the previous steps and apply the style labeled None to remove the lines again.

If you do decide to keep rule lines or gridlines displayed permanently, you can change their color to match that of your text and visuals on your page. From the Rule Lines menu, click Rule Line Color and then click the color you want.

Using Tables to Organize Information

Anyone who's ever used various Microsoft Office programs like Word, Excel, and PowerPoint to create documents, spreadsheets, or presentations knows how useful tables can be to organize information and group information together in logical, meaningful ways.

Whether you're organizing information for yourself or for other people, you can use tables in OneNote to present data in a familiar, easy-to-understand, row-and-column format.

SHOW ME   Media 7.2—Using Tables

Access this video file through your registered Web Edition at
my.safaribooksonline.com/9780132182447/media.

Even though OneNote has excellent table support, I must point out that its approach to table creation and formatting differs quite a bit from its other Microsoft Office counterparts. As I've mentioned before, such seemingly inconsistent design choices aren't the work of programmers who want to drive you crazy. Like many things in OneNote, it has to do with the complexity of the OneNote canvas and the freedom it provides from the typical lines and cells that constrain other types of electronic documents.

Because OneNote is also primarily a tool that lets you focus on your thoughts and ideas, the creation of tables is much simpler, compared with other programs. The intent behind this feature design is for the interface to get out of your way so you can concentrate on what you're thinking and writing about.

While even intentional inconsistencies between computer programs can increase the initial learning curve by a bit, the payoff comes later, when you've learned how to use the feature and you see how it saves you time. If you prefer to go the long, more comfortable route when working with tables, OneNote also includes the "normal" commands on the ribbon to let you create tables on your pages in more traditional ways.

Creating a Table

To create a table in the most straightforward way, follow these steps:

1. On any page, click where you want to create a table.

2. On the ribbon, click the Insert tab.

3. In the Tables group, click Table.

4. On the pop-up menu that appears, click the Insert Table command at the bottom of the menu.

5. In the small Insert Table dialog box that appears (see Figure 7.6), enter the number of columns and rows you want to start with and then click OK.

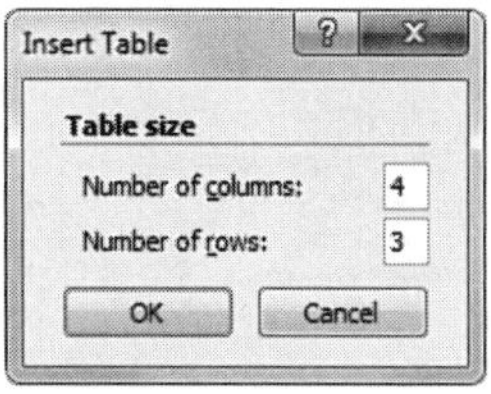

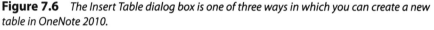

Figure 7.6 *The Insert Table dialog box is one of three ways in which you can create a new table in OneNote 2010.*

If you prefer to visually draw a table grid before filling its cells with information, do the following:

1. On any page, click where you want to create a table.

2. On the ribbon, click the Insert tab.

3. In the Tables group, click Table.

4. On the pop-up menu that appears, slowly move the mouse pointer over the table grid from the upper-left corner toward the lower right until the text over the table grid indicates the table size. For example, a 4 × 3 table would create a table with 4 columns and 3 rows (see Figure 7.7).

5. When the text confirms the dimensions you want, click the left mouse button to create the table.

If you want to create tables more quickly, you can take advantage of the fast method that I mentioned in the introduction to this chapter. This method bypasses the user interface entirely and lets you create a new table even while you're in the middle of typing notes.

Here's how it works:

1. On any page, click where you want to create the new table.

2. Start typing the text that you want to appear in the first table cell (the left-most column and the topmost row).

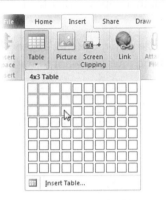

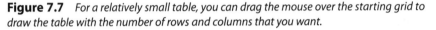

Figure 7.7   *For a relatively small table, you can drag the mouse over the starting grid to draw the table with the number of rows and columns that you want.*

3. On your keyboard, press the Tab key. OneNote creates a new table, puts the text you typed on the current line into the first cell, and then creates the next column.

4. To continue the table until it has the dimensions you want, press the Tab key whenever you want to create a new column or press the Enter key to create a new row.

If the information that you want to include in your notes already exists in a table format in another program, like the spreadsheet cells in a Microsoft Excel workbook or a table in a Microsoft Word document, you can copy any selection from these and other programs and paste the table or grid selection into your notes. Note that any tables and spreadsheet cells that you paste into OneNote might not come over exactly as they appear at their source. OneNote lacks some of the sophisticated formatting choices that the Quick Galleries in Word, Excel, and other Office programs offer. This is because tables in OneNote are primarily intended to organize information instead of dressing it up with fancy formatting styles for the purpose of presentation.

If you need to include a fully formatted table in your notes—the same way it appears in its original spreadsheet or document—consider taking a screen clipping of the table portion you want and then inserting it into your notes. Though you can't edit the information in screen clippings, this workaround provides a quick-and-easy way to include related information from other sources in your notes.

After you have created a table in OneNote, an entire new toolbox of commands awaits you on the ribbon. To display it, click any cell in your table to activate the cursor and then look for the yellow Table Tools tab that appears directly over the Layout tab on the ribbon (see Figure 7.8). When you click this yellow tab, 15 table-related commands become available for you to use. If you work a lot with tables in OneNote, the extra clicks to reach these commands on the ribbon might become tedious. For this reason, most of these commands are also available by right-clicking any cell in a table and then clicking the Table command on the shortcut menu (only the three cell alignment commands are exclusive to the Table Tools ribbon tab). I'll describe each of these commands in more detail in the following step-by-step procedures.

Figure 7.8   *When the cursor is located inside of a table cell, OneNote adds a yellow Table Tools tab over the Layout tab on the ribbon. Clicking this tab reveals the table-specific formatting tools.*

  LET ME TRY IT

Inserting a New Row in a Table

To insert a new table row above the current row, do the following:

1. In your table, click any cell in the row over which you want to create the new row.

2. On the ribbon, above the Layout tab, click Table Tools.

3. In the Insert group, click Insert Above.

To insert a new table row below the current row, do the following:

1. In your table, click any cell in the row under which you want to create the new row.

2. On the ribbon, above the Layout tab, click Table Tools.

3. In the Insert group, click Insert Below.

These and several other table commands can be applied instantly by using keyboard shortcuts, allowing you to avoid clicking your way through the ribbon interface. To see which shortcuts are available, see "Using Keyboard Shortcuts to Modify Tables" later in this chapter.

 LET ME TRY IT

Inserting a Line Break Within the Current Table Row

If you want to create a new line of text in a table without forcing it onto a new row in the table, you can insert a line break into any cell. OneNote will expand the current row of cells to make room for the new line of text.

To insert a line break within the current table row, follow these steps:

1. In your table, click the cell where you want to insert a line break.

2. On your keyboard, hold down the Shift key and then press Enter.

3. Type the text you want to appear below the previous line of text in the same cell.

You can also use the Shift+Enter line break shortcut to space out your table cells vertically. This can make large tables or tables with complex data a little easier to read.

The Shift+Enter keyboard shortcut is also the only way to manually resize table rows (other than typing more text to expand their size) because you cannot use the mouse to modify table row borders the way you can with column borders (see "Resizing a Table Column" later in this chapter).

 **LET ME TRY IT**

Inserting a New Column in a Table

To insert a new table column to the left of the current column, do the following:

1. In your table, click any cell in the column next to which you want to create the new column.

2. On the ribbon, above the Layout tab, click Table Tools.

3. In the Insert group, click Insert Left.

To insert a new table column to the right of the current column, do the following:

1. In your table, click any cell in the column next to which you want to create the new column.

2. On the ribbon, above the Layout tab, click Table Tools.

3. In the Insert group, click Insert Right.

 **LET ME TRY IT**

Resizing a Table Column

When you type text into the cells in a table, the rows and columns of the table will adapt to the size and length of the text in and around those cells. Although you can only manually expand table rows by using line breaks (see "Inserting a Line Break Within the Current Table Row" earlier in this chapter), you can manually adjust the width of a column with your mouse.

To resize a table column, do the following:

1. Move the mouse pointer over the right border of any cell whose column you want to expand or contract.

2. When the mouse pointer changes to the resize cursor (see Figure 7.9), click and drag the column border to the left or right until it is the size you want and then release the mouse button.

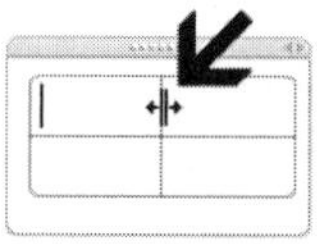

Figure 7.9 *Moving the mouse over the vertical border between two table columns changes the pointer to the resize cursor. Clicking and dragging the mouse at this point will change the dimensions of the column to the left of the pointer.*

Although you can select individual cells in OneNote tables for the purpose of copying and formatting them, OneNote 2010 does not offer a way to specify a precise size measurement of any parts of a table. This is because tables in OneNote are primarily intended to organize information on your notes pages. Because table cells automatically adapt to their contents, setting cell-based properties typically isn't necessary.

If the precise dimensions of a table are critical for some reason, you can work around the lack of table properties in OneNote by creating a table grid in another Office program (or even a drawing program), formatting its cells with the exact dimensions you want, and then inserting a picture of this table grid as a picture or screen clipping. After the picture is inserted on your notes page, position it where you want it to appear, right-click the picture, and then click Set Picture as Background. Now you can click anywhere over the picture and type text into the cells that appear behind the text. To precisely position note containers over the grid in the picture, hold the Alt key while dragging a note container to align it.

 LET ME TRY IT

Selecting an Entire Table

You can quickly select all of the text in a table by doing the following:

1. Click any cell in your table.

2. On the ribbon, above the Layout tab, click Table Tools.

3. In the Select group, click Select Table.

To select a table more quickly, right-click any table cell, click Table on the shortcut menu that appears, and then click Select Table.

An entirely different way to select a table or parts of a table is to use the progressive Select All command in OneNote, which is available through the Ctrl+A keyboard shortcut. Although this command is not exclusive for use with selecting tables, its unique behavior, compared with the Select All command in other programs, is especially apparent when you try it out within a table.

Click in any cell in your table and then press Ctrl+A. OneNote selects the current cell. Pressing Ctrl+A again will extend the current selection to the entire row in which the previously selected cell is located. If you press Ctrl+A once more, OneNote will select the entire table. Finally, pressing Ctrl+A a fourth time will keep the current table selected and also select the note container that the entire table is placed in.

When your table is selected, you can format all its cells with the font, font size, text color, or cell alignment you want.

LET ME TRY IT

Selecting a Column in a Table

You can quickly select a column in a table by doing the following:

1. Click any cell in your table.

2. On the ribbon, above the Layout tab, click Table Tools.

3. In the Select group, click Select Columns.

> To select a column more quickly, right-click any table cell, click Table on the shortcut menu that appears, and then click Select Columns.

If the plural form in the Select Columns command seems out of place, it's because you can use this command to select multiple columns, not just the current column. To do this, click any cell in the first column that you want to select, hold down the Shift key, and then click any cell in the last column that you want to select. When you now use the Select Columns command, either on the ribbon or on the right-click menu, OneNote will select all of the columns between and including the columns of the two cells you selected.

After any column is selected, you can format it with the font, font size, font style, text color, or cell alignment you want.

LET ME TRY IT

Selecting a Row in a Table

You can quickly select a row in a table by doing the following:

1. Click any cell in your table.

2. On the ribbon, above the Layout tab, click Table Tools.

3. In the Select group, click Select Rows.

> To select a row more quickly, right-click any table cell, click Table on the shortcut menu that appears, and then click Select Rows.

If the plural form in the Select Rows command seems out of place, it's because you can use this command to select multiple rows, not just the current row. To do this, click any cell in the first row that you want to select, hold down the Shift key, and then click any cell in the last row that you want to select. When you now use the Select Rows command, either on the ribbon or on the right-click menu, OneNote will select all of the rows between and including the rows of the two cells you selected.

After any row is selected, you can format it with the font, font size, font style, text color, or cell alignment you want.

 LET ME TRY IT

Selecting a Single Cell in a Table

You can quickly select any cell in a table by doing the following:

1. Click any cell in your table.

2. On the ribbon, above the Layout tab, click Table Tools.

3. In the Select group, click Select Cell.

To select a cell more quickly, right-click any table cell, click Table on the shortcut menu that appears, and then click Select Cell. An even faster way to select a single table cell is by triple-clicking it.

 LET ME TRY IT

Aligning Text Within a Table Cell

After you have selected any cell, row, or column in your table, you can change the alignment of text or objects within the selected cells.

To align text within a table cell, do the following:

1. Select the cells whose text you want to align.

2. On the ribbon, above the Layout tab, click Table Tools.

3. In the Alignment group, click the alignment you want (Align Left, Center, Align Right).

To change the alignment of cells more quickly, select the cells you want, and then on the Home tab, click the arrow next to the Paragraph Alignment button. On the pop-up menu that appears, click Align Left, Center, or Align Right. The buttons in these two different locations do the same thing. Keyboard shortcuts are also available for two of these commands: Press Ctrl+L to align text in the selected cells to the left or press Ctrl+R to align it to the right. A keyboard shortcut for centering text within selected table cells is not available.

 **LET ME TRY IT**

Showing and Hiding Table Borders

When you create a table in OneNote, its cells are divided by a visible grid to help keep the information in the table cells visually separated. In most cases, this makes the information easier to read.

If you use tables as a page layout or spacing tool for information or objects on your notes page, you can hide the table borders.

To hide table borders, do the following:

1. Click any cell in the table whose borders you want to hide.

2. On the ribbon, above the Layout tab, click Table Tools.

3. In the Borders group, click Hide Borders.

The Hide Borders command is an On/Off toggle, which means you can restore table borders by repeating the previous steps. Clicking the Hide Borders command again when it is selected (the button on the ribbon will appear orange) turns off the option.

To hide table borders more quickly, right-click any table cell, click Table on the shortcut menu that appears, and then click Hide Borders. To quickly show the borders again, repeat the same steps. Clicking Hide Borders on the shortcut menu again turns off the option.

Because table borders disappear completely when you do this, it's the very last thing you should do after you have formatted the table contents the way you want them to appear.

When the borders of a table are hidden, you can still navigate through or select its individual cells, if necessary. Click anywhere in the borderless table to activate any cell and then use the directional arrow keys on your keyboard to go to the cell you want. You can also use the mouse to interact with any part of a borderless table. For example, moving the mouse pointer over an invisible column border will display the column resize pointer. In most cases, though, it's simply easier to temporarily display the borders again if you need to reformat any part of a table.

 LET ME TRY IT

Deleting an Entire Table

To delete an entire table, do the following:

1. Click any cell in the table you want to delete.

2. On the ribbon, above the Layout tab, click Table Tools.

3. In the Delete group, click Delete Table.

To delete a table more quickly, right-click any of its cells, click Table on the shortcut menu that appears, and then click Delete Table.

If you select this command by accident, remember that the Undo command on the Quick Access Toolbar (or the Ctrl+Z keyboard shortcut) can instantly restore the entire table.

 **LET ME TRY IT**

Deleting a Column in a Table

To delete a column within a table, do the following:

1. Click any cell in the column you want to delete.

2. On the ribbon, above the Layout tab, click Table Tools.

3. In the Delete group, click Delete Columns.

To delete a column more quickly, right-click any of its cells, click Table on the shortcut menu that appears, and then click Delete Columns.

If the plural form in the Delete Columns command seems out of place, it's because you can use this command to delete multiple columns at once, not just the current column. To do this, click any cell in the first column that you want to delete, hold down the Shift key, and then click any cell in the last column that you want to delete. When you use the Delete Columns command, either on the ribbon or on the right-click menu, OneNote will delete all of the columns between and including the columns of the two cells you selected.

 LET ME TRY IT

Deleting a Row in a Table

To delete a row within a table, do the following:

1. Click any cell in the row you want to delete.

2. On the ribbon, above the Layout tab, click Table Tools.

3. In the Delete group, click Delete Row.

To delete a row more quickly, right-click any of its cells, click Table on the shortcut menu that appears, and then click Delete Rows.

If the plural form in the Delete Rows command seems out of place, it's because you can use this command to delete multiple rows at once, not just the current row. To do this, click any cell in the first row that you want to delete, hold down the Shift key, and then click any cell in the last row that you want to delete. When you use the Delete Rows command, either on the ribbon or on the right-click menu, OneNote will delete all of the rows between and including the rows of the two cells you selected.

LET ME TRY IT

Using Keyboard Shortcuts to Modify Tables

When you're comfortable with the way tables work in OneNote, learn the various keyboard shortcuts (see Table 7.1) that let you create and modify tables and their cell contents. They provide the easiest and fastest way to organize information on any page in your notes.

Table 7.1   Keyboard Shortcuts for Tables in OneNote

To Do This	Press
Start a new table from typed text	Tab
Insert a new column in a table with a single row	Tab
Insert a new row below the current row (when the cursor is at the end of the last cell)	Enter
Insert a line break in the current cell	Shift+Enter
Insert another paragraph in the current cell	Alt+Enter
Insert a column to the left of the current column	Ctrl+Alt+E
Insert a column to the right of the current column	Ctrl+Alt+R
Insert a new row above the current row (when the cursor is at the beginning of any row)	Enter
Delete the current empty row in a table (when the cursor is at the beginning of the row)	Delete (press twice)
Align cell text to the left	Ctrl+L
Align cell text to the right	Ctrl+R
Delete a selected table	Delete

Navigating Notebook Content with Links

In the previous chapter, you learned the basics of working with links in OneNote. Typically, links are used to point to related information that does not need to be stored as part of your notebook. For example, you might link to a specific Wikipedia article that discusses something in greater detail than its brief description in your notes.

When it comes to organizing your notes and notebooks, however, the link functionality in OneNote offers a convenient way to link pages, sections, and entire notebooks together. The practical uses for this are virtually endless—from wiki creation to giving shared notebooks a real navigation system.

For example, corporate trainers can distribute reading materials electronically by sharing such content in notebooks where the pages and sections are linked for easy cross-referencing. A reader of the notebook can easily jump to various locations in the notebook by simply clicking the links.

SHOW ME   Media 7.3—Navigating Notebooks with Links
Access this video file through your registered Web Edition at
my.safaribooksonline.com/9780132182447/media.

The following procedures show you how you can use the commands that OneNote provides to create navigation links to various parts of your notebook content and how you can use the wiki syntax while typing notes to link to existing pages and sections or to dynamically create new pages that you want to link to.

LET ME TRY IT

Creating a Link to a Specific Notes Page

To create a link that will open a specific page in your notebook, follow these steps:

1. Navigate to the page that the link should open when it is clicked and then right-click its page tab near the right side of the OneNote program window.

2. On the shortcut menu that appears, click Copy Link to Page (see Figure 7.10).

3. Go to the notes page where you want the link to appear, click to activate the cursor, and then press Ctrl+V to paste the link.

When pasting links to pages, OneNote automatically copies the page title into the link text so you don't have to type it again. It also formats the link in blue, underlined text to indicate that it is clickable.

After the link has been pasted, clicking it will immediately open the page it points to. To return to the previous page in your notebook, click the Back button on the Quick Access Toolbar near the upper-right corner of the OneNote program window.

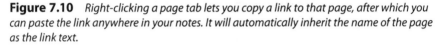

Figure 7.10 *Right-clicking a page tab lets you copy a link to that page, after which you can paste the link anywhere in your notes. It will automatically inherit the name of the page as the link text.*

In addition to creating a link to any page in any of your notebooks, you can also create a link to any specific paragraph of text or to an object on a page. To do this, move the mouse pointer over the text or object you want to link to and then right-click the four-headed arrow icon that appears next to it. On the menu that appears, click Copy Link to Paragraph. After you paste the copied link into your notes text, clicking it takes you to that specific position on the page where the text or object is located.

 LET ME TRY IT

Creating a Link to a Specific Notebook Section

To create a link that will open a specific section in your notebook, follow these steps:

1. Navigate to the section that the link should open when it is clicked and then right-click its section tab under the ribbon.

2. On the shortcut menu that appears, click Copy Link to Section (see Figure 7.11).

3. Go to the notes page where you want the link to appear, click to activate the cursor, and then press Ctrl+V to paste the link.

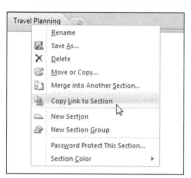

Figure 7.11 *Right-clicking a section tab lets you copy a link to that section, after which you can paste the link anywhere in your notes. It will automatically inherit the name of the section as the link text.*

When pasting links to sections, OneNote automatically copies the section title into the link text so you don't have to type it again. It also formats the link in blue, underlined text to indicate that it is clickable.

After the link has been pasted, clicking it will immediately open the section it points to. To return to the previous section in your notebook, click the Back button on the Quick Access Toolbar near the upper-right corner of the OneNote program window.

 LET ME TRY IT

Creating a Link to a Specific Notebook

To create a link in your current notebook that will open another notebook you have open, follow these steps:

1. On the navigation bar near the left side of the OneNote program window, right-click the icon of the notebook that the link should open when it is clicked.

2. On the shortcut menu that appears, click Copy Link to Notebook (see Figure 7.12).

Figure 7.12   *Right-clicking a notebook icon on the navigation bar lets you copy a link to that notebook, after which you can paste the link anywhere in your notes. It will automatically inherit the name of the notebook as the link text.*

3. Go to the notes page in the notebook where you want the link to appear, click to activate the cursor, and then press Ctrl+V to paste the link.

When pasting links to notebooks, OneNote automatically copies the notebook's name into the link text so you don't have to type it again. It also formats the link in blue, underlined text to indicate that it is clickable.

After the link has been pasted, clicking it will immediately open the notebook it points to. To return to the previous notebook, click the Back button on the Quick Access Toolbar near the upper-right corner of the OneNote program window.

If the notebook you want to link to isn't shown on the navigation bar, click the File tab, click Open, and then either click the notebook from the Recently Closed Notebooks list or click the Open Notebook button.

 **LET ME TRY IT**

Creating Wiki-Style Links to Other Locations in Your Notebook

If you're familiar with wiki editing and it's something you plan to do with OneNote, you'll be happy to learn that OneNote supports the bracket syntax that lets you create navigational links to your pages, sections, and notebooks without using the interface.

To create a link to an existing place in your notebook, do the following:

1. In your notes, where you want the link to appear, type [[(two left brackets) to begin the link.

2. Immediately following the opening brackets, type the name of the page, section, or notebook that you want to link to. This text must exactly match the name of your link target.

3. To end the link, type]] (two right brackets). As soon as you type the last bracket, the text will change to a blue, underlined, clickable link that will point to the page, section, or notebook name that you specified.

It's important to note that, while wiki link names can have spaces between words, there should be no space immediately following the opening pair of brackets and preceding the closing pair of brackets.

If the name of your link target exists, the link that will point to it will appear underlined with a solid line, just like a normal link. If you type the title of a page or the name of a section or notebook that doesn't exist, OneNote creates a new, blank page with the name you typed for the link and places this page in the current section of the notebook that you're presently working in. Blank pages that are created and linked to in this way are formatted with a blue, broken underline (see Figure 7.13) to signal that, while the target page has been created, you'll need to add content to this page at some point in the future.

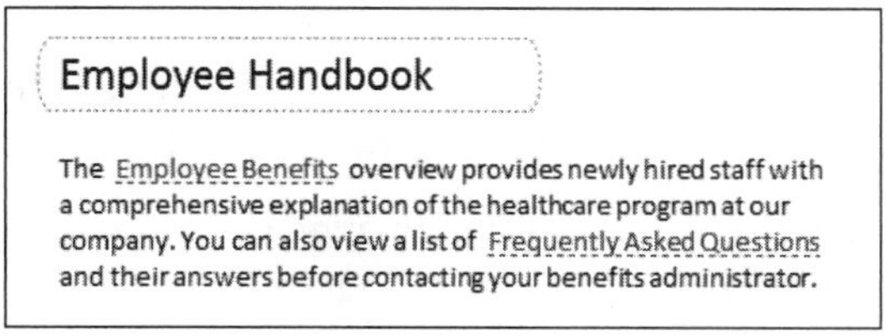

Employee Handbook

The Employee Benefits overview provides newly hired staff with a comprehensive explanation of the healthcare program at our company. You can also view a list of Frequently Asked Questions and their answers before contacting your benefits administrator.

Figure 7.13 *Typing the title of a page that does not yet exist in your notebook as a wiki link will cause OneNote to create a new, blank page with that title so that you remember to add content to the page later. To help you spot empty pages that you have linked to, the link underline appears as a dotted line.*

If OneNote creates a new, blank page as the target of a wiki link and you then delete this page, the link to that page remains. If you click the link in your notes, OneNote opens the deleted page in the notebook's Recycle Bin, from which you can move it back into your notebook. The opportunity to restore pages in this way expires after 60 days from the day the page was originally deleted.

If you have both a section and a page in your notebook that have the same name, automatic wiki links will favor the page first. If you want to create a navigational link to both the page and the section that share the same name, you can use the wiki link syntax to create the link to the page and then use the manual link creation for the section by right-clicking the section tab, clicking Copy Link to Section, and then pasting that link into your notes at the location you want it to appear. Similarly, because pages are given preference, you cannot create a new section by typing a new name as a wiki link, as this will create a new page. To create a new section that you can then link to, right-click any existing section tab at the location the new section should appear, and then click New Section on the shortcut menu.

As is the case with manually created navigational links, wiki links that you create from typed text are automatically maintained even if you move pages and sections around in your notebook after the links have been created. Similarly, your navigational links won't break if you change the names of the pages, sections, or notebooks to which they point. OneNote automatically updates and maintains them as needed.

If, for some reason, you prefer to create navigational links by selecting their destination from a list, you can use the quick filing menu to create a link. To do this, click in the line of text where you want to create your link and then press Ctrl+K to display the Link dialog box. In the lower half of the dialog box, navigate to and then select the destination of the link. When you click OK, OneNote inserts a formatted link to the page, section, or notebook that you selected.

Now that you know how to organize information in your notebooks by adding optional navigation, it's time to learn how you can move things around when needed.

Organizing the Pages and Sections in a Notebook

One of the many benefits of your electronic notebooks compared with their paper-based counterparts is the ability to change the structure of your notebook, even after the notes have been created. This is something that you simply cannot do with paper.

Because you can easily change and update the content in your notebooks in OneNote, you might also need to change the location of specific pages or entire notebook sections that contain them. I'll show you how to do this in the following procedures.

SHOW ME   Media 7.4—Organizing Pages and Sections
Access this video file through your registered Web Edition at
my.safaribooksonline.com/9780132182447/media.

Before you get started with copying or moving pages and sections, however, remember a related organizational feature covered in Chapter 4, "Notebooks, Sections, and Pages." There, you learned that you can organize page tabs and section tabs by clicking and dragging them where you want them to appear.

For example, to alphabetize your section tabs, you can click one section tab at a time and then horizontally drag it behind other section tabs until all of the section tabs in the notebook appear in alphabetical order. When you drag a section tab to a different location, all of the pages stored in that section will automatically travel with it.

Likewise, you can organize the order of appearance for the pages in any particular notebook section by clicking one page tab at a time and then dragging it up and down in the column of page tabs until each tab appears where you want it.

You can also click and vertically drag the notebook icons on the navigation bar to position your open notebooks in the order you want them to appear.

LET ME TRY IT

Displaying the Hierarchy of a Notebook on the Navigation Bar

When you're ready to organize the pages and sections of your notebooks, you'll want to expand the navigation bar at least temporarily to display the full hierarchy of sections within each notebook:

1. Near the right side of the OneNote program window, locate the navigation bar on which the icons that represent your open notebooks appear.

2. At the top of the navigation bar and just under the ribbon, click the small chevron arrow that points to the right. This is the Expand Navigation Bar toggle button. The navigation bar (see Figure 7.14) expands to show the sections contained within each notebook (see Figure 7.15).

Figure 7.14   *The navigation bar can be expanded by clicking the small arrow button at the top of your list of notebooks.*

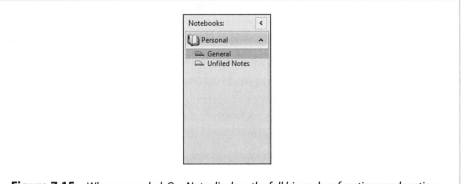

Figure 7.15   *When expanded, OneNote displays the full hierarchy of sections and section groups within each notebook. The arrow button you used to expand the navigation bar can be clicked once more to collapse the navigation bar again.*

As time goes on, your notebook will likely grow by several sections and pages. Displaying the hierarchy of each notebook by expanding the navigation bar lets you see exactly where your content is located and decide where you might want to copy or move information. Expanding the navigation bar also makes it easier to move or copy pages and sections by dragging them to their new destinations with the mouse.

To collapse the notebook hierarchy again at any point, click the small chevron arrow again, which will then point to the right.

LET ME TRY IT

Moving or Copying a Notes Page

You can move or copy any existing page to another section in the current note-book or to a section in a different notebook.

To move or copy a notes page, do the following:

1. Right-click the page tab of the page you want to move or copy to another location and then click Move or Copy on the shortcut menu.

2. In the Move or Copy Pages dialog box that opens, navigate to the section where you want the page to go. The notebook you're currently working in will appear with an open book icon, but you can also expand any other notebooks that you have listed and click to select a target section.

3. When you have clicked to select the target section you want, click either the Move or the Copy button at the bottom of the dialog box.

As the name of these commands implies, copying a page will leave it in its original location but also place an exact duplicate of it in the location you choose. This can be useful for authors who want to keep multiple versions of a set of notes for the purpose of draft management. Moving a page rips it out of its present location and places the original page in the new location you specify.

Typically, the Move command is a preferred notebook organizational tool for relo-cating your pages and sections because it puts the original set of your notes pages in their rightful places.

When you feel more familiar with the Move and Copy interface in OneNote, you can also use the mouse to click and drag page tabs from one location to the next. Clicking and dragging a page will move it, whereas holding the Ctrl key while drag-ging a page tab to another location will make a copy of the page.

As with most commands in OneNote 2010, you can use the Undo command on the Quick Access Toolbar (or the Ctrl+Z keyboard shortcut) to correct any mistakes you make while using the Move or Copy command to reorganize your notes pages.

If you followed along with the introduction to screen clipping and side notes in Chapter 6, "Collecting and Researching Information," you'll remember some pointers about the Unfiled Notes section, that virtual junk drawer where you can freely collect all of the information that you bring into OneNote that might not yet belong in a particular place in your notes. You might still be structuring your notebook the way you want, or you're not sure yet if you'll be keeping and using that information. Occasionally cleaning out any notes from the Unfiled Notes section is an important organizational task if you prefer to keep your notes organized, especially when sharing them with other people at some future point.

If, by the end of this chapter, you decide to rely more on instant search than organization of your notes, you may let things fall where they may. However, if you opt to put notebook organization to good use, keep the Unfiled Notes section in mind.

 LET ME TRY IT

Moving or Copying a Notebook Section

You can move or copy any existing notebook section to a different notebook. This is useful when you're ready to split out one or more sections into their own notebook, such as when a brainstorming idea turns into an actual project.

To move or copy a notebook section, do the following:

1. Right-click the section tab of the section you want to move or copy to another notebook and then click Move or Copy on the shortcut menu.

2. In the Move or Copy Section dialog box that opens, click the name of the notebook where you want the section to go. (The notebook you're currently working in will appear with an open book icon; the others will be marked with a closed book icon.)

3. When you have clicked to select the target notebook you want, click either the Move or the Copy button at the bottom of the dialog box.

Moving or copying a section from one location to another includes all of the pages and subpages that a section contains. If you copied a section and do not want the copied version to include all of the pages, open the copy of the section at its new location and then delete the pages you do not want to keep. Doing this is faster than bringing over the individual pages into a new section.

You can also use the mouse to click and drag section tabs from one location to another. Clicking and dragging a section with your mouse will move it, whereas holding the Ctrl key while dragging a section tab to another location will make a copy of the section and the pages it contains.

If you make a mistake, remember the Undo keyboard shortcut (Ctrl+Z).

 LET ME TRY IT

Merging One Notebook Section into Another

Another useful organizational tool in OneNote 2010 is the ability to merge one section with another. Doing so will copy all of the pages in the starting section and move them to another section that you specify. When the pages have been successfully merged at their destination, OneNote deletes the original section. Merging sections is faster than copying single pages from a section you plan to delete to a new section that already contains pages.

To merge sections, do the following:

1. Right-click the section tab of the section you want to merge into another, and then select Merge into Another Section on the shortcut menu.

2. In the Merge Section dialog box that opens, click the name of the section into which you want to merge the current section. (The notebook you're currently working in will appear with an open book icon; the others will be marked with a closed book icon.)

3. To merge the section with one in the current notebook, click its section tab. To merge the section with one in another notebook, click the + symbol next to the notebook you want and then click the target section.

4. When you have clicked to select the target section you want, click the Merge button at the bottom of the dialog box.

OneNote will warn you that the section merge that you're about to undertake cannot be undone with the Undo command on the Quick Access Toolbar, nor with the Ctrl+Z shortcut, so you must acknowledge that you're certain about continuing. In the warning dialog box, click the Merge Sections button to merge the two sections or click Cancel to leave things as they currently are.

 LET ME TRY IT

Combining Multiple Sections into a Section Group

As your notebook grows more large and complex over time, it might become cumbersome to quickly navigate between a large number of section tabs, especially when certain section tabs are ordered in such a way that makes scrolling between them time consuming.

Although you could split up a large notebook by moving some of its sections to a second notebook, you may prefer to keep all of your notes and information pertaining to a particular subject in a single notebook. You can manage section clutter by organizing at least some of your sections into section groups, which let you group together one or more notebook sections that are then kept visually separate from the main navigation of your notebook.

You can think of section groups much like folders on your hard drive. Each folder can have multiple files in it or store additional folders that, in turn, contain another level of content. You can give a meaningful name to each section group to remind you of that subset of notes that each section contains. Section groups you've created can be accessed to the far right of the row of section tabs underneath the ribbon or in the expanded hierarchical view in the navigation bar. When you click a section group icon, the master row of notebook sections near the top of the OneNote program window is hidden from view, and OneNote will display only the sections that the selected section group contains. In such a condensed view, the immediate benefit is that you don't have to click past or dig through all of the sections in your notebook. By moving a handful of sections into each section group, you'll have easy access to those section tabs while that section group is displayed.

To create a new section group in your current notebook, do the following:

1. Right-click any existing section tab and then click New Section Group on the shortcut menu.

2. While OneNote has the temporary name highlighted, type a new, meaningful name for the new section group and then press Enter.

3. You can now click and drag sections over a section group icon to place it there, or right-click a section tab and then use the Move or Copy command on the shortcut menu to put a section into one of the section groups that you have created.

To further illustrate the use of section groups, imagine that your notebook is your entire collection of recipes, and each of your notebook sections represents one letter of the alphabet. In each of those sections, you keep all of the recipe pages whose dishes start with that particular letter of the alphabet (the page holding your recipe for apple crisp is in the section labeled A, and so on).

Although such a notebook could be considered to be well organized, 26 sections is a lot of tabs to scroll back and forth among—even on the largest of computer monitors. You might consider putting an even amount of sections into about 4 or 5 section groups each, so that you can easily click between the section group icons and quickly access the smaller group of section tabs that each section group contains. As before, each notebook section would still represent one letter of the alphabet and contain all of its recipe pages, but navigating between the sections would be much easier now because of the reduced tab clutter.

To navigate to a specific section group, find and click its name in the same place where regular section tabs ordinarily appear. When your view has switched to the contents of that section group, you can click the individual section tabs in that group to access the pages in that section. To go back up a level, click the green arrow icon that appears to the far left of the section tab row until you're back at the top section level.

Using section groups is entirely optional. If splitting huge notebooks into smaller ones makes more sense to you, then use that approach to make your notes more manageable. If you'd prefer to stay in a single notebook, but you want to simplify viewing and navigating between sections that have started to scroll off the screen, consider grouping multiple sections into fewer section groups.

If your notebook contains section groups, you can link to them in the same way you can link to pages, regular sections, and other notebooks, which you learned earlier in this chapter. To copy the link to a specific section group, right-click the section group's name and then click Copy Link to Section Group on the shortcut menu that appears. You can then paste the copied link where you want it to appear in your notes. When you click the link, it will immediately take you to that particular section group.

Similarly, the functionality of sections that have been placed into section groups remains the same. You can move or copy sections out of section groups or merge them with the pages in other sections, regardless of whether those sections are also part of a section group.

 **LET ME TRY IT**

Deleting Unwanted Pages or Sections

This last organizational option in OneNote might seem obvious, but I'm including it here for completeness.

To remove notes you no longer care about, do either of the following:

1. To delete a page you no longer want or need, right-click its page tab and then click Delete on the shortcut menu.

2. To delete a section or section group you no longer want or need, right-click its section tab and then click Delete on the shortcut menu.

Now that you've learned about the various options you have available to organize the content in your notebooks and the structure of your notebooks themselves, let's continue by learning about what you can do with your content to help prioritize it, categorize it, and help to find it more easily in a notebook search.

Prioritizing and Categorizing Notes with Tags

You might have seen tags on websites before, where they are often used on blogs and news sites to group similarly themed content into categories. By clicking the category tag, you can quickly see a list of content that's available in that category. Tags have many other, similar uses. For example, when you import photos from your digital camera into an image-editing program, it may let you apply tags to your photos to describe what appears in them (the tags would consist of keywords like landscapes, pets, children, and so on) before the pictures are added to your collection. As your photo album grows to hundreds or perhaps thousands of pictures down the road, it would become increasingly harder to find, say, all of your pictures of your dog. By using tags to categorize and search for files, you can quickly locate and display all of the items that are associated with a particular tag.

Tags can also be used to indicate the priority of an item. In Microsoft Outlook, for example, using the Important or Low Priority markers for the e-mail messages that you send is a useful way of tagging the priority of the content in such messages, thus making it easier for the recipient to decide which items require immediate attention and which ones can wait.

In OneNote, tags are an optional way for you to categorize and prioritize selected notes, and you can also use note tags to aid in quickly locating and displaying specific, important information again whenever you need it. Before you get to OneNote's powerful search features, however, take a closer look at using tags.

 SHOW ME   Media 7.5—Tagging Notes
Access this video file through your registered Web Edition at
my.safaribooksonline.com/9780132182447/media.

In OneNote, a tag consists of an icon that will appear next to your notes text to mark the note (see Figure 7.16). Each tag also has a description that indicates its category or purpose (for example, Important, Idea, Client Request, and so on).

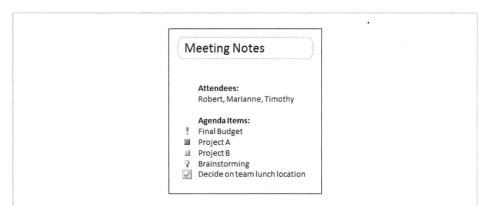

Figure 7.16 *Note tags are small icons that you can apply to the left of selected text paragraphs or to other objects on a page, such as a picture, to indicate the tagged item's priority, classification, or follow-up status. OneNote can search your notes for tags to help you find high-priority follow-up items instantly.*

For example, if you tag all of the distinct ideas that come up during a brainstorming session with your team, it's much easier to scan your notes and look for the lightbulb icon that represents the Idea tag. To see the descriptive name of a tag, move the mouse pointer over the tag's icon once it has been applied to a part of your notes.

 LET ME TRY IT

Applying a Tag to a Note

To apply a tag to a note, follow these steps:

1. Open or create a page with a couple of paragraphs of notes.

2. Click the first line of any paragraph of text on the page. This lets OneNote know which paragraph you want to tag with an icon.

3. On the Home tab, in the Tags group, click the yellow star icon that is labeled "Important." OneNote places the yellow star icon in the left margin of the current paragraph. If you move the mouse over the star icon, a ToolTip appears to let you know that this is the note tag for indicating important notes.

To see all available tags in OneNote, click the Home tab and then, in the Tags group, click the small downward-facing arrow at the bottom of the tags list box. A ToolTip will say "More" if you hover over this arrow (see Figure 7.17). When you click this button, OneNote displays the full collection of available note tags and reveals the command for customizing your own tags.

Figure 7.17 *To access the full list of available note tags and to gain access to additional tag commands, click the More button in the lower-right corner of the Tags list.*

Tagging isn't just reserved for typed text. You can tag handwritten notes, inserted files and printouts, pictures, screen clippings, scanned images, and any other objects that you've placed on your notes page.

Though tagging your notes is entirely optional, it's quite useful in a variety of situations, depending on how you collect and then want to use the information in your notebooks. You can use tags to flag important notes for follow-up (for example, the action items assigned to you in a meeting). You can also use tags to categorize information in your notes (for example, to identify all of the ideas during brainstorming and all the questions that have been asked about them). Finally, you can also use tags to identify multiple projects that are associated with specific follow-up items or reminders and list these in separate or combined to-do lists. OneNote does all the work, leaving you to spend your time focusing on your notes and information, your thoughts and ideas, instead of flipping through all of your pages, trying to find specific information in your notebook. Applying tags and the ability to fully customize these tags is yet another way in which OneNote beats paper notebooks every time.

 **LET ME TRY IT**

Using the To Do Tag

Though most note tags in OneNote 2010 are static icons, there is one tag that's interactive—the To Do tag. Initially, it appears as a blank check box, but you can click this box to place a check mark in the box to indicate that a task has been completed.

The To Do tag is best applied to follow-up reminders, such as action items that were assigned to you during a business meeting, things your teacher told you to study for your next test, or the chores you've been assigned at home.

To create a to-do list with this tag, insert the To Do tag at the beginning of every line item in your list and then click the items you have completed. When all of the items on your list have been completed, you can delete the list from your notebook, or you can keep it as a record of your accomplishments.

 LET ME TRY IT

Search for Tagged Notes

The real power of tagging notes is the ability to search for specific tags and instantly retrieve the notes that are associated with them. This becomes more and more useful over time, as your notebook grows in size and complexity.

To begin looking for tagged notes, do the following:

1. On the Home tab, in the Tags group, click the Find Tags button, which is located just to the right of the tags list.

2. In the Tags Summary pane that opens near the right side of the OneNote program window, OneNote will display a list of all tagged notes in the current notebook (see Figure 7.18). This initial view lets you step through all of your tagged notes so you can review them and remind yourself about any important items that you might have forgotten about.

3. To review the results list, use the scrollbar in the task pane (if displayed) to go through all of the tags that OneNote found. To go to a tagged note on its original page, click its entry in the results list.

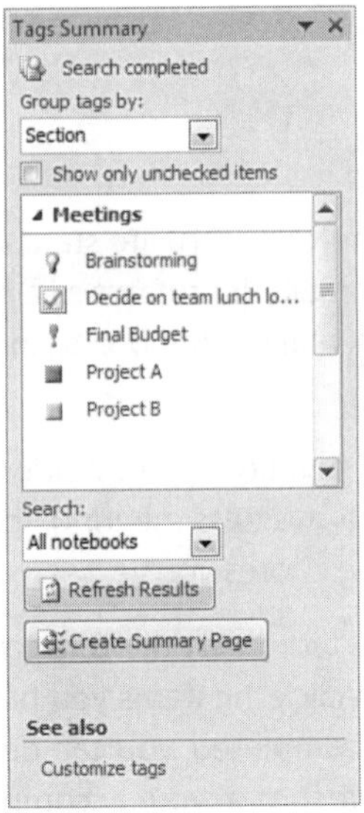

Figure 7.18   *The Tags Summary task pane displays all tagged notes that are found within the constraints of the search scope (in this example, the list of tags represents all of the tagged notes that exist in all open notebooks). To go to the page where a tagged note appears, click the note in the results list.*

You can customize the display of the tagged notes results list by changing the Group tags drop-down at the top of the Tag Summary task pane to a different sort option. For example, you could choose to display the tagged notes by the name of the sections they appear in. When you change this filter, the results list is instantly updated with your new display preference.

If you have a large number of tags applied to copious amounts of text, you might want to change the search scope to narrow your results to what you're really looking for. At the bottom of the Tag Summary task pane, under Search, click the drop-down menu and then change the default search scope ("This notebook") to one of the other options you want. For example, you could narrow the results list to only show tags in the current section or only tags applied to notes you've taken today. Likewise, if you're having trouble finding a tagged note again, you can temporarily change the search scope to include tagged notes in all notebooks.

Finally, if the results list is showing you the tagged notes you were looking for, you have the option of creating a tag summary page, which causes OneNote to take the note tag search results and copy them over to a new page, which you can then use to create lists of your tagged (i.e., categorized and prioritized) notes and follow-up items.

The multifaceted benefits of tagging your notes will become more evident over time, when your notebooks will contain more and more notes in a larger variety of subjects.

LET ME TRY IT

Removing a Tag from a Note

When a tag is no longer needed to mark a specific part of your notes, you can remove it. This is recommended if you don't want to keep seeing old tagged notes in your current results when the search scope is fairly broad.

To remove a tag, do the following:

1. Navigate to the note that contains the tag you want to remove. (If you still have your tags displayed in the Tag Summary task pane, you can click the search result containing that note and tag to quickly jump to it.)

2. Click the note text that contains the tag you want to remove.

3. On the Home tab, in the Tags group, click the small downward-facing arrow at the bottom of the tags list box. A ToolTip will say "More" if you hover over this arrow (see Figure 7.17).

4. At the bottom of the pop-up menu that appears, click Remove Tag.

LET ME TRY IT

Customizing Note Tags

If some of the tag icons and their descriptions don't quite match your needs, you can modify any existing tag or create your own.

To customize a note tag, do the following:

1. On the Home tab, in the Tags group, click the small downward-facing arrow at the bottom of the tags list box. A ToolTip will say "More" if you hover over this arrow (see Figure 7.17).

2. At the bottom of the pop-up menu that appears, click Customize Tags.

3. In the Customize Tags dialog box that opens, do one of the following:

   - To customize an existing tag, select it in the list and then click Modify Tag.

   - To create a brand new tag, click New Tag.

4. After you have modified or created a tag by specifying the name, icon, and optional highlight color you want (see Figure 7.19), return to the Customize Tags dialog box and then use the up and down arrows near the upper right of the tags list to move a selected tag up or down in the list. For example, you could move the tags you create and modify to the top of the list so they appear before all of the others.

Figure 7.19 *When you want to modify an existing tag that comes with OneNote 2010, this dialog box lets you change the tag's name, icon, and colors. When you're happy with your customization results, click OK to save your changes.*

5. Click OK to save your changes.

If you use OneNote on more than one computer and you want to use the note tags that you've created or customized on all of your computers, you can copy a single file that stores this information. On the computer where you created or modified your custom note tags, find the Preferences.dat file that is located in C:\Users\<username>\AppData\Roaming\Microsoft OneNote\14.0\ and copy this file to the same location on any of your other computers running Microsoft OneNote 2010.

Alternately, if you only have one or two custom tags you want to transfer to another computer, you can quickly do so by applying each custom tag to some notes text and then e-mailing that page to yourself on your other computer. There, open the page in OneNote 2010 and then right-click any custom note tag. On the shortcut menu that appears, click Add to My Tags. Repeat this for any additional tags. When this is done, the custom tags will be available in the Tags list on the other computer. Note that this method only works for tags that contain an icon. If you created custom tags that only change the highlight color of text, for example, you'll need to do it the long way and transfer your preferences file.

When you're done trying out the tagging features, close the Tag Summary task pane by clicking the X in the upper-right corner of the task pane.

Searching for tagged notes is only part of OneNote's powerful search capability. I've saved the best for last—the ability to search for and instantly find virtually anything in your notes.

Searching Notes

If you're wondering why I've waited to talk about one of OneNote's coolest features until the end of this chapter, it's because to really demonstrate the power of the Search function in OneNote you need at least a bit of content on the pages in your notebook(s). Hopefully, if you've been following along and tried some of the features along the way, you should have enough stuff in your practice notebook to give the search features a whirl. If not, you can always return to this chapter after your notebook has grown a bit.

The other reason I didn't delve right into searching is because I wanted to first point out the various organizational options you have available in OneNote, some of which can make searching easier or more efficient. By learning about all of the ways in which you can stay organized in OneNote, you can now better decide whether you think those features are quick and easy enough for your particular style of organization, or if you know in your heart that you'd rather toss everything into a single notebook and rely entirely on the search features to retrieve information again when you need it.

There is no right or wrong decision—OneNote fully supports both styles of note-taking and personal organization, so go with what feels most natural to you.

SHOW ME   Media 7.6—Searching Notes
Access this video file through your registered Web Edition at
my.safaribooksonline.com/9780132182447/media.

You've seen how fast and simple OneNote can search for tagged notes. Before you perform a regular notebook search for the first time, take a quick look at a couple of options that can affect the results and speed of your searches.

LET ME TRY IT

Turning Audio Search On or Off

If you frequently record audio or video clips with OneNote 2010, you have the option to include spoken words in these clips in your notebook searches. OneNote can recognize your search text in spoken audio, provided that the volume and sound quality is fairly good and that the recording does not have too much ambient noise. Audio search is supported for spoken English, French, German, Italian, Japanese, Korean, Spanish, as well as traditional and simplified Chinese.

Audio searching is initially turned off, so if you want to include your audio notes right from the start, follow these steps:

1. Click the File tab and then click Options.

2. In the OneNote Options dialog box, click the Audio and Video category in the list on the left.

3. On the right, under Audio Search, click to select the check box labeled Enable Searching Audio and Video Recordings for Words. (If you have no audio clips in your notes yet, you don't need to enable this option.) When you click the check box, OneNote displays a confirmation message to remind you of the system requirements for audio search (see Figure 7.20).

4. Click OK.

As the label of the check box indicates, audio search works with both audio clips and the audio portion of video clips that you record with or import into OneNote.

Although audio search is a remarkably useful feature, it is turned off by default for a reason. Depending on their length, audio files and the audio portion of video files can result in very large file sizes. When audio search is enabled, OneNote must scan these files completely to see whether the search text can be recognized. If you're using OneNote 2010 on a slow computer or your notebooks contain several large audio or video files, you might want to keep audio search disabled for your routine text searches unless you really need it.

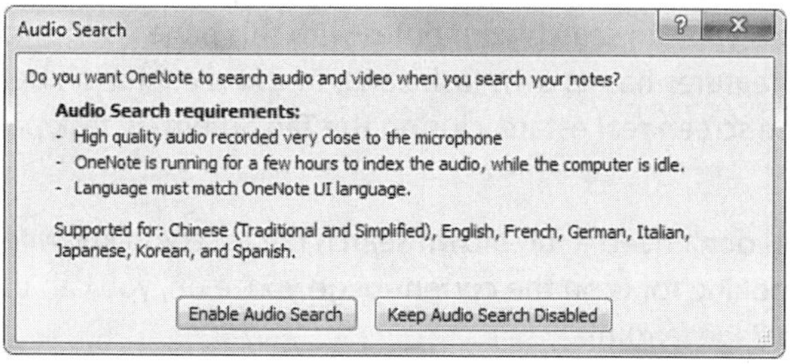

Figure 7.20 *When you first enable Audio Search from the OneNote Options dialog box, this confirmation message appears to let you know of the system requirements for this feature.*

 LET ME TRY IT

Turning Text Recognition in Pictures On or Off

You might remember that OneNote 2010 has built-in text recognition for pictures and screen clippings. This option is turned on by default, which means that if your search text is found in any of the pictures or screen clippings in your notes, OneNote will include that text in your search results.

If you want to turn this feature off, do the following:

1. Click the File tab and then click Options.

2. In the OneNote Options dialog box, click the Advanced category in the list on the left.

3. On the right, scroll down to the Text Recognition in Pictures heading near the end of the list.

4. To disable finding text in pictures, click to select the check box labeled Disable Text Recognition in Pictures. If the option is currently disabled and the box is checked, you can reenable this functionality by clicking to deselect this check box again.

5. Click OK.

LET ME TRY IT

Searching for Text on the Current Page

First, if the Tag Summary task pane is still shown on the right side of the OneNote program window, close it by clicking the X in the upper-right corner of the task pane. Although you can search your notes with this pane visible, you'll see that one of the search features has its own task pane. To avoid confusion between the two and save some screen real estate, closing the Tag Summary task pane is a good idea.

Whenever you don't need a full-blown search because you know for certain that what you're looking for is on the current page you're on, you can use OneNote's quick Find on Page feature.

To search for text on the current page, do the following:

1. If necessary, open or navigate to the page that you want to search.

2. On your keyboard, press Ctrl+F (for Find).

3. Near the right side of the OneNote program window just below the ribbon, look for the yellow Find on Page prompt (see Figure 7.21) and then type the word or phrase for which you want to search. For example, to find all occurrences of the word *meeting*, type **meeting** into the Search box (without quotes or punctuation).

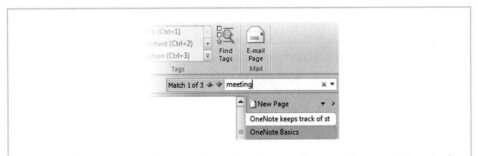

Figure 7.21 *Pressing Ctrl+F opens the Find on Page interface near the upper-right side of the OneNote program window. When you type a search term in the box, OneNote instantly counts and displays the number of matches. You can use the blue arrow keys to navigate up and down the occurrences that OneNote found in your notes.*

4. As you type the search text, OneNote highlights all instances of it on the current page. If the page has a large amount of text on it and it would take

a while to scroll through the results, click the blue arrows that are displayed in the Search box to step through the number of matches OneNote has found in the text. Click the blue down arrow in the Search box to go to the next match or click the up arrow to return to a previous match.

5. When you're done, press Esc.

If your practice notebook doesn't yet have enough sample notes content to try out the search features, you can either switch to the Guide notebook that OneNote created when you started OneNote for the first time and search for text there, or you can paste a few paragraphs of text from another document or web page onto your current notes page and then search for words that you know have at least one or two matches. That way, you can see how search results show up in a single page search.

 LET ME TRY IT

Searching for Text with Instant Search

The second level of searching in OneNote is called Instant Search. It is not limited to a single page but instead searches through all of the notes in all of your notebooks. As the name suggests, it does this instantly.

To start an Instant Search, do the following:

1. On your keyboard, press Ctrl+E.

2. OneNote activates the Search box near the right side of the OneNote program window and displays a pop-up window that represents a partial view of all of the notebooks and sections you have available (see Figure 7.22). Any notes that contain the text you're searching for will be highlighted in this list of notes.

3. In the Search box where the cursor is blinking, type a word or phrase to search for. Note that, just below the Search box, the blue text indicates that you're currently searching for your text in all notebooks. (If you want, you can click Change to change your search scope by telling OneNote where to search.)

4. As with the single page search in the previous procedure, OneNote instantly finds results based on every letter you type into the Search box. Finish typing the search text until you find what you're looking for.

Figure 7.22   *Pressing Ctrl+E opens the main search window, which displays highlighted search results within your notebook structure, provides access to change the search scope, and lets you open the Search Results pane.*

5. When OneNote has highlighted the result you want in the pop-up window, click the result in the list, and OneNote will fetch the note containing the matching search result.

6. To open the page containing one of the other matches, click its highlighted search result in the list. When you're done searching, press Esc to dismiss the search interface.

You can initiate a new Instant Search at any time by pressing Ctrl+E or by typing something into the Search box. Note that every time you initiate a new search by pressing Ctrl+E, OneNote automatically reverts to searching all available notebooks, even if you changed the search scope in a previous search. If you want OneNote to remember your preferred search scope selection, first click the word *change* in the blue link under the Search box and narrow your search. For example, to only search for results in the current section, you can click This Section on the shortcut menu. Once you have selected a new search scope, you can make it permanent by clicking the word *change* in the blue link under the Search box once again and this time clicking Set this Scope as Default on the shortcut menu. When you do this, OneNote will remember your preference across sessions, which means that if you shut down OneNote and run it again later, your first search initiated with Ctrl+E or by typing into the Search box will be limited to your previously selected search scope. You can change it back to All Notebooks when you're done limiting your searches to specific places.

The functionality in the Search pop-up window isn't limited to just displaying your notebook structure or your matching search results. You can click any item in the list to quickly navigate to that location and review your notes there. However, only pages with occurrences of matching search text will be highlighted in the pop-up window.

 LET ME TRY IT

Searching for Text with the Search Results Task Pane

If you want to use the entire height of the OneNote window to review and filter your search results, you can open the optional Search Results task pane. It provides a bit more detail about every matching search result, which is useful when you have several notes that have similar text or when you want to see the date of the page containing the matching note.

To search for text with the Search Results task pane, do the following:

1. On your keyboard, press Ctrl+E to start a new instant search.

2. In the Search box near the right side of the OneNote program window, where the cursor is blinking, type a word or phrase to search for.

3. When you're done typing and you see at least one matching search result highlighted, press Alt+O (that's the letter O, not the number zero).

4. OneNote opens the Search Results task pane (see Figure 7.23). Here, you can click through the search results to display each page containing the text you were looking for. Each search result in the list contains a short excerpt of the text, as well as the creation date of each page.

5. If you want to change the search scope for the currently displayed results, click the top drop-down menu near the top of the Search Results task pane and choose a new search scope. For example, you can narrow your scope from All Notebooks to only look in This Section.

6. From the drop-down menu immediately below the search scope, you can change the way the search results are sorted by date and instead sort them by the sections in which matching notes appear or by the page titles of matching pages.

Figure 7.23   *The Search Results task pane appears near the right side of the OneNote program window when you press Alt+O after a notebook search. The task pane gives a small text preview of each search result and provides a time stamp for each note. You can narrow or expand your search scope in this pane and sort the results in the list.*

7. When you're done with the Search Results task pane, you can dismiss it by either clicking the X in the upper-right corner of the task pane or by pressing Esc.

> If you create a new note that contains the text you previously searched for and the Search Results task pane is still displayed, it will not automatically update itself to include the new occurrence. To refresh the results, press Ctrl+E to initiate a new search and then search for the same word again.

 **LET ME TRY IT**

Troubleshooting Problems with Search

The search features in OneNote depend on the Instant Search component in the latest versions of Microsoft Windows. If you installed OneNote 2010 on a Windows 7 or Windows Vista computer, the search features should work as intended without any action on your part.

However, if you're using OneNote 2010 on a computer that you're sharing with other people, it's possible that another person has turned on or off one or more search features. Similarly, if you're still using an outdated operating system like Windows XP, you might need to manually install one of the search components.

To verify that OneNote has everything it needs to use Instant Search features, complete either or both of the following procedures.

To verify that the Instant Search component is installed, do the following:

1. Click the File tab and then click Options.

2. In the OneNote Options dialog box that opens, click the Advanced category on the left.

3. On the right, scroll down to the Search heading and look for a button labeled Install Instant Search. If this button can be clicked, then you did not have Instant Search installed. Complete the installation by following any onscreen prompts.

4. Click OK.

If the Install Instant Search button appears grayed out, it means that this component is already properly installed and that you don't need to do anything else here. In this case, click OK to close the OneNote Options dialog box.

If you verified that Instant Search was installed but you see a Warning dialog box a few minutes after you start OneNote (see Figure 7.24), a secondary component may be turned off in Windows.

Figure 7.24   *If this warning appears a few moments after you've launched OneNote 2010, you won't be able to take advantage of the Instant Search speed in OneNote unless you turn the Windows Search service back on.*

You can restart this component by doing the following:

1. In Windows 7, click the Start button.

2. In the Search box at the bottom of the Start menu, type the word **Services** and wait for the word to appear near the top of the search results window on the Start menu.

3. In the search results list, highlight the word *Services* (do not highlight other results, such as Component Services), and then press Enter.

4. Maximize the Services window that appears.

5. In the list, scroll down until you see Windows Search in the Name column and then double-click the words *Windows Search*.

6. In the Windows Search Properties dialog box that opens, make sure that the Startup type option is set to Automatic (Delayed Start). If it isn't, click the drop-down menu and select this option from the list.

7. If the Service Status further below is set to Stopped, click the Start button underneath this text.

8. Click OK to close the Windows Search Properties dialog box.

9. Restart OneNote 2010.

Unlike the Instant Search component, which must be installed, the Windows Search service does not have to be running if you're content with slower searches in OneNote. For example, if your computer or laptop is equipped with a Solid State Drive (SSD) instead of a regular hard drive, it's possible that Windows Search indexing was turned off by the manufacturer. SSD drives are memory chip-based hard drives with no moving parts. Because of this, their performance is so fast that search indexing is usually not necessary. If you have an SSD drive and you want to keep search indexing disabled, you can click the Don't Show This Again check box in the Warning dialog box (see Figure 7.24) to tell OneNote that you've acknowledged the warning and that you're fine with normal searching instead of Instant Searching. The high performance of an SSD hard drive will more than make up for the difference.

I hope that this chapter has given you a good idea about the powerful ways in which you can organize information and instantly recall any of that information whenever you need to. The benefits that all of these features avail you make it easy to understand why keeping all of your stuff in OneNote is your best step to improving your personal organization at work, at school, or at home—even if you're not a particularly organized person.

You can choose to use OneNote's organizational features to help you and others use and benefit from the information that you've collected with OneNote. If you don't want to bother with organizing your notes, it's perfectly fine to rely exclusively on search. The benefits of OneNote's search feature may well keep amazing you, even after you've used it for a while. It's the best reason for keeping all of your notes, research, and information in OneNote, even if that information originated in other places.

In the next chapter, you'll learn about shared notebooks. When collaborating with other people in the same notebook, the organizational options you've learned about in this chapter can come in handy. You can also greatly benefit from OneNote's search features in shared notebooks when trying to find and view information that others have created or modified.

Learn how to keep important notes protected with the tips covered in this chapter.

Security Features in OneNote

Before the age of electronic note-taking, notebook protection meant having a tiny little padlock on your leather-bound journal. Much like present-day car alarms, they provided little more than a false sense of security. Let's face it: If someone really wanted to read your private notes, a good whack on the lock was probably all that was needed to breach the feeble guardian. The only saving grace was that the damage inflicted to the cover would leave no doubt in your mind that your secrets were no longer safe.

In Chapter 9, "Sharing Notes with Other People," you'll learn more about one of OneNote's most versatile and useful features—sharing your notes and notebooks with other people. Before opening up your notes to the joys and risks of other readers and coauthors mingling in your notebook files, let me introduce you to the security features in OneNote 2010. These features not only provide a strong layer of protection from prying eyes, but they also provide a way to recover from disaster should your most important notes be accidentally lost, overwritten, or deleted.

As with all computer-based housekeeping tasks, all of the procedures and tips offered in this chapter are entirely optional. Assigning a password to private files is simple enough, but a backup strategy takes a bit more forethought and effort. In the end, it's all very much like insurance: When everything goes according to plan, you feel justified for not having bothered with it. But when disaster strikes, you wish you'd been more prepared.

I won't lecture you here about the importance of backing up your computer files regularly and testing your restoration procedures. But if you do decide to make OneNote your information repository so you can enjoy all of the conveniences and benefits that come along with doing this, I promise you that learning how to protect your notes will be time well spent.

Keeping Private Notes Private

What makes people consider their notes to be personal or private? Only you can answer that for yourself. Different people have different comfort levels when it comes to sharing information. This is true even in the social networking age, when we've seemingly gotten used to sharing just about everything about ourselves with others.

No matter how you use OneNote, it's likely that some of your notes will, at some point, contain personal or private information that you don't want others to see or know about. For example, you could create a notebook section dedicated entirely to keeping track of personal security information—such as account numbers, passwords, street addresses, e-mail addresses, phone numbers, website credentials, and so on. By protecting such information with a single password in OneNote, you're better protected from forgetting something important.

There are many other reasons to protect some notes and not others. For example, while you probably wouldn't care if someone were to stumble upon your to-do list or your vast recipe collection, you'd probably be concerned quite a bit more about others seeing a confidential business plan or the details of a project that's under a nondisclosure agreement. No matter what's behind your own, personal want or need for privacy, having a place where you can keep all of your information together and protecting that place can be very important.

 SHOW ME   Media 8.1—Protecting Notes with Passwords
Access this video file through your registered Web Edition at
my.safaribooksonline.com/9780132182447/media.

The following procedures illustrate how easy it is to work with password protection in OneNote 2010.

 **LET ME TRY IT**

Locking a Notebook Section with a Password

If you're not already somewhat familiar with how password protection works on computers, be sure to practice the following procedures with a dummy section that you don't really care about. If necessary, create a new section in your notebook and then type some text on the single page it contains. You can use this section for practice and, if you make a mistake while learning about password protection, you won't lose any important information.

To assign a password to any section in a notebook, do the following:

1. Navigate to the notebook containing the section that you want to protect with a password.

2. Right-click its section tab and then click Password Protect This Section on the shortcut menu.

3. Near the right side of the OneNote program window, the Password Protection task pane appears (see Figure 8.1). Under the Current Section heading near the top of the task pane, click Set Password.

Figure 8.1   *The Password Protection task pane in OneNote 2010 lets you manage the optional security for the current notebook section.*

4. In the Password Protection dialog box that opens, type the password you want into the Enter Password box (see Figure 8.2). As you type the password, its characters are shown as bullets to prevent anyone from seeing your password. It's important to note here that passwords in OneNote are case sensitive, which means that when you type any letters of the alphabet in either upper- or lowercase, you must type them again exactly as they were entered to unlock that section again. Take care, therefore, that

the Caps Lock key is not pressed and that you always enter passwords very carefully.

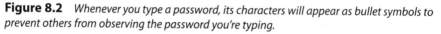

Figure 8.2   *Whenever you type a password, its characters will appear as bullet symbols to prevent others from observing the password you're typing.*

5.   In the Confirm Password box, type the same password again that you typed into the Enter Password box in step 4. Here, too, your password confirmation will appear on your screen as bullets. The passwords you typed into both fields must match each other exactly before OneNote applies the password to the section.

6.   Click OK to save your password and to protect the current section.

The effectiveness and reliability of password-based security in computer programs offered in today's software marketplace can dramatically vary. Unlike some programs, which lock only the "front door" to a collection of sensitive data, OneNote actually securely encrypts all of the information in your notebook sections that you choose to protect with a password. For this reason, it is imperative that you take great care when thinking up and entering new passwords that will lock notebook sections containing important or critical information. No one at Microsoft will be able to help you unlock OneNote sections whose passwords you've forgotten. (For that matter, neither can the author nor the publishers of this book.)

Although it's generally a good idea to use strong and unique computer passwords that your family members, schoolmates, or work colleagues can't guess, make sure that you don't use overly long and complicated passwords that you yourself won't be able to remember. If you need to, write down the passwords you use and keep them in a safe and secret location.

Although it is not possible to password protect entire notebooks in OneNote 2010, you can protect all of the contents in a notebook by assigning the same password to each section. To see how to lock all notebook sections at once, see "Locking All Protected Sections in a Notebook" later in this chapter.

As soon as OneNote has successfully protected the current section with a password, it will explicitly confirm this in the text shown under the Current Section heading in the Password Protection task pane (see Figure 8.3).

Figure 8.3   *The protection status of the section you're currently viewing is displayed just under the Current Section heading in the Password Protection task pane.*

When a section is password protected, you can continue to view it for a while. After a certain amount of time, or if you navigate away from the current section, you will need to enter the section password to return to it.

 **LET ME TRY IT**

Unlocking a Protected Section

When a section in your notebook has been protected with a password, you must enter that password whenever you want to return to that section again to look at its pages.

To unlock a section, do the following:

1. Click the tab of the password-protected section that you want to view.

2. When you see the password protection screen (see Figure 8.4), click the screen or press Enter.

3. In the Protected Section dialog box that appears, type the password for the section, and then click OK. Remember that passwords in OneNote are case sensitive. Upper- and lowercase characters must be entered exactly as you typed them when you first created the password for the current section.

Figure 8.4   *Whenever you navigate to a protected section in your notebook, you can click the screen or press the Enter key to display the dialog box that unlocks the section with the correct password.*

If you enter the wrong password or you typed the right password incorrectly, OneNote displays a "Password is incorrect" warning in the Protected Section dialog box and clears the Enter Password field so you can try again.

When you type the correct password, OneNote unlocks the section and displays all of its pages.

Unlocked and unprotected sections are two different things. An unprotected section has no password assigned to it and can be viewed by anyone with access to the notebook in which it is stored, whereas an unlocked section still has a password assigned to it.

By default, a password-protected OneNote section stays unlocked for up to 10 minutes of inactivity after you have entered its correct password. After this time, the section will automatically lock itself again. This timeout can provide an additional layer of security, for example, if you're called away from your computer while viewing a protected section, especially if that computer has no password-protected screensaver.

 **LET ME TRY IT**

Locking All Protected Sections in a Notebook

If you've applied passwords to multiple sections in your notebook and you want to lock them all again after viewing them, you can do so with a simple command.

With one or more of your protected sections unlocked, do either of the following:

- If the Password Protection task pane is visible near the right side of the OneNote program window, click the Lock All button under the All Protected Sections heading (see Figure 8.5).

- On your keyboard, press Ctrl+Alt+L to lock all protected sections.

Figure 8.5   *If you have multiple protected sections open and you want to immediately lock them all, you can either press the Lock All button in the Password Protection task pane or use the Ctrl+Alt+L keyboard shortcut.*

 **LET ME TRY IT**

Changing the Password for a Protected Section

Changing passwords is very important if you think your original password has been compromised. This can happen if you become aware of someone having watched your keyboard while you entered a valid password or when someone with whom you shared a password should no longer have access to the protected information (for example, when a colleague at work leaves a confidential project to go work on another team).

Provided that you have the correct password for a protected section, you can change it at any time by doing the following:

1. Navigate to and then unlock the protected section whose password you want to change.

2. In the Password Protection task pane, click Change Password (see Figure 8.6).

3. In the Change Password dialog box that appears, first type the current password into the Old Password box.

4. In the Enter New Password box, type a new password for the current section. Remember that passwords in OneNote are case sensitive.

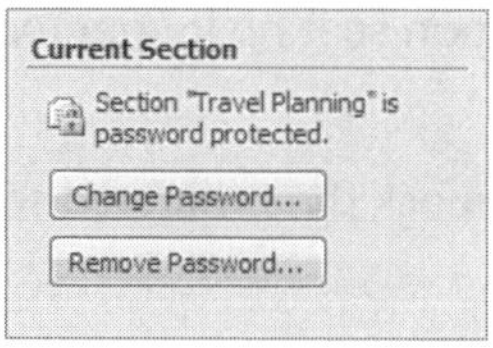

Figure 8.6 *If the password for a protected section should become compromised, you can click the Change Password button in the Password Protection task pane to assign a new password to that section.*

5. In the Confirm Password box, type the new password again. Only if this confirmation matches the new password will OneNote change the password for the current section.

If you type the original password incorrectly into the Old Password box, or if the new password and its confirmation don't match, OneNote doesn't change the current password but clears the password fields in the Change Password dialog box so you can try again.

When the old password, new password, and new password confirmation match, OneNote will change the password for the current section. Depending on the speed of your computer, a progress bar may briefly appear while OneNote is changing the password. When the dialog box disappears, the password will have successfully been changed. At that point, the old password for that section will no longer unlock it. You will have to use the new password to view the section again.

If you closed the Password Protection task pane and you want to display it again, right-click the tab of any unprotected section and then click Password Protect This Section on the shortcut menu. When the task pane appears again, navigate to the protected section that you want to work with by clicking its section tab.

LET ME TRY IT

Removing the Password for a Protected Section

When the notes in a protected section are no longer considered to be secret or sensitive in nature, you can opt to remove the password protection from that section. Removing a password may also be a temporary convenience whenever you need to do lengthy editing work in multiple protected sections and you become annoyed with their automatic timeout. Of course, in the latter case, be sure to reapply password protection to such sections again when your work is finished.

To unprotect a protected section so it no longer requires a password to be viewed, do the following:

1. Navigate to and then unlock the protected section whose password you want to remove.

2. In the Password Protection task pane, click Remove Password (refer to Figure 8.6).

3. In the Remove Password dialog box that appears, type the current password for the section and then click OK.

If you enter the current password incorrectly, OneNote won't remove the current password. When you enter the current password correctly, the password is removed from the current section. You can verify this by looking at the confirmation text under the Current Section heading near the top of the Password Protection task pane.

When you no longer need the Password Protection task pane, you can regain some screen space by closing it. To do so, click the small X in the upper-right corner of the task pane to dismiss it. If you want to follow along with the rest of the procedures in this chapter, however, you might want to keep it displayed for now.

 LET ME TRY IT

Setting Password-Protection Preferences

OneNote will keep protected sections unlocked for up to 10 minutes of inactivity after you've entered the correct password. If this amount of time proves to be too long or too short to suit your needs, you can change this setting by doing the following:

1. Click the File tab and then click Options.

2. On the left side of the OneNote Options dialog box that appears, click the Advanced category.

3. On the right side of the dialog box, scroll down to the Passwords heading (see Figure 8.7).

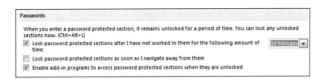

Figure 8.7 *Under the Passwords heading in the Advanced category of the OneNote Options dialog box, you can change how and when OneNote locks password-protected notebook sections.*

4. Make sure that the check box in front of the first option ("Lock Password Protected Sections After I Have Not Worked in Them for the Following Amount of Time") is selected, and then click the drop-down menu next to this option to select a security timeout that suits you. You can choose from a minimum of 1 Minute all the way up to 1 Day.

Independent of the first option, you can also tell OneNote to lock protected sections immediately after you click away from them:

1. Click the File tab and then click Options.

2. On the left side of the OneNote Options dialog box that appears, click the Advanced category.

3. On the right side of the dialog box, scroll down to the Passwords heading (see Figure 8.7).

4. Make sure that the check box in front of the second option ("Lock Password Protected Sections as Soon as I Navigate Away from Them") is selected.

Finally, if you use any add-in programs with OneNote 2010 that provide additional functionality, you can tell OneNote to let such programs access your protected notebook sections as long as these are unlocked. To do this, follow these steps:

1. Click the File tab and then click Options.

2. On the left side of the OneNote Options dialog box that appears, click the Advanced category.

3. On the right side of the dialog box, scroll down to the Passwords heading (see Figure 8.7).

4. Make sure that the check box in front of the third option ("Enable Add-In Programs to Access Password Protected Sections When They Are Unlocked") is selected.

If you don't use add-in programs with OneNote 2010 or if you don't even know what they are, you can leave the third option selected, as it is when OneNote is first installed. Because permission is only given to sections that you yourself have unlocked with a valid password, you needn't worry about any unauthorized access to your notes.

Whenever you choose to protect sensitive or confidential notes with a password, be aware of the following important information:

If you store extremely confidential information in a notebook, such as trade secrets or mission-critical business plans, it is highly recommended that you first create a new section, password protect it, and only then add the confidential notes to new pages in that section. Protecting a section after it has existed on your computer for a while might leave automatic backups of those sections freely available on your computer. (The remaining part of this chapter explains in more detail how backups are created and how they might contain various versions of previously created notes.)

When protected sections in your notebook are locked, the notes on their pages are not included in the results of any notebook search. This is an intentional security feature to prevent others from seeing your confidential notes without a valid password. However, this also means that you'll need to remember to first unlock all of your protected sections to include their pages in your notebook searches.

Lastly, if any of the pages in a section that you're protecting with a password contain one or more audio and/or video recordings, only the notes will be protected. The clips on such pages will not be protected or encrypted. If this concerns you, you should first delete such clips from your notes before password protecting sections containing such pages.

Backing Up Your Important Notes

I once overheard a colleague say to another: "If you don't back up your computer, you deserve to lose all your stuff. It means you don't really care about it." A bit harsh? Hmm, perhaps. Then again, the topic of computer backups usually requires a bit of tough love for the uninitiated.

Security comes at the expense of convenience. The task of backing up your most important computer files is no exception. If you choose the easy path by never bothering with backups, you greatly increase your chances of being greatly inconvenienced when the unthinkable happens—such as a hard drive crash. Such things occur without warning and never at convenient times. The fallout from lost and especially irreplaceable data can be enormously painful. In most cases, people won't even realize all that they've lost. Only as the days, weeks, and months pass, whenever they desperately search for a file they were sure they still had, will the damage become evident. Data loss is the gift that keeps on giving—the gift that nobody wants.

Although backing up your computer is simply a good idea, doing so regularly is a *great* one. It gives you a way of going back in time and restoring lost data to the last time you backed up. The longer you wait to refresh your backup, the more painful unexpected data loss will be. The more often you back up your files, the less it will hurt when everything is lost. As I said at the beginning of this chapter, it's all quite a bit like insurance: While the platters on your hard drive spin happily, you feel justified for not having bothered with backups. But when they finally come crashing down, you wish you'd been more prepared.

 SHOW ME Media 8.2—Backing Up Important Notes
Access this video file through your registered Web Edition at
my.safaribooksonline.com/9780132182447/media.

In Chapter 7, "Organizing and Searching Notes," I told you that OneNote will never nag you about organizing your notes if that's not your cup of tea. The same is true for backing up your notes. Therefore, it falls on you to decide whether you want to be protected from data loss or not. If you're using OneNote just for yourself, you probably have only yourself to answer to. However, after you begin sharing notes with others, as I cover in Chapter 9, you'll see how quickly the loss of important information can impact a whole team—even an entire organization. Just like no one can help you remember a forgotten password, no one can help you if you lose critical information and you didn't keep any backups.

Even if you're not yet sold on backing up your notes, I urge you to read on and at least let me introduce you to the easy backup features that OneNote 2010 makes available to you. It's much less of a pain than you might think.

 **LET ME TRY IT**

Selecting a Backup Location

Remember what I said about cheap little padlocks on leather-bound journals and car alarms? They provide a false sense of security. The same is true if you use the default location that OneNote 2010 selects for automatic backups. This is because

OneNote's backup system defaults to the same drive on which you install OneNote itself, which is also where you'll typically create and store your notes.

The trouble with this is that, if your hard drive crashes, not only your original notes will be lost, but your "backups" as well. If you keep this configuration, you might as well not have bothered with backups at all. Although keeping backups on the same drive as your primary files does provide a handy way to undo damage resulting from human errors, such as if you accidentally delete a section you still needed, the real solution is to designate a location other than your primary hard drive as OneNote's backup folder. This location could be another hard drive in your computer, an external hard drive connected to your computer, or even a USB drive that you temporarily connect to create a manual backup and which you then keep in a safe location.

To select a folder that OneNote should use for backups, follow these steps:

1. Click the File tab and then click Options.

2. On the left side of the OneNote Options dialog box that appears, click the Save & Backup category (see Figure 8.8).

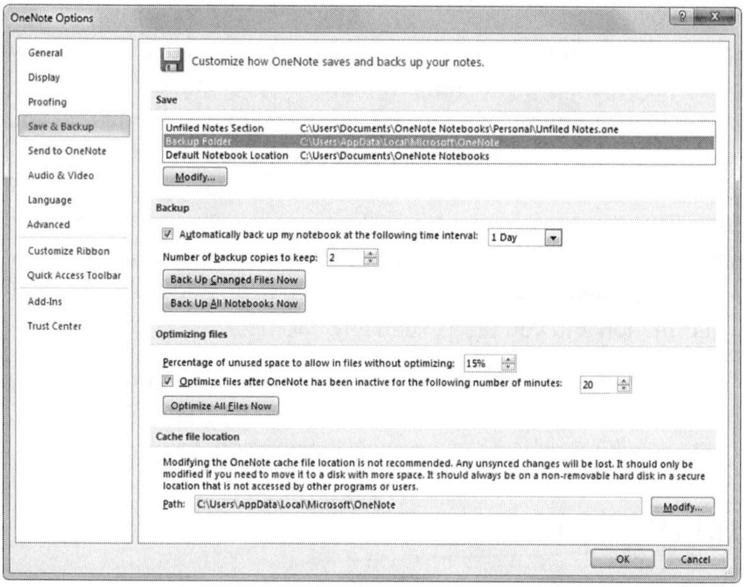

Figure 8.8 *The Save & Backup category in the OneNote Options dialog box lets you control where and how often OneNote should create automatic backups of your notebooks. Here, you can also create instant backups, which is useful when you want immediate security after creating or modifying a large amount of important notes.*

3. On the right side of the dialog box, under the Save heading, click the second line in the list with the prefix "Backup Folder" and then click the Modify button below it.

4. In the Select Folder dialog box that opens, navigate to a location other than your primary hard drive where OneNote should keep your backups. If you want automatic backups to be saved here at regular intervals, you'll need to select a drive that's always available, such as a second or external hard drive, or a file share on your network to which you have read and write access.

5. If necessary, create a new folder called OneNote Backups at this new location and then navigate to it.

6. Click Select to accept the new location and close the Select Folder dialog box. OneNote updates the Backup Folder path in the list with the new location you specified.

7. If you want to save the new location, you must click OK at the bottom of the OneNote Options dialog box. If you click Cancel, OneNote will revert to the previous backup location.

After you've set a reliable (and preferably permanent) secondary location as your backup folder, you can already rest a bit easier. If you accept the factory settings, OneNote will now create a backup of your open notebooks once every 24 hours and it will keep two days' worth of backups at any one time. After that, the oldest backup will be overwritten with a fresh one. If this does not suit your needs, you can easily adjust both the time interval for automatic backups as well as the number of backup sets that OneNote should keep on hand.

 LET ME TRY IT

Changing the Automatic Backup Time Interval

To have OneNote create automatic backups more frequently than just once a day, do the following:

1. Click the File tab and then click Options.

2. On the left side of the OneNote Options dialog box that appears, click the Save & Backup category (see Figure 8.8).

3. On the right side of the dialog box, under the Backup heading, make sure that the check box in front of the first option ("Automatically Back Up My

Notebook at the Following Time Interval") is selected, and then click the drop-down menu next to this option to select a backup frequency that suits you. You can have OneNote create a fresh backup every single minute or wait up to 6 weeks between one automatic backup and the next.

4. You must click OK at the bottom of the OneNote Options dialog box to save your changes. If you click Cancel, OneNote will revert to the previous settings.

If you want to completely turn off automatic backups for some reason, simply deselect the check box labeled Automatically Back Up My Notebook at the Following Time Interval in step 3. To turn automatic backups back on after you've turned them off, reselect the check box.

If you change the time interval to have OneNote create automatic backups more often than once a day, keep in mind that you might also want to change the number of backup sets that are kept in your backup folder. If you keep the factory setting of just two backups at any one time, it can severely limit your restoration options. Read on for an elaboration of this problem.

 LET ME TRY IT

Changing the Number of Backups to Keep

Imagine that you've set up OneNote to make an automatic backup of your work every hour on the hour. Although this might seem like a highly safe option, it might not be. Leaving the number of backups to keep at just two sets (the OneNote default setting) means that you might not be able to undo any accidental deletions or overwritten notes that you might discover some 3–4 hours after such an error has occurred. After just 2 hours, all of your backup sets will have been overwritten with those fresh, hourly backups you wanted, and those new backups will each contain the mistakenly overwritten notes (or lack the pages that were accidentally deleted). This would make your two backup sets entirely useless.

To avoid this, remember to also increase the number of backups you want OneNote to keep whenever you choose to increase the frequency of your automatic backups. The only cost for doing this is hard drive space. If you create more backup sets more often, it might require a significant amount of free space in your backup location.

If you're backing up to a spacious secondary drive or network share that's dedicated to your OneNote backups and nothing else, keeping a large number of backups shouldn't be much of an issue. However, if your notes contain a lot of significantly large attachments, or a significantly large number of images or audio and video clips, you might need to first double-check how much space is needed for each backup set of all your notes. You can do this by opening Windows Explorer and looking at the file sizes of your notebooks by checking them in their primary storage location on your hard drive (typically, in the subfolders found in the OneNote Notebooks folder, which, in turn, is tucked away in your Documents [or My Documents] folder).

To increase or decrease the number of backup sets OneNote should keep at any one time, do the following:

1. Click the File tab and then click Options.

2. On the left side of the OneNote Options dialog box that appears, click the Save & Backup category (see Figure 8.8).

3. On the right side of the dialog box, under the Backup heading, replace the number shown in the field following the second option ("Number of Backup Copies to Keep") with the number of backup sets you want to save in your backup location. The oldest of these sets will be overwritten at the time interval you specified in the option immediately above. If you have the space available for it, you can keep up to a staggering 99,999 backup sets.

4. You must click OK at the bottom of the OneNote Options dialog box to save your changes. If you click Cancel, OneNote will revert to the previous settings.

If you change the number of backup sets to keep after you've had OneNote open for a while, you might see a warning that your configuration changes won't take effect until you restart OneNote (see Figure 8.9). In this case, it is highly recommended that you exit and restart OneNote as soon as possible so that your next automatic backup will be complete.

Figure 8.9 *This dialog box may appear if you're modifying the number of backups that OneNote should keep after you've been editing notes for a while. Click OK to dismiss this notification and then exit and restart OneNote.*

No magic formula can tell you what you should set your backup time interval and number of backup sets to. It really depends on the importance of your notes and how often you may need to recover from critical mistakes, which is likely to happen more often than complete data loss due to technical failures. If you have the space available in your backup location, creating many backups more often may be the best insurance policy, especially if you frequently work with very sensitive or mission-critical information. For less serious work, you can certainly choose to reduce the frequency of your backups, but consider still keeping a larger number of backup sets than just the two that OneNote starts out with. The more sets you have available to restore notes from, the better your chances of recovering exactly those notes that you cared about and somehow lost or overwrote.

 LET ME TRY IT

Immediately Backing Up All Changed Files

If you've created or changed a significant amount of important notes and you don't want to wait for the next automatic backup interval, you can immediately create a backup of all of your changed files:

1. Click the File tab and then click Options.

2. On the left side of the OneNote Options dialog box that appears, click the Save & Backup category.

3. On the right side of the dialog box, under the Backup heading, click the Back Up Changed Files Now button. After a moment, you should see a confirmation message that tells you that the backup was created successfully (see Figure 8.10).

4. At the bottom of the OneNote Options dialog box, click OK.

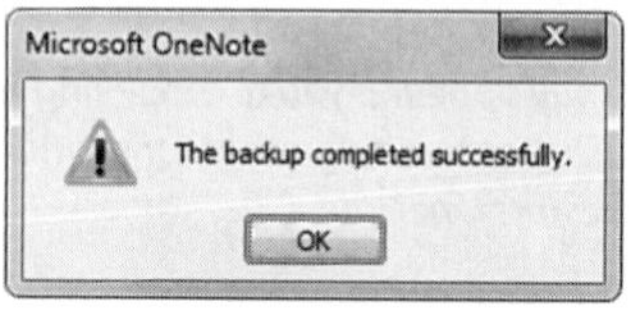

Microsoft OneNote

The backup completed successfully.

OK

Figure 8.10 *OneNote displays this confirmation whenever it successfully completes a backup that you've manually initiated.*

LET ME TRY IT

Immediately Backing Up All Notebooks

Similar to the previous procedure, you can create a manual, immediate backup of all of your notebooks whenever you want or need to. This is most useful if you've created or changed a significant amount of important notes across multiple notebooks and you don't want to wait for the next automatic backup interval.

To create an immediate backup, do the following:

1. Click the File tab and then click Options.

2. On the left side of the OneNote Options dialog box that appears, click the Save & Backup category.

3. On the right side of the dialog box, under the Backup heading, click the Back Up All Notebooks Now button. After a moment, you should see a confirmation message that tells you that the backup was created successfully (see Figure 8.10).

4. At the bottom of the OneNote Options dialog box, click OK.

 **LET ME TRY IT**

Copying Your Notebooks to a USB Drive

Finally, there's a quick-and-dirty way to create a complete, manual backup of all of the notebooks stored on your computer's hard drive. If you're still experimenting with the automatic backup settings I discussed in the previous procedures, you might want to create a complete, manual backup set of all of your notebooks.

Typically, I don't recommend this option as a valid backup method because it creates a separate version of all of your notes. If you create too many copies of all of your notes, you might confuse yourself about which set is most current. However, I'm including this here as a final backup tip because it's really the simplest and fastest way to an instant notebooks' insurance policy.

To back up all of your notebooks to a USB drive, do the following:

1. Connect your USB drive to your computer. For the highest reliability, connect USB drives only to the ports on your computer, not to USB hubs or USB extension cords.

2. In Windows Explorer, navigate to your Documents (or My Documents) folder.

3. Right-click the folder labeled OneNote Notebooks and then click Copy on the shortcut menu.

4. Navigate to the contents of your USB drive. Right-click over a blank area in the window (not over any existing folders there), and then click Paste on the shortcut menu. OneNote will copy the entire OneNote Notebooks folder from your hard drive to your USB drive.

If you might confuse yourself with having multiple OneNote Notebooks folders appearing on multiple drives, consider renaming the copied folders on your USB drive by appending the date of the backup to the folder name. Alternately, you could also create a Readme text file in the same location, in which you briefly describe the purpose of the manual backup (for example, "Backup of all note-books before major revisions on September 1, 2011").

If you opt for this method of creating quick, manual backups of all of your OneNote files, be sure never to move or rename the original OneNote Note-books folder (nor its subfolders) in your Documents (or My Documents) folder.

Restoring Notes from a Backup

After you've created at least one set of notebook backups, you can use these files to restore your notes to that previous version if your most current version of those notes becomes lost or corrupted, or if parts of it were overwritten or deleted due to human error.

 SHOW ME   Media 8.3—Restoring Notes from a Backup
Access this video file through your registered Web Edition at
my.safaribooksonline.com/9780132182447/media.

Although the task of restoring notes itself is fairly quick and easy, it's important not to breeze through this process, especially if you're looking through multiple versions of the same notes. No one but you can accurately decide which notes (and which version of them) contain the things you care about, the things you lost, and the things you need to restore.

LET ME TRY IT

Opening a Set of Notes from a Backup Folder

To open notes from a backup, do the following:

1. Click the File tab, click Info, and then click Open Backups. OneNote opens the default backup location.

2. Double-click the folder matching the name of the notebook whose notes you want to restore.

3. In the folder of the backed-up notebook, click the section file containing the notes you want to restore, and then click Open.

4. OneNote may prompt you whether you want to open only the selected section or also the notebook that the section is part of (see Figure 8.11). If you see this dialog box, click either Open Notebook or Open Section to proceed.

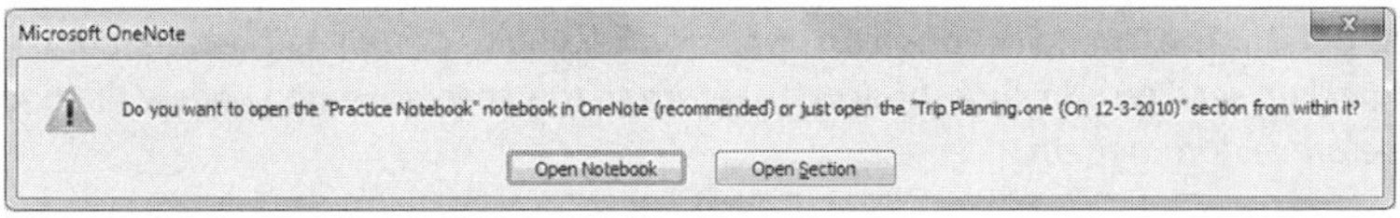

> Microsoft OneNote
>
> ⚠ Do you want to open the "Practice Notebook" notebook in OneNote (recommended) or just open the "Trip Planning.one (On 12-3-2010)" section from within it?
>
> [Open Notebook]   [Open Section]

Figure 8.11 *When opening a backed-up section file (a file ending with a *.one file extension), OneNote may display this dialog box. In most cases, opening the associated notebook of a backed-up section (and not just the section alone) will give you more context about the version of the old notes you're looking at and whether or not they are indeed the notes that you want to restore.*

5. When OneNote opens sections from a backup file, they are placed in a special Open Sections area, which appears under the Unfiled Notes icon at the bottom of the navigation bar. You can examine the notes here to make sure that they are the version you want to restore. To return to this area at any time after clicking away, click the Open Sections icon again (see Figure 8.12).

Figure 8.12 *The Open Sections icon appears after you've double-clicked a section file from a backup set. You can click this icon to return to this special area to review the backup notes before restoring them.*

 **LET ME TRY IT**

Restoring an Entire Section from a Backup

After you've reviewed the notes that you opened from one of your backup sets, you can restore them by copying an entire section and its pages to your current, most up-to-date notebook on your primary hard drive.

To restore an entire section, do the following:

1. If necessary, open the notebook to which you want to restore a set of backed-up notes.

2. Click the Open Sections icon at the bottom of the navigation bar to display the section or sections that you opened from a backup set (see Figure 8.12) and then click the section containing the notes pages you want to restore.

3. To restore the currently selected backup section to its proper notebook, right-click its section tab, and then click Move or Copy on the shortcut menu.

4. In the Move or Copy Section dialog box, click to select the icon of the notebook to which you want to restore the section and its pages, and then click Copy. (You cannot choose Move because doing so would leave you with an incomplete backup folder of those notes.)

5. Navigate to the notebook to which you copied (restored) the backup section. When you see the restored section, it will still contain the date stamp of the backup as part of the section name. When you no longer need this information, right-click the section tab, click Rename on the shortcut menu, and then either delete the date stamp or type a new name for the section and then press Enter.

6. When you're done examining the backup in the Open Sections area, right-click each of the open section tabs and then click Close on the shortcut menu.

 LET ME TRY IT

Restoring Selected Pages from a Backup

If you don't want to restore an entire section of notes but merely one or more specific pages within a backed-up section, you can restore those pages to your current, most up-to-date notebook on your primary hard drive.

To restore selected pages, do the following:

1. If necessary, open the notebook to which you want to restore a set of backed-up notes.

2. Click the Open Sections icon at the bottom of the navigation bar to display the section or sections that you opened from a backup set (see Figure 8.12) and then click the section containing the notes pages you want to restore.

3. On the right side of the currently selected backup section, click the tab of the page you want to restore. If you want to restore multiple pages from this section, hold the Ctrl key on your keyboard and click the page tabs that you want to include in the restoration.

4. Right-click any one of the selected page tabs and then click Move or Copy on the shortcut menu.

5. In the Move or Copy Pages dialog box, expand the target notebook and click to select the section to which you want to restore the selected pages, and then click Copy. (You cannot choose Move because doing so would leave you with an incomplete backup folder of those notes.)

6. Navigate to the notebook to which you copied (restored) the backup pages to inspect that they were restored correctly.

7. When you're done examining the backup in the Open Sections area, right-click each of the open section tabs and then click Close on the shortcut menu.

When you no longer need a specific backup set of your notes, or if you need to delete a backup set after a successful restoration for security reasons, you can delete its folder in the backup location that you specified (see "Selecting a Backup Location" earlier in this chapter). Unless hard drive space or security is an issue, you generally don't need to manually clean up backup sets, as the oldest ones will eventually be overwritten with new versions.

It's up to you to decide how much you want to invest in the security and reliability of your notes and of the information that you create and keep in OneNote.

If you come to rely on this great program as your primary information repository (or more simply put, an ever-expanding extension of your brain), consider committing to the few extra steps it takes to protect your notes from prying eyes, from technical failures, and from those all-too-common human errors that can ruin a perfectly good day. You'll be glad you did.

Sharing Notes with Other People

Whenever I mention the sharing capabilities in OneNote 2010 to people who are
new to electronic note-taking, I invariably get one of two responses: an immediate
nod of approval—or sheer, visible horror.

For those of us who grew up before the Internet was everywhere, the latter reac-
tion is understandable. In the age of social networking, it may well be common-
place to share literally everything, everywhere, all of the time—our thoughts, our
current activities, our pictures, our videos, our music. But for many, there was a
time when a notebook or journal was considered a very personal thing, no matter
what was kept inside.

Before you skip over this chapter and assume the worst, keep in mind that "sharing" in the computer world can mean and imply many different things. In the real
world, sharing something typically means that you must give up at least part (or
all) of that something so that someone else can possess it or benefit from it. If you
give half of your chocolate bar to a friend, you lose that half. If you let a friend bor-
row a book, you can't read that book yourself until your friend returns it to you.
Similarly, for things not easily duplicated, such as a handwritten note that you
might have passed to another student in class, he or she will be the only person to
end up with that note. Likewise, if you send someone a handwritten letter in the
mail, you'll no longer have access to the original after it leaves your possession.

The benefits of the electronic equivalents to these examples are immediately obvious. Passing notes in class has been replaced by texting on cell phones. Now, both
the sender and the recipient have an instant copy of the original note available to
them, and they can even build a "conversation" by sending more notes back and
forth. Similarly, sending a letter in an e-mail lets you keep an instant copy of everything in your Sent Items folder, so that you can refer to it again at any time you
want or need to.

Taking and sharing notes electronically has similar benefits. If you share your notes
pages or an entire notebook with a classmate, you don't lose the ability to use
those notes while your friend is using them, even if you both use them at the same

time. You both can benefit from the information, no matter who authored it and no matter who has the original. If you use OneNote for your study group, for example, it's easy to see how several people can benefit from information that may have originated in just one place. If every student in a shared notebook contributes to a particular page or section, all can benefit from the notebook, which results from the shared effort. In other words, OneNote lets you instantly share your thoughts, ideas, plans, brainstorms, and other collections of information so that both you and others can share the benefit (see Figure 9.1). No matter what you share with OneNote, you always retain your own full use of that information.

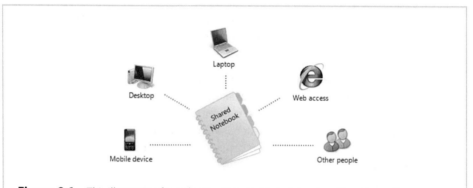
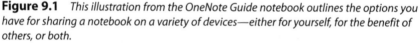

Figure 9.1   *This illustration from the OneNote Guide notebook outlines the options you have for sharing a notebook on a variety of devices—either for yourself, for the benefit of others, or both.*

If you're still worried about protecting the privacy of your notes, you can take comfort in the fact that OneNote lets you fully control what you share. The concept of privacy may be evolving, but there's no question that some types of information will and should always be regarded as sensitive, private, or personal. As you saw in Chapter 8, "Security Features in OneNote," the password-protection features in OneNote let you apply your own privacy preference to the individual sections in any of your digital notebooks. This level of control remains in place even if you decide to share the rest of your notebook with others—be it colleagues at work, classmates in school, or your friends and family at home. And, as you'll see later in this chapter, sharing your notes in the cloud lets you apply even more control over who can view and use notes that you share. OneNote 2010 gives you the best of both worlds: protecting your personal information while still enjoying the many benefits of sharing notes.

This chapter first covers how you can share static snapshots of your notes for others, which is a quick way to distribute a copy of your information without giving others access to your source material. An example of this is passing out printed notes to your co-workers or e-mailing the members of your study group a copy of your teacher's instructions about a homework assignment that you jotted down in class.

Next, this chapter shows you how you can set up and use a shared notebook, either as a way for you to access your notebooks across multiple computers (and, thus, sharing it with yourself) or as a way to collaborate with other people where multiple authors can view and edit the same set of notes.

Finally, this chapter gives you a brief overview of the wonderful OneNote Web App that works together with your free Windows Live SkyDrive account, which lets you instantly share notes online with anyone in the world, including people who don't have the full version of OneNote 2010.

 SHOW ME   Media 9.1—Printing and Publishing Copies of Notes
Access this video file through your registered Web Edition at
my.safaribooksonline.com/9780132182447/media.

Printing Your Notes

Although OneNote is designed to help you "go green" by making it easier to cut down on your paper use, there might still be times when you need to print out a page or a set of notes to give to someone. You can print from OneNote 2010 as easily as with any other Office program.

 LET ME TRY IT

Previewing Notes Before Printing

Although OneNote uses a page metaphor to store and organize notes in a section, pages printed from OneNote can appear quite different than they do in traditional page-based documents used by other programs, such as Microsoft Word. In a word processor, the page typically matches that of a piece of paper. In OneNote, however, any single page can technically scroll on forever, depending on how you take notes and organize them.

To give you an idea about how your notes will look when printed out on paper, you can save paper by first previewing any print job.

To preview your notes before printing, do the following:

1. In your notebook, navigate to the page you want to print.

2. Click the File tab, click Print, and then click Print Preview.

3. In the Print Preview and Settings dialog box that opens, inspect the image under the Print Preview heading (see Figure 9.2). Here, you can see how the first page in your printer will be filled by OneNote if you print the current notes page with the settings shown. Underneath the page image, OneNote tells you how many physical pages will be needed to print the current OneNote page.

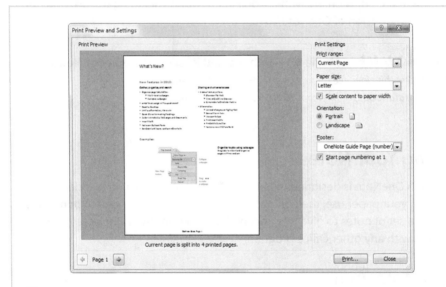

Figure 9.2 *The Print Preview dialog box shows you how notes pages will appear when printed to standard size pages on paper. You can cycle through all of the pages here and make any necessary adjustments to the print settings.*

4. In the lower-left corner of the dialog box, use the Next Page and Previous Page buttons to cycle through all of the page previews to make sure the notes will be printed the way you want. If necessary, adjust any of the Print Settings on the right side of the dialog box and then re-inspect the previewed pages.

5. If you don't want to print the previewed pages, click Close to exit Print Preview without printing. Alternately, if the previewed pages look all right to you and you want to print them out, click Print. In the Print dialog box that opens, select your printer, and then click Print.

A main benefit of electronic notes pages is that, unlike paper, they can go on for as long as you want or need them to. However, if you'll be printing notes frequently and you want to match your notes pages to the dimensions of a particular paper size, you can customize the automatic settings that OneNote uses for normal pages. Click the View tab on the ribbon and then, in the Page Setup group, click Paper Size. In the Paper Size task pane that opens, change the Size from Auto to the size that you want and then set any additional options that may become available. If the result is not what you want, remember that you can use the Undo button on the Quick Access Toolbar (depending on how many page settings you've changed, you might need to press Undo multiple times).

In the Paper Size task pane, you can also set the print margins that OneNote should use when printing out the notes on the current page. Additionally, you can create a custom page size in this task pane and then save the resulting page as a template that you can use for all new pages you create.

As it is in other Office programs, using the Print Preview feature in OneNote 2010 is entirely optional.

 LET ME TRY IT

Printing Notes

To print notes without previewing them first, do the following:

1. In your notebook, navigate to the page you want to print.

2. Click the File tab, click Print, and then click Print again.

3. In the Print dialog box that opens, select your printer and then click Print.

Depending on the make and model of your printer, the Print dialog box provides access to additional printing options for your printer. After selecting your printer in the list, click the Preferences button. In the Printing Preferences dialog box that opens, make any selections you want and then click OK.

If you need to print notes often, you can add a Print button on the Quick Access Toolbar in the upper left of the OneNote program window. To learn how, see Chapter 12, "Customizing OneNote 2010."

Although printing notes is a perfectly legitimate and often necessary way of sharing information with others, it can also serve as an unintentional crutch for new

OneNote users who are reluctant or hesitant to commit to making the switch to electronic note-taking. If you find that you're printing out many or most of your notes for yourself instead of others, try to remind yourself of the many advantages electronic note-taking offers over traditional, paper-based notes by reviewing all that you've learned so far in this book. Although you can certainly choose to not fully embrace all of what OneNote has to offer, you'll be cheating yourself out of many of the benefits that come with a life less cluttered with stacks of paper everywhere.

Next, take a look at sharing copies of your notes through a more environmentally friendly way: your e-mail program.

Sharing Notes in E-mail

Perhaps the easiest way to share a copy of any page in your notes is to send it in an e-mail. If you have an e-mail program like Microsoft Outlook 2010 installed on your computer and properly configured, OneNote provides an easy interface for sending notes in e-mail.

If you don't use Outlook or you use a web-based e-mail service like Hotmail, you can still send and share notes with a few extra steps.

Before getting started with OneNote's e-mail features, first get up to speed about what's required.

Requirements for Using E-mail Features in OneNote

Using e-mail integration features in OneNote—such as sending notes in an e-mail message or sending invitations to shared notebooks—requires a copy of Microsoft Outlook 2010 that's installed and configured on your computer. If you installed OneNote 2010 as part of Microsoft Office Home and Business 2010, Professional, Professional Plus, or Professional Academic, you already have Outlook 2010 available, but you must first properly configure it (see Figure 9.3).

If you installed the standalone version of OneNote 2010, or as part of Microsoft Office Home and Student 2010 edition, you'll need to either purchase Outlook 2010 separately, or you can configure and use another Windows-based e-mail application to use some of OneNote's e-mail features.

The way OneNote works with your e-mail program also depends on the version of Windows you are using. For example, whereas Windows XP and Windows Vista included basic e-mail clients (see Figure 9.4), Windows 7 no longer offers this feature (see Figure 9.5) because of the ever-increasing popularity of web-based mail programs. If you fall into the latter category, you can still share notes and invite others to shared notebooks by following some additional, manual steps that I'll provide in context with some of the procedures in this chapter.

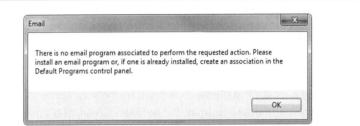

Figure 9.3 *If you have Microsoft Outlook 2010 installed on the same computer as OneNote 2010, you can use the e-mail integration features. If you see this error message, it means that you merely installed Outlook, but that you still have to properly configure it with your e-mail account information. After Outlook is configured to send and receive mail, all OneNote/Outlook integration features will be enabled, including e-mail.*

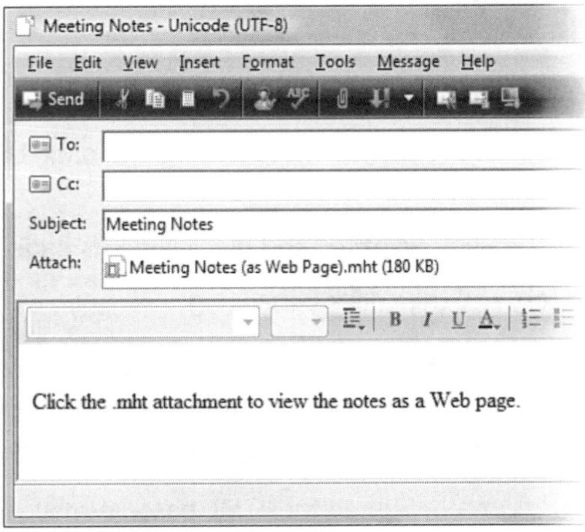

Figure 9.4 *If you're running an older version of Windows, such as Windows Vista (shown here), you can use its integrated Windows Mail client with OneNote. However, note that you're limited to sending notes as separate web page attachments because older mail clients can't render OneNote pages like Outlook can. Only Microsoft Outlook 2010 offers the full set of integration features with OneNote 2010.*

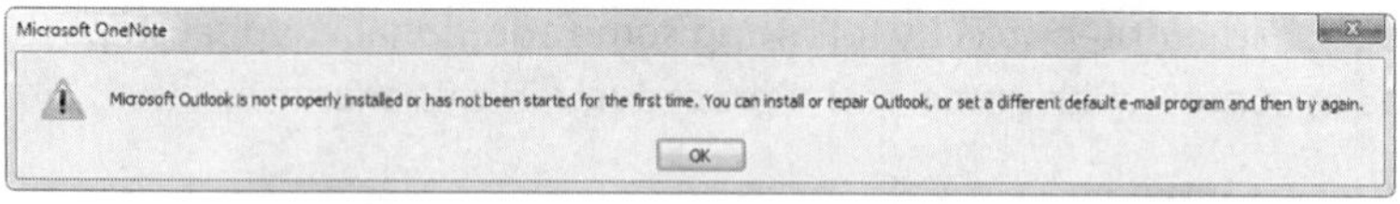

Figure 9.5 *If you have no e-mail program installed on your computer, you might see this dialog box when trying to use OneNote's e-mail features to send or share notes. To resolve this error, install a program like Microsoft Outlook 2010.*

If you don't use a locally installed e-mail program on your computer because you prefer web-based e-mail like Hotmail, Yahoo! Mail, Gmail, or a similar service, you can't use the shortcuts to the mail integration features in OneNote (such as the E-mail Page button on the ribbon). However, in most cases, you can go through a few simple steps to achieve the same result. I'll point these out throughout the rest of this chapter, where applicable.

Sending Notes in an Outlook Message

If you're using Microsoft Outlook 2010 or a similar e-mail program on your computer, sending a copy of any notes page is as simple as clicking a button on the ribbon.

To send notes in an Outlook message, do the following:

1. In any notebook, click the section that contains the page that you want to send.

2. Navigate to the page you want to send by clicking its page tab.

3. Click the Share tab, and then click E-mail Page.

Outlook 2010 will open a new message and place the contents of the notes page into the body of the message. It will also use the page title and place it into the Subject field of the message, which you can keep or modify as needed.

As long as you have Outlook configured for HTML-based e-mail, notes pages you send from OneNote will be rendered exactly as they appear in your notebook, letting recipients of the e-mail message view the page as if they had access to your notes.

Notes pages sent in e-mail are copies of the original pages in your notebook. If you change the contents of a notes page after sending a copy of it, only your notebook will reflect those changes; the sent copy will not be modified for the recipient. To share an updated page of your notes with someone, simply send them a new copy of that page.

LET ME TRY IT

Sending Notes as an Outlook Attachment

If you're using Outlook 2010 to send notes in e-mail, you can opt to include a copy of a notes page as a file attachment. This is a good option if you're not sure if the recipient of your message has Outlook 2010 or another HTML-based e-mail program. It is also useful if the recipient has a copy of OneNote 2010 and you want them to be able to view and use your notes page in OneNote instead of e-mail.

If you want OneNote to include page attachments whenever you click the E-mail Page button on the ribbon, do the following:

1. Click the File tab, and then click Options.

2. On the left side of the OneNote Options dialog box that appears, click the Advanced category.

3. On the right side of the dialog box, scroll down to the E-mail Sent from OneNote heading (see Figure 9.6).

Figure 9.6 *On the Advanced tab in the OneNote Options dialog box, the top check box lets you tell OneNote to include a file attachment of notes you send in e-mail. This lets the recipient open the copy of the notes in OneNote 2010.*

4. Select the Attach a Copy of the Original Notes as a OneNote File check box, and then click OK.

5. In your notebook, click the section that contains the page that you want to send and then navigate to the page by clicking its page tab.

6. Click the Share tab, and then click E-mail Page.

With this option configured, Outlook 2010 opens a new message and places the contents of the notes page into the body of the message, just like before. However, it will now also include a file attachment containing a copy of your original notes page. If your recipient has OneNote 2010 installed on his or her computer, he or she can double-click the attachment and view the notes page in OneNote instead of just in the e-mail message. This is useful when you want someone to review your notes and perhaps send back corrections or additions that you might want to add to your original notes.

If you don't know if the recipient has Outlook and whether or not he or she will be able to see the message in HTML format, you can use an alternate way to generate an e-mail message that contains both a OneNote file attachment and a copy of the notes in *.mht web page format that the recipient can view in Internet Explorer.

Do the following:

1. Navigate to the page you want to send as an attachment.

2. Click the File tab, click Send, and then click E-mail Page as Attachment.

Outlook 2010 will open a new message and place the contents of the notes page into the body of the message. It will also attach a copy of the page in OneNote format and include a separate copy of the notes as an *.mht file that recipients without Outlook or OneNote can view in Internet Explorer as a web page.

Although it's a more passive way to collaborate with others, e-mailing notes back and forth is a perfectly acceptable way to share your notes with others without giving them access to your notebook.

> When sending notes pages as file attachments, be sure you know the notebook format you're working in. If you send a notes page created in OneNote 2010 to someone who still uses OneNote 2007, they won't be able to open the attachment. To get around this, you'll first need to convert a copy of your original page to the OneNote 2007 format. For more information, refer to Chapter 2, "Upgrading from a Previous Version."

The following procedures outline how you can send notes in e-mail when using e-mail programs other than Microsoft Outlook or when using web-based e-mail like Hotmail.

 **LET ME TRY IT**

Sending a Copy of One or More Pages in an E-mail

When using any e-mail program other than Outlook, you can create a file attachment of one or more OneNote pages, and then attach that file to a new e-mail message.

To send a copy of one or more pages in an e-mail, do the following:

1. In any notebook, click the section that contains the page or pages that you want to send.

2. Navigate to the first page by clicking its page tab. If you want to select additional pages, hold down the Ctrl key on your keyboard, and then click once on the page tab of each additional page that you want to include. Release the Ctrl key when you've clicked the tab of the last page to be included.

3. Click the File tab, and then click Save As.

4. Under the heading 1. Save Current, leave Page selected.

5. Under the heading 2. Select Format, click OneNote 2010 Section (*.one).

6. Click Save As.

7. In the Save As dialog box that opens, navigate to the folder on your computer where you want to save the file containing your selected pages, type a descriptive title into the File Name field (for example, *Meeting Notes for the Week of April 16th*), and then click Save.

8. In your e-mail program, open a new message and then attach the *.one file you created.

When OneNote creates the file containing the pages you selected, it opens the contents of that file in a special display area called Sections Opened During This Session (see Figure 9.7). This lets you quickly verify that all of the pages you wanted were included in the section file you saved.

To return to your original notes, either click the round Back arrow button on the Quick Access Toolbar (see Figure 9.8), or click the icon of the notebook to which you want to return.

 **LET ME TRY IT**

Sending a Copy of a Section in an E-mail

If you want to send all of the pages in any particular section of your notebook, you can create a file attachment of an entire notebook section, and then attach that section file to a new e-mail message.

Figure 9.7   *The Sections Opened During This Session icon appears at the bottom of the navigation bar after you've manually created a file attachment of one or more pages of notes. In this temporary display area, you can review the contents of saved section files that are not part of any notebook.*

Figure 9.8   *On the Quick Access Toolbar, click the Back button to return to your original notes after examining the pages from which you created a file attachment.*

To send a copy of a section in an e-mail, do the following:

1. In any notebook, click the section that you want to send.

2. Click the File tab and then click Save As.

3. Under the heading 1. Save Current, click Section.

4. Under the heading 2. Select Format, click OneNote 2010 Section (*.one).

5. Click Save As.

6. In the Save As dialog box that opens, navigate to the folder on your computer where you want to save the file containing your selected pages, type a descriptive title into the File Name field (for example, *July Project Notes*), and then click Save.

7. In your e-mail program, open a new message, and then attach the *.one file you created.

You can use the preceding steps to send entire sections in Outlook e-mail, too.

 LET ME TRY IT

Sending a Copy of an Entire Notebook in an E-mail

If you want to send all of your notes in a particular notebook, you can create a file attachment of the entire notebook, and then attach that notebook file to a new e-mail message.

To send a copy of an entire notebook in an e-mail, do the following:

1. Navigate to any page in the notebook you want to send.

2. Click the File tab and then click Save As.

3. Under the heading 1. Save Current, click Notebook.

4. Under the heading 2. Select Format, click OneNote Package (*.onepkg).

5. Click Save As.

6. In the Save As dialog box that opens, navigate to the folder on your computer where you want to save the notebook file, type a descriptive title into the File Name field (for example, *Robert's Psychology Class Notebook*), and then click Save.

7. In your e-mail program, open a new message, and then attach the *.onepkg file you created.

You can use the preceding steps to send entire notebooks in Outlook e-mail, too.

A OneNote Package (*.onepkg) file makes it easy for the recipient to install an entire OneNote notebook on his or her computer. Double-clicking the package file opens the Unpack Notebook Wizard, which lets the recipient specify what the notebook should be called and where it should be opened.

As mentioned previously, when sending notes pages, sections, or entire notebooks as file attachments in e-mail, be aware of the notebook format you're working in. If you send notes created in OneNote 2010 to someone who still uses OneNote 2007, he or she won't be able to open the attachment. For more information about converting notes between formats, refer to Chapter 2.

Publishing Your Notes Online

Because OneNote provides such a flexible canvas for capturing ideas and streams of consciousness, you might want to share copies of your notes electronically with people whom you don't know or converse with in e-mail. For example, you could use OneNote to draft blog posts and then publish those notes as web pages. Or, you could save your notes in a portable file format so that people can download and read your notes on a variety of computer platforms and devices. Alternately, you can also take your thoughts and ideas that you jot down in OneNote and then send them to Microsoft Word whenever you need to use the information in a more formal document that you'll share with others.

 LET ME TRY IT

Saving Notes as a Web Page

Sharing your notes as a web page lets people view and read them exactly as they appear in your notebook, even if they don't have OneNote installed. This is a good option if you have formatted your notes extensively, either for visual appeal or to organize the information on your pages.

To save notes as a web page, do the following:

1. Navigate to the notes that you want to save as a web page.

2. Click the File tab and then click Save As.

3. Under the heading 1. Save Current, choose what you want to include (the current page, the current section and its pages, or the entire notebook you're currently in).

4. Under the heading 2. Select Format, click Single File Web Page (*.mht).

5. Click Save As.

6. In the Save As dialog box that opens, navigate to the folder on your computer where you want to save the web page containing the notes you selected, type a web page title into the File Name field (for example, *My Science Project*), and then click Save.

If you now double-click the *.mht file you saved, it will open in Internet Explorer and show you what the notes will look like when you upload the page to your web server or FTP server.

The *.mht file extension is a web page format understood by Microsoft Internet Explorer. If you're using a different web browser as your default browser (for example, Mozilla Firefox), you can still view *.mht files on your computer by right-clicking their icon, clicking Open With, and then clicking Internet Explorer.

 LET ME TRY IT

Saving Notes as a PDF or XPS File

The best way to preserve page fidelity in portable files that others across different platforms can open and view reliably, no matter what type of computer or device they're using, is to create a copy of your notes in Adobe's Portable Document Format (PDF) or in Microsoft's XML Paper Specification (XPS) format.

Both of these formats are read-only document files that can be viewed, searched, and printed. Of these, Adobe's PDF file format is perhaps the most widely used in the world.

To save notes as a PDF or XPS file, do the following:

1. Navigate to the notes that you want to save as a portable file.

2. Click the File tab and then click Save As.

3. Under the heading 1. Save Current, choose what you want to include (the current page, the current section and its pages, or the entire notebook you're currently in).

4. Under the heading 2. Select Format, click either PDF (*.pdf) or XPS (*.xps) to create a file in either format.

5. Click Save As.

6. In the Save As dialog box that opens, navigate to the folder on your computer where you want to save the file containing the notes you selected, type a title into the File Name field (for example, *My Research Notes*), and then click Save.

You can share PDF and XPS files by attaching them to e-mail messages, by publishing them on your website or blog, or by uploading them to an FTP server so people can download the files.

One benefit of sharing PDF or XPS files on a website or FTP server is that you can overwrite the files with newer versions of your notes at any time so that more recent visitors will receive the most up-to-date information that you're sharing.

> Both PDF and XPS files require software to be able to read these formats. For PDF files, you can download the free Adobe Reader (formerly called Adobe Acrobat Reader) for your computer. To view PDF files on other devices such as your cell phone, on the Amazon Kindle, or on the Apple iPad, simply download a PDF reader app for your device. XPS files are also viewable on multiple platforms with free software, which is already preinstalled on Windows Vista and on any edition of Windows 7.

 LET ME TRY IT

Saving Notes as a Microsoft Word File

If you were a dedicated note-taker before OneNote came along, you already know that many thoughts, ideas, plans, and schedules start as a few scribbles on a piece of paper. You took that information and eventually moved it elsewhere to flesh it out more and perhaps prepare it to be read and evaluated by others.

OneNote's role in giving life to your ideas and plans is no different. Though you can keep, format, organize, and use everything you care about in OneNote, there will likely be many times when you need to present a more formal document to someone, such as your boss or your teacher.

When your notes are taking shape and are ready to be moved into a Microsoft Word document for more advanced formatting and word processing, OneNote provides a direct path to its Microsoft Office counterpart.

To save your notes as a Microsoft Word file, do the following:

1. Navigate to the notes that you want to save as a Word document.

2. Click the File tab, and then click Save As.

3. Under the heading 1. Save Current, choose what you want to include (the current page, or the current section and its pages). Note that you cannot save an entire notebook as a Word document.

4. Under the heading 2. Select Format, click either the Word Document (*.docx) option to save the file in a newer format that can be used by Microsoft Word 2010 and Word 2007, or click the Word 97–2003 Document (*.doc) option to save the file in an older format that can be read by Microsoft Word 97, Word 2000, Word XP, and Word 2003.

5. Click Save As.

6. In the Save As dialog box that opens, navigate to the folder on your computer where you want to save the file containing the notes you selected, type a name into the File Name field (for example, *Curriculum Vitae*), and then click Save.

Because OneNote does not by default use page dimensions typically used by a word processor, you might want or need to adjust the margins and the selected view in Microsoft Word after opening a document file that was created from your OneNote notes.

Although all of the sharing options I've discussed so far in this chapter are effective ways to give others access to information you've created or collected, none of these methods provide a way to really collaborate with each other in real time. Let's proceed to learn about the features in OneNote that make it possible to do just that.

Collaborating with Others in Shared Notebooks

When the first version of OneNote first came onto the scene in 2003, its capabilities were quite limited. Although already a powerful tool for electronic note-taking, OneNote 2003 only let you have a single notebook and that notebook was trapped on your computer's hard drive. Not at all a bad start for such a revolutionary program, but people soon wanted the ability to do more.

First, they wanted the option to not only view but fully edit their notebook from another computer. Although you could set up a shared folder on a hard drive to accomplish this over a network, the computer had to remain switched on at all times or access to the notebook from elsewhere on the network was lost. A single power outage could quickly defeat such an elaborate setup.

Second, people wanted the ability to give others access to their notebooks so that the latest, newest information would always be seen by all participants in real time, meaning the screen would refresh automatically with new information whenever someone else added a new paragraph of notes, a new picture, or anything else on a page.

When OneNote 2007 was released, it had a feature called Live Sharing Sessions, which was a step in the right direction. Once two or more computers were connected, their users could edit notebooks together and really collaborate on ideas, even if they were a city or an ocean apart. The downside to this feature was the need to futz around with TCP/IP addresses and ad hoc passwords for each participant and session. If used in meetings, a Live Sharing Session could take up a significant amount of set-up time before everyone was connected and ready to go.

As a result, OneNote developers scrapped the Live Sharing Sessions and let the shared notebook features come into full maturity in OneNote 2010. Now it's finally possible to do everything people want to do when working together with others: Share information in real time, see each other's changes and updates clearly marked, and retain a complete set of notes that can be viewed and edited even if the connection is temporarily broken for any of the participants (for example, while on an airplane).

OneNote handles all of the updating and synchronizing automatically, letting even groups of authors focus on their thoughts and ideas instead of having technology get in the way of it all.

 SHOW ME   Media 9.2—Taking Notes Together with Other People
Access this video file through your registered Web Edition at
my.safaribooksonline.com/9780132182447/media.

The shared notes features in OneNote 2010 allow you to use your network to create and keep one or more notebooks in a shared location (for example, a personal file share on a file server, or a subweb on a SharePoint site) and then let authorized participants use those notes together in that location.

After a shared notebook is set up, using it is as easy as any other OneNote notebook that you've used on your own hard drive. The following section covers some of the less-obvious additional features that are available when you're in shared mode. If you have access to a file share on the network at your company, your school, or your organization, I encourage you to try out these features to get a real sense of what shared notebooks in OneNote can do.

 **LET ME TRY IT**

Creating a New Shared Notebook

The best way to get started with a shared notebook is to create a fresh, new notebook in the location to which you and the intended participants (authors) have access.

If you don't already have a file share on your network in which you can create and change files, contact your Help Desk or system administrator to help you get set up on your network. If your support staff is not yet familiar with OneNote and shared notebooks, simply explain that you need a file share with read/write permissions and then also list the names of your co-workers, faculty, or teachers and students who will need full permissions to this location on the network.

Once you have permission to create and change files on your network, do the following:

1. Click the Share tab.

2. In the Shared Notebook group, click New Shared Notebook. (You can also get here by clicking the File tab, clicking New, and then clicking Network.)

3. Under the heading 1. Store Notebook On, click Network (see Figure 9.9).

4. Under the heading 2. Name, type a meaningful description for the notebook (for example, *Team Research Notes*). Remember that the notebook name should make sense to all participants.

5. Under the heading 3. Network Location, click Browse and then navigate to the file share on your network where you and the other authors have full access permissions to create, open, and change files. If you're creating your shared notebook on a SharePoint site, enter the full http:// address of the SharePoint folder where the shared notebook should be created.

6. Click Create Notebook.

7. When prompted to invite others to the notebook via e-mail (see Figure 9.10), click No, Thanks. (I'll explain why in a moment.)

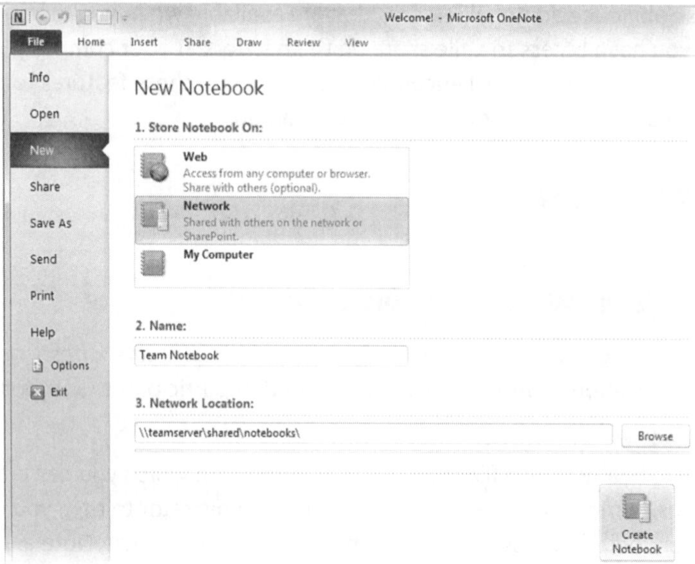

Figure 9.9   *Creating a new shared notebook is as easy as 1, 2, 3. Decide on a platform, a descriptive name, and the location of your new shared notebook, and then click the Create Notebook button.*

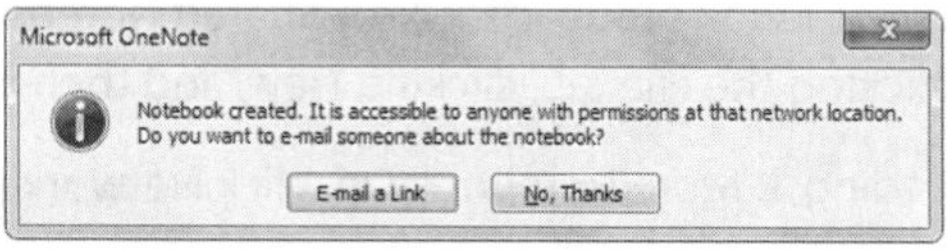

Figure 9.10   *This dialog box appears after you create a new shared notebook on your network. You can either generate an invitation e-mail right away or do it later, after you've created some content that you want the other participants to see (for example, a welcome page with instructions).*

When OneNote creates the shared notebook, it prompts you whether or not you want to invite someone else to your notebook (see Figure 9.10). You can choose to send invitations right away or do it later.

There are some advantages to doing this later, especially if you're still new to working with shared notebooks, so choose to decline this option for now by clicking No, Thanks. I'll cover this in more detail under "Inviting Others to Your Shared Notebook" later in this chapter.

When a shared notebook has been created, it is placed as an open notebook icon on the navigation bar, the same way new notebooks on your hard drive appear after you've first created or opened them.

While you are connected to a shared notebook on a network, you can leave it open at all times, even when you close OneNote or shut down your computer. Unlike other file-sharing programs, where participants must check files in and out and lock them for editing and require everyone to wait their turn, the beauty of shared notebooks in OneNote is that you'll never lock the file, even when you're actively adding new notes to the notebook or changing any of the information that's already there.

Another benefit of hosting a shared notebook in a file share on your network instead of in a folder on your computer is that others can continue to use the shared notebook, adding and changing information as needed, even when you turn off your computer at night or shut down your laptop computer between meetings. Whenever anyone connects to a shared notebook again by starting OneNote, its pages will be automatically refreshed, so that all participants will always see all of the latest information.

Before we learn more about shared notebook features, let's first look at how you can convert any notebook that already exists on your computer's hard drive into a shared notebook.

 LET ME TRY IT

Sharing an Existing Notebook

If you're already working in a notebook on your hard drive and you've already created or collected a significant amount of notes and information and you now want to invite co-workers or class members to co-author in the notebook by adding and managing their own information in the notebook, you can easily promote a normal notebook to a shared notebook.

To share an existing notebook, do the following:

1. Open the notebook on your hard drive that you want to share and then click the Share tab.

2. In the Shared Notebook group, click Share This Notebook. (You can also do this by clicking the File tab and then clicking Share.)

3. Under the heading 1. Select Notebook, make sure the notebook you want to share is selected.

4. Under the heading 2. Share On, select Network.

5. Under the heading 3. Network Location, click Browse and then navigate to the file share on your network where you and the other authors have full access permissions to create, open, and change files. If you want to share your notebook on your shared notebook on a SharePoint site, enter the full *http://* address of the SharePoint folder where the notebook should be shared.

6. Click Share Notebook.

7. When OneNote acknowledges that the notebook is now shared at the location you chose (see Figure 9.11), click OK.

Figure 9.11   *When you see this confirmation, a notebook that was previously only accessible by you has been changed to a shared notebook. You'll also see this confirmation when you change the location or file share path of a shared notebook in the Notebook Properties dialog box.*

Adding or Changing Notes in a Shared Notebook

Taking notes in a shared notebook is no different from starting a newly created notebook on your computer's hard drive: Just click on a page and start typing!

If any other notebook authors are connected to the shared notebook while you're already typing anywhere in it, your notes will automatically appear on their screens (and theirs on yours) and all notes will be continuously refreshed every few minutes so that everyone can see each other's latest changes, additions, and deletions.

Even if two or more people are editing the same notes page or even the same paragraph of notes at the same time, OneNote silently manages the split-second differences between the time new information was added and existing information was changed or deleted by someone else to avoid "note collisions." This clever way of monitoring changes is what makes real-time note-taking in OneNote such a useful thing. Nobody has to worry about the technology; everyone can just focus on their thoughts and ideas.

 **LET ME TRY IT**

Inviting Others to Your Shared Notebook

If you followed the steps under "Creating a New Shared Notebook" a little earlier in this chapter, you probably saw the dialog box that appears after a shared notebook has been created (see Figure 9.10). Although clicking the E-mail a Link button in this dialog box is a convenient way to begin sharing a notebook immediately by telling others where to access it, you may want to click the No, Thanks button instead, so you can first add some content to the shared notebook. Generally, it's best to send shared notebook invitations to others later, after you've verified that the shared notebook is accessible by everyone on your team (and on your network) and when you can be sure that the recipients will know what to do with your notebook once they successfully connect to it.

Personally, I always choose to send invitations later, after I've added some preliminary structure and content to the shared notebook, which helps the other participants to know in which sections they should add pages and to which pages they can add information. I also tend to include a welcome page that gives authors some instructions about what to do in the notebook and what's already available, which can be helpful for people who aren't yet very familiar with shared notebooks or with OneNote (see Figure 9.12).

You can easily create a welcome page by adding content to the first page in the first section of your shared notebook, which new participants will see when they first connect to your shared notebook. The welcome page could contain a brief welcome message from you that lets others know they're in the right place and remind them what sorts of information will be stored in the notebook. You could also provide a simple Table of Contents on the page, consisting of clickable links to all of the sections in the notebook. This is especially useful for novice users, who'll already know how to click text links even if they don't immediately know to click through the notebook sections. Remember, you can easily create links to specific sections and pages by right-clicking the notebook's section or page tabs and using the Copy Link To commands on the shortcut menu. See "Navigating Notebook Content with Links" in Chapter 7, "Organizing and Searching Notes," if you need a refresher about this useful feature.

Once you've created the basic section structure of your notebook and customized the first page with a welcome message and other information, you're ready to let others know about your shared notebook. If you have an e-mail program installed on your computer, you can have OneNote generate the invitation, which you can then send to the other authors.

Figure 9.12 *In a new shared notebook, consider adding a welcoming message and shortcuts on the first page of the first section that new participants will see when they first open the shared notebook. A simple welcome page like this can take the mystery out of getting started with a shared notebook and help to orient new authors.*

To invite others to your shared notebook, do the following:

1. Open the shared notebook. If it's already open on the navigation bar, click its icon there, the same way you would switch to any other notebook that you have open.

2. Click the File tab to open the Info tab in the Backstage View. Here, you see a list of all of your open notebooks.

3. In the list of notebooks, find (and scroll down to, if necessary) the shared notebook you currently have open.

4. Underneath the name and location of the shared notebook, click the Invite People to This Notebook link.

5. On the next screen that is displayed, OneNote will confirm that this notebook is already shared. At the bottom of the text you see here, click the E-mail Others About the Notebook link.

6. OneNote creates a new e-mail message containing the link the recipients of the message can click to automatically open the shared notebook in their copy of OneNote 2010 on their computer. Add the appropriate recipients to the e-mail message and then click Send.

The steps for inviting other participants to a shared notebook are the same for brand-new shared notebooks and for existing notebooks that you decide later to share with others.

Like all the e-mail integration features in OneNote 2010, the e-mail invitation feature requires a properly installed and configured copy of Microsoft Outlook 2010 or a comparable e-mail program on your computer (see "Requirements for Using E-mail Features in OneNote" earlier in this chapter). If you don't have such software installed, you can still invite others by creating a new e-mail message manually and then including the notebook's file path in your message. To copy and paste the notebook location, click the File tab in OneNote, and then click Info. Under your shared notebook's name, click to select the location path shown. When the text is highlighted in blue to indicate that it's selected, press Ctrl+C to copy it. Switch to the e-mail message you're composing and then press Ctrl+V to paste the text. Now just add a note that recipients should double-click the "Open Notebook" file they find in this location. When they do so, the shared notebook will open in OneNote 2010 on their computer.

If you've never shared a notebook before and want to avoid any possible technical problems before sending mail to a large number of people, first send this invitation e-mail to a friend at work who can try out the link to make sure everything works as expected. Networks can be complicated things, and depending on how your company, school, or organization administers and secures it, you might need to first verify that the people you'll invite to your shared notebook actually have network access to that location. If the test with your friend goes well, you can follow the previous steps to generate a new invitation e-mail for all of the authors.

When sharing notebooks with other people who are using OneNote, be sure to find out which version they are using. Shared notebooks are supported in both OneNote 2007 and in OneNote 2010. Although OneNote 2010 can read 2007 notebook files, the reverse is not the case.

If your shared notebook is in OneNote 2010 format and you send a shared notebook invitation to someone who still uses OneNote 2007, they might not be able to access or use the shared notebook. However, if you convert your shared notebook to the older OneNote 2007 format, you and other OneNote 2010 users won't be able to take advantage of some of the new features that were introduced in OneNote 2010. Before you upgrade or downgrade the file format of your shared notebook, refer to the information in Chapter 2, "Upgrading from a Previous Version."

LET ME TRY IT

Synchronizing a Shared Notebook

Shared notebooks are automatically synchronized whenever OneNote detects that you or any other author has made a change to the notebook's contents. The purpose of synchronization is to let all participating notebook authors continuously see the most recent changes that have been made to the contents, organization, and structure of the shared notebook.

When a shared notebook is synchronized, it appears the same in all locations from which it is accessed. Because shared notebooks are typically updated quite frequently, synchronization attempts can occur each time OneNote detects an addition, a change, or a deletion in the shared notebook. This would be cumbersome to manage manually, which is why this process is entirely automatic in OneNote 2010.

Just like you never have to click a Save button in OneNote while you're working in your computer-based notebooks, you don't have to manually synchronize any changes that you've made to a shared notebook. Similarly, you won't need to manually synchronize a shared notebook to see changes made by others. As long as your computer maintains a healthy connection to your shared notebook on your organization's network or on the Web, you don't need to take any action to keep your notes in sync.

Notebook synchronization happens quietly in the background, so you won't need to stop working in the shared notebook during synchronization. If someone else is editing the same page as you, their notes will appear and update on your screen from time to time so you can see their work and they can see yours.

Before you learn about those rare occasions when you might have to take action, it's important to understand the symbols that can appear over the navigation bar icons of shared notebooks to which you connect (see Figure 9.13).

When you connect to a shared notebook, its navigation bar icon provides continuous clues about the connection and synchronization status of the notebook. Besides indicating the location of a shared notebook, a navigation bar icon can communicate the following four distinct synchronization statuses:

- OneNote is currently synchronizing changes to the shared notebook (see Figure 9.14).

- OneNote has finished synchronizing changes to the shared notebook (see Figure 9.15).

- OneNote could not fully synchronize changes to the shared notebook (see Figure 9.16).

Figure 9.13   *Similar to the way regular notebook icons appear on the navigation bar as shown here, the icons for shared notebooks let you check the location and status of each of your shared notebooks at a glance.*

Figure 9.14   *When OneNote is in the process of synchronizing changes to a shared notebook—made by you or by other authors—a green, spinning, double-arrow symbol temporarily appears over the shared notebook icon. (The version on the left is used if your shared notebook is stored on a network. The version on the right is used if it is stored on the Web.) When you see either of these two icons, your shared notebook is functioning properly.*

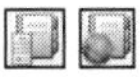

Figure 9.15   *When OneNote has finished synchronizing changes to a shared notebook (made by you or by other authors), no status symbol appears over the shared notebook icon. (The version on the left is used if your shared notebook is stored on a network. The version on the right is used if it is stored on the Web.) When you see either of these two icons, your shared notebook is functioning properly.*

Figure 9.16   *When OneNote has attempted to synchronize changes to a shared notebook but encountered one or more errors, a yellow warning symbol appears over the shared notebook icon. (The version on the left is used if your shared notebook is stored on a network. The version on the right is used if it is stored on the Web.) Though some errors can resolve themselves during a future synchronization attempt, you should check the OneNote error log if this warning symbol persists or appears often.*

- OneNote cannot connect to the shared notebook (see Figure 9.17) and therefore cannot synchronize any changes.

Figure 9.17   *When OneNote cannot connect (or can no longer connect) to a shared notebook, a red, slashed circle symbol appears over the shared notebook icon. (The version on the left is used if your shared notebook is stored on a network. The version on the right is used if it is stored on the Web.) If your connection was temporarily interrupted for known reasons, these errors can resolve themselves during a future synchronization attempt. However, if this warning persists or appears often, you should check the OneNote error log.*

If you don't remember the various status icons and their meanings at first, don't worry. You can quickly view the location and synchronization status of a shared notebook by resting the mouse pointer over the notebook's icon on the navigation bar. In the ToolTip that appears, you can see the name of the notebook, its location path on your network or on the Web, and its synchronization status in plain English.

To check errors that a shared notebook may have encountered (see Figures 9.16 and 9.17), you'll need to check the OneNote error log.

To check the OneNote error log, do the following:

1. Go to any page in the shared notebook that you want to troubleshoot, click the File tab and then click Info.

2. On the far right on this screen, under the thumbnail image of the current page of the notebook you have open, click the View Sync Status button (see Figure 9.18).

Figure 9.18   *On the File tab, in the Info screen, clicking the View Sync Status button opens the Shared Notebook Synchronization dialog box where you can view the error log to see what might be keeping your shared notebook from synchronizing or connecting.*

3. In the Shared Notebook Synchronization dialog box that appears, make sure that the first option, Sync Automatically Whenever There Are Changes, is selected.

4. Click the Errors tab and look for any symptoms and troubleshooting suggestions (see Figure 9.19).

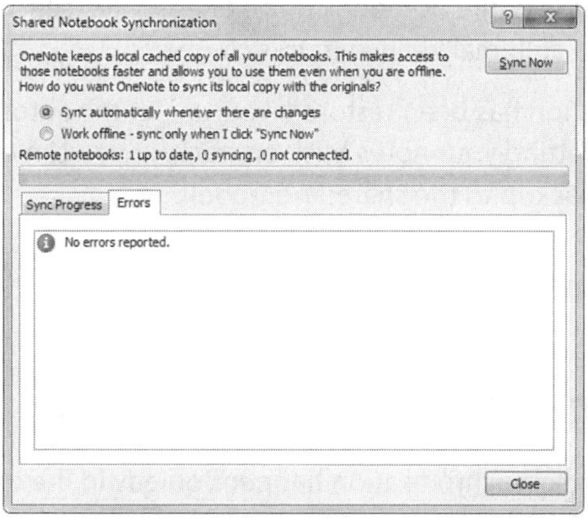

Figure 9.19   *Whenever a shared notebook encounters a connection problem or a synchronization error, information about the issue will appear on the Errors tab in the Shared Notebook Synchronization dialog box. Here, you can make sure you're not accidentally working in offline mode, and you can manually synchronize the shared notebook to try and resolve temporary network congestion.*

5. If you suspect the problem was a temporary network congestion issue, click the Sync Now button to try synchronizing the shared notebook again manually. If this does not resolve the problem, try this again later, or contact your Help Desk or network administrator to further troubleshoot the network connection or synchronization issue.

For faster access to the Shared Notebook Synchronization dialog box, right-click the navigation bar icon of any shared notebook, and then click Notebook Sync Status on the shortcut menu that appears.

It's important not to panic if you're encountering any temporary connection issues with any of your shared notebooks. Networks are complicated and fickle. It's quite normal for most shared notebooks to run into temporary hiccups now and then.

Your changes to shared notebooks that cannot sync aren't lost; they're just waiting to be added the next time you can successfully connect. Any unsynchronized changes that you've worked on are still stored in the version of the shared notebook that's on your computer.

If you're worried or need to urgently share your notes with someone in preparation for a meeting or a presentation, you can always send yourself or others a copy of those notes in an e-mail. If you want to create a quick backup, you can save a copy of your version of the entire notebook as a *.onepkg file (see "Sending a Copy of an Entire Notebook in an E-mail" earlier in this chapter).

Once your connection has been restored, you can let the automatic synchronization take care of getting your notes back on track, or you can copy or move any pages from your backup to the shared notebook.

 LET ME TRY IT

Working Offline in a Shared Notebook

Automatic notebook synchronization happens quietly in the background, so you won't need to stop working in the shared notebook, even if other authors are adding or changing information in the same notebook at the same time.

If other people are editing the same page as you, their notes will appear and update on your screen from time to time so you can see their work and they can see yours. If you find this distracting or annoying and you'd prefer to think about only your own notes on the current page, you can opt to work offline and have OneNote synchronize your changes later.

To temporarily stop automatic synchronization of your shared notebook, do the following:

1. Right-click the navigation bar icon of the shared notebook you want to stop synchronizing, and then click Notebook Sync Status on the shortcut menu that appears.

2. In the Shared Notebook Synchronization dialog box that appears, click Work Offline—Sync Only When I Click "Sync Now."

3. Click Close.

While you're working in offline mode, a red, slashed circle will appear over the notebook's navigation bar icon (see Figure 9.17). This is to signal you that the connection is temporarily severed and that your changes to the shared notebook will not appear to others until the next time the notebook is synchronized.

To resume normal synchronization of a shared notebook, do the following:

1. Right-click the navigation bar icon of the shared notebook you want to resume synchronizing, and then click Notebook Sync Status on the shortcut menu that appears.

2. In the Shared Notebook Synchronization dialog box that appears, click Sync Automatically Whenever There Are Changes.

3. Click Sync Now.

When the shared notebook has finished synchronizing, click Close.

> Although manual synchronization typically isn't necessary, the Sync Now button in the Shared Notebook Synchronization dialog box can be useful if you're in a hurry to shut down your computer after adding or pasting a large amount of notes on a shared page. Clicking the Sync Now button lets you save large changes without having to wait for the next automatic synchronization. Once your manual synchronization has finished, you can trust that the other authors will be able to see your recent changes and you can then shut down your computer.

Now that you've learned the basics of notebook synchronization, it's time to learn more about working with the contents of shared notebooks and the features that are unique to them.

 LET ME TRY IT

Showing or Hiding Author Information

Notes that you yourself have added or changed will look the same as in any other notebook. However, if you want to know which other authors have added information, you can opt to temporarily or permanently display this information by doing the following:

1. While in any section of a notebook, click the Share tab.

2. In the Shared Notebook group, take note of the Hide Authors button (see Figure 9.20). The button appears orange by default, which means that the initials of authors who have added or changed notes on the current page are currently not displayed.

Share
Draw
Review
View
New Shared Notebook
Share This Notebook
Recent Edits
Find by Author
Hide Authors
Shared Notebook

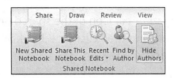

Figure 9.20 *To reveal the initials of authors who have added or changed information on pages in a shared notebook, turn off Hide Authors mode by clicking the button on the far right of the Shared Notebook group on the Share tab. When the button no longer appears orange, authors' initials will be shown in shared notes.*

3. To exit the selected Hide Authors mode, click the Hide Authors button. It no longer appears orange and the initials of any page authors are revealed.
4. To view more information about a change made by a particular author, rest the mouse pointer over the initials displayed next to a paragraph of text. You'll see the author's full name and the date and time that his or her edits took place.

When you inspect the page now, you may see lines next to paragraphs of notes marked with the initials of any of the other authors (see Figure 9.21). If you see no initials, it either means that no author has edited the page, or that it was you who edited it. (Your own initials are never shown to you, only to others.)

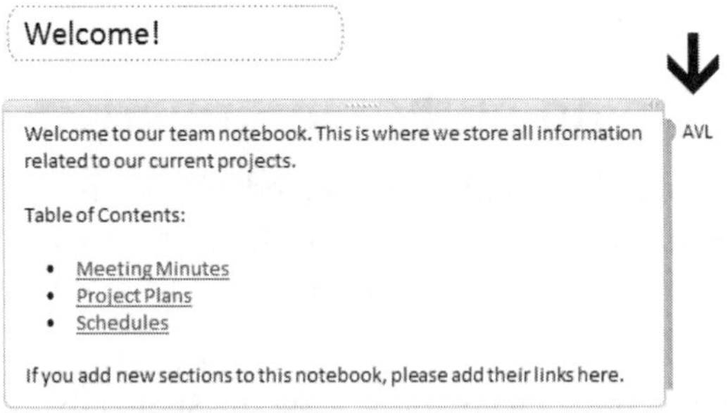
Welcome!
Welcome to our team notebook. This is where we store all information related to our current projects.
Table of Contents:
Meeting Minutes
Project Plans
Schedules
If you add new sections to this notebook, please add their links here.
AVL

Figure 9.21 *When the Hide Authors option is turned off, the initials of shared notebook authors who have made additions or changes to the notebook content will appear next to the locations of their edits. If you rest the mouse pointer over any initials you see, OneNote will display the full name of the author and the date and time of his or her edits.*

Author information is useful to be kept visible while you're editing complex notes and you want to visually keep a separation between the contributions of any of the other people taking notes in the shared notebook.

If any of the other authors' initials or full names aren't accurate, ask them to correctly enter this information in the personalization fields in their copy of OneNote 2010. Click the File tab, click Options, click General, and then verify the name and initials shown under the heading "Personalize Your Copy of Microsoft Office." If a correction is necessary, be sure to click OK after making any changes to save the new settings.

If you no longer want or need to know which authors contributed which notes, do the following:

1. Click the Share tab.

2. In the Shared Notebook group, click the Hide Authors button. It will once again appear orange, meaning that it is selected and the authoring information is hidden.

Remember that even if you work in Hide Authors mode, you can still easily see who created any particular paragraph of notes at any time. Move the mouse pointer over a line of text, and then right-click the four-headed arrow icon that appears just to the left of the text. On the shortcut menu that appears, look at the very end of the menu to see the name of the author and the date and time when the note was created.

Because this book is aimed at beginners, I won't go into all of the technical details of everything that can occur while taking notes together in the same space. Suffice it to say that even when a rare conflict in editing occurs, OneNote will inform you in plain English what it needs to know from you and how it should handle certain updates. Similarly, there is fail-safe functionality that prevents others from erasing notes you care about, something I'll briefly touch on in some of the upcoming procedures in this chapter.

LET ME TRY IT

Catching Up on Unread Notes

Each new shared notebook created with OneNote will assume that its authors will want a way to easily view what's been added or changed since the last time the shared notebook was accessed. Such notes are called unread notes.

Catching up on unread notes is useful if you need to carefully review the accuracy or relevance of new notebook content that others have added or changed, or when you've been disconnected from the notebook for a time and want to catch up on the newest information. For example, imagine your company has employees in opposite time zones in another country. While you're sleeping at night, they add new information to the shared notebook. When you come to work the next day and reconnect to the shared notebook, you can quickly review the new notes that were added or changed by your international colleagues by stepping through all of the unread changes. They can do the same with notes that you'll add during your workday.

To review unread notes in a shared notebook, do the following:

1. Open the shared notebook whose changes you want to view.

2. On the Share tab, in the Unread group, click Next Unread. OneNote switches to the next unread page in the shared notebook. If the Next Unread button is not available, it means that there are no new unread notes or that you've reached the last page of unread notes.

3. To mark a page as read, click the Mark as Read button on the ribbon, and then click Mark as Read on the shortcut menu (see Figure 9.22). For a faster way, you can use the Ctrl+Q keyboard shortcut.

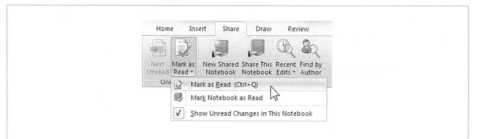

Figure 9.22   *The shortcut menu that appears when you click the Mark as Read button lets you mark unread pages as read, mark read pages as unread, and mark entire notebooks as read. Here, you can also turn this feature off entirely.*

After a page is marked as read, it will no longer be included in the Next Unread cycle. If you want to remind yourself to review a particular page again the next day or the next time you connect to the shared notebook, you can mark a page as unread again by following the preceding steps and clicking Mark as Unread in step 3. You can also use the keyboard shortcut again: Ctrl+Q toggles a page between its read or unread state.

When a shared notebook contains one or more unread pages, the notebook's name will appear bold on the navigation bar to signal you that there are new notes added or changed by others that you haven't yet seen. If you don't care to review each individual page during any given pass, you can mark the entire notebook as read. On the Share tab, in the Unread group, click the Mark as Read button, and then click Mark Notebook as Read on the shortcut menu.

To turn this feature off entirely, click the Mark as Read button and then deselect the option Show Unread Changes in This Notebook. If you change your mind, click the button again and then click the same command again.

 LET ME TRY IT

Searching Shared Notes by Author

If you don't want to cycle through all of the pages in a large, shared notebook to see what's new, you can instead monitor what information was added or changed by a particular notebook author.

To search shared notes by author, do the following:

1. Open the shared notebook whose changes you want to view.

2. On the Share tab, in the Shared Notebook group, click Find by Author.

3. In the Search Results task pane that opens, click the small triangle that appears to the left of an author's name to view the names of the pages he or she has edited and when those changes were made (see Figure 9.23).

4. If you need to narrow your search results, use the first drop-down menu near the top of the task pane.

5. If you want to toggle between authors' names and the modification dates of their notes, use the second drop-down menu near the top of the task pane.

Figure 9.23   *When you click the Find by Author button on the Share tab, OneNote displays a special version of the Search Results task pane, which lets you view the pages that each author in a shared notebook added or changed and when. At the top of this task pane, you can also narrow your search scope or choose to display the results by modification date instead.*

6. To jump to any particular page of notes, click its light blue page title in the search results list.

> If you want to change the alphabetical order of the authors listed in the Search Results task pane, click the small A–Z (or Z–A) button next to the arrow that appears next to the second drop-down menu at the top of the task pane.

When you're done with the Search Results task pane, you can close it by clicking the *X* in the upper-right corner.

 LET ME TRY IT

Viewing Recent Edits in Shared Notes

Similar to the author search function in the previous steps, OneNote can also quickly create a list of notes that have recently been edited in a shared notebook.

This is useful if you want to narrow your review of new or changed notes by others to a specific span of time. For example, imagine you were on vacation for a week or two. When you return to the office, you can opt to view only the notes that were added or changed in the past 7 or 14 days.

To view recent edits in shared notes, do the following:

1. Open the shared notebook whose changes you want to view.

2. On the Share tab, in the Shared Notebook group, click Recent Edits.

3. From the menu that appears, select the date range you want. Alternately, if you want a complete list of all of the pages in the shared notebook and have them sorted in a list that's organized by date, click All Pages Sorted by Date.

> If you want to change the sort order of the dates shown, click the small A–Z (or Z–A) button next to the arrow that appears next to the second drop-down menu at the top of the task pane.

 **LET ME TRY IT**

Viewing and Managing Multiple Versions of a Changed Page

OneNote 2010 includes a useful history feature to keep track of changed pages in your shared notebooks. This makes it easy to keep track of notes that shouldn't have been changed or deleted.

If you use shared notebooks in a creative process, this option also lets you see the thought process of others by reviewing any previous versions of a page and comparing them with the current or final version of the page.

To view previous versions of a page, do the following:

1. Open the shared notebook whose history you want to view.

2. On the Share tab, in the History group, click the small arrow next to the Page Versions button.

3. On the menu that appears, click Page Versions. This option is a toggle that turns the page history display on or off. If any previous versions of pages exist, they will be shown as gray tabs immediately underneath the current version of the pages (see Figure 9.24). Tabs indicating a previous version of a page don't show the page title but the edit date and author of each version that OneNote remembers.

To view the contents of an older version of the page, click the page tab with the modification date and author's name you want. While viewing a previous version of a page, OneNote displays an orange bar under the section tabs and over the top of the page. If you click this bar, a shortcut menu appears that lets you decide what to do with this version of the page (see Figure 9.25).

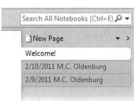

Figure 9.24 *The Page History feature lets you compare the most current page in a shared notebook with a prior version that you or someone else previously edited. If older versions of any particular page are available, clicking the Page Versions command makes them appear immediately underneath the current page tab.*

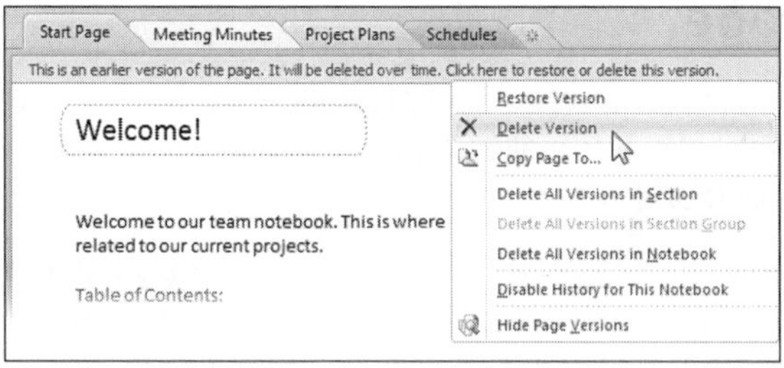

Figure 9.25 *When you click any gray page tab to view the previous version of a page it contains, OneNote displays an orange bar over the page to warn you that you're looking at an older version of the page. Clicking the bar lets you access a similar version of the shortcut menu that appears when you click the Page Versions button on the ribbon. You can use these menu commands to manage your shared notebook's page history.*

The shortcut menu that appears when you click the orange bar is nearly identical to the shortcut menu that appears when you click the arrow next to the Page Versions button on the ribbon. It doesn't matter where you use a history menu command, but because working with page versions can take greater care and concentration than working with normal pages, you might want to deliberately switch to a specific page version and then use the menu from the orange bar on that page. This way, you can be sure that you're working with the particular page version that you want to manage.

If, after clicking the orange bar, you click the Restore Version command on the shortcut menu, the older version of the page will be immediately promoted as the current page. The version that was current before you began managing the page history will, in turn, be demoted as the most recent older version of the page. If you do this by accident, remember that you can use the Undo command on the Quick Access Toolbar (or press Ctrl+Z on your keyboard).

If you prefer, you can use the Copy Page To command on the shortcut menu to save the information elsewhere in the shared notebook or in another notebook. This option is useful if you want to save older information in a safe location when you're not sure if that version should become the most current or final version of the page.

To permanently discard a specific previous version of a page, click its gray tab and then click the orange bar. On the shortcut menu that appears, click Delete Version. Alternately, you can also click Delete All Versions in Section, Delete All Versions in Section Group (if there is a section group in the shared notebook), or Delete All Versions in the Notebook to remove any unwanted page history.

Although you can use the Undo (Ctrl+Z) command to change your mind about any page history you've deleted, this is only possible within the same OneNote editing session. If you shut down OneNote and then return to the shared notebook, any deleted page history is gone forever. Note that you also cannot undo someone else's deletion of page history in a shared notebook.

If you want to completely disable the history features in OneNote, click the Disable History for This Notebook command on the shortcut menu that appears when you click the arrow next to the Page Versions button on the ribbon or when you click the orange bar that appears at the top of a previous page version that you're viewing. Note, however, that disabling the notebook history will also disable the Notebook Recycle Bin, which is described in the following procedure.

LET ME TRY IT

Viewing the Contents of the Notebook Recycle Bin

If you've been using Microsoft Windows for any amount of time, you're probably well aware of the Recycle Bin that appears on your computer's desktop. In Windows, the Recycle Bin gives you a last chance to salvage any files that you've deleted before they are permanently and irrevocably destroyed.

Similarly, OneNote 2010 employs a Notebook Recycle Bin for shared notebooks, which lets you review and restore important pages or sections that were discarded either by you or by another author working in a shared notebook.

To view and recover deleted sections or pages, do the following:

1. Open the shared notebook for which you want to view the Notebook Recycle Bin.

2. On the Share tab, in the History group, click the small arrow next to the Notebook Recycle Bin button.

3. On the menu that appears, click Notebook Recycle Bin. See Figure 9.26.

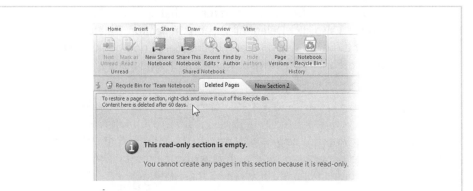

Figure 9.26   *When deleting pages or sections from a shared notebook, they're placed in the Notebook Recycle Bin. Deleted pages appear in the special Deleted Pages section, whereas deleted sections appear next to the Deleted Pages tab. To save, delete, move, or copy any deleted page or sections from the Notebook Recycle Bin, right-click the page or section tab and then make a selection from the shortcut menu that appears.*

As the orange bar over pages in the Notebook Recycle Bin indicates, deleted content automatically disappears permanently after 60 days. Though you can delete content from the Notebook Recycle Bin sooner than that, there's no option in OneNote 2010 to extend the two-month grace period.

If you want to empty the Notebook Recycle Bin and permanently discard any pages or sections it contains, click the small arrow next to the Notebook Recycle Bin button on the ribbon, and then click Empty Recycle Bin on the shortcut menu that appears.

The Notebook Recycle Bin is turned on by default, but you can turn this feature off if you don't want to use it. Click the Disable History for This Notebook command on the shortcut menu that appears when you click the small arrow next to the Notebook Recycle Bin button on the ribbon. Note, however, that disabling the

Notebook Recycle Bin will also disable the page history features in OneNote, which is described in a previous part of this chapter.

 **LET ME TRY IT**

Closing a Shared Notebook

When you no longer need to work in a specific shared notebook, you can close it and thus remove it from your navigation bar.

As with regular notebooks, closing a shared notebook does not delete it, nor does it revoke notebook access from the other authors. It merely removes it from your navigation bar to avoid clutter.

To close a shared notebook, do the following:

1. Before closing a shared notebook, you should synchronize it once more to prevent any final edits you've made from getting stuck on your computer. Although this is unlikely to happen, it's a best practice to manually synchronize notebooks once before you close them.

2. On the navigation bar, right-click the shared notebook you want, and then click Notebook Sync Status on the shortcut menu that appears.

3. In the Shared Notebook Synchronization dialog box that opens, click Sync Now.

4. When the notebook has finished synchronizing, click Close.

5. On the navigation bar, right-click the shared notebook once more, and then click Close This Notebook on the shortcut menu.

Note that closing a shared notebook does not delete it, nor does it revoke any of the other authors' access to the shared notebook. If you want to delete a shared notebook, you must do so in the shared location in which it is stored. If you want to merely stop sharing a notebook to prevent all others from editing it further, you must move it from its current shared location and place it in a new folder that only you can access. As with all shared computer files, it is strongly recommended that you create and keep a complete backup of any shared notebook that you decide to move or delete. If necessary, refer back to Chapter 8, "Security Features in OneNote" to review the backup features in OneNote 2010.

Sharing Notes in the OneNote Web App

The free OneNote Web App is one of the cool new features in OneNote 2010. It lets you view and edit OneNote notebooks in a computer-based or mobile web browser. By storing one or more shared notebooks on a free, secure Internet file storage service (or "in the cloud," as we're fond of saying these days), you can share your notes across multiple computers, laptops, cell phones, and other devices—no matter where in the world you are.

As with shared notebooks on a regular network, this can be very beneficial when you want to simply access your private notes from anywhere. For example, while you may frequently be out of range of your company's network, you can easily retain access to your important notes by placing them online and then accessing them in the web browser of your mobile phone.

The OneNote Web App also provides a great solution for sharing specific notebooks with other people—either as a way for them to view your notes from anywhere or for the purpose of collaborating together on shared research and projects. This is very useful when working with people who are outside of your company's or school's network (for example, a contractor or contract firm that you've hired for temporary work, or a friend in your study group who goes to another school), and it's also a great way to share your notes with people who don't yet have the full version of OneNote 2010.

 SHOW ME   Media 9.3—Sharing Notes on SkyDrive
Access this video file through your registered Web Edition at
my.safaribooksonline.com/9780132182447/media.

Naturally, the free OneNote Web App has only a limited set of features compared with the full version of OneNote 2010, but it supports the basics of note-taking and cross-platform sharing, which are typically all you need to stay on the same page when working with others online.

 **LET ME TRY IT**

Creating a Free Windows Live SkyDrive Account

If you don't already have a free Windows Live, Hotmail, or Xbox LIVE account, you must create one before you can use the OneNote Web App or any of the other Office 2010 Web Apps.

Signing up is simple and free. Do the following:

1. Type *http://www.skydrive.com* into your web browser's Address bar and then press Enter.

2. When the Windows Live SkyDrive home page appears (see Figure 9.27), click the Sign Up button and then follow the steps to create a new account.

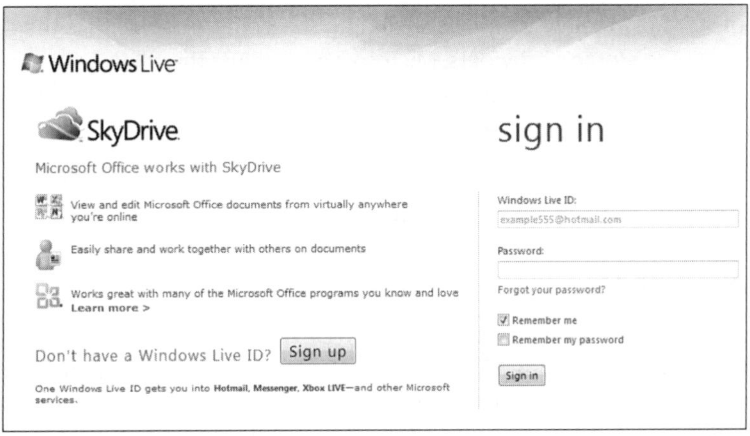

Figure 9.27   *SkyDrive is a free file storage service that lets you store your computer files online so that you and anyone you authorize can access them from virtually anywhere. SkyDrive runs on Microsoft's Windows Live service, so you can either use your existing Hotmail or Windows Live account, or create a new one.*

If the screenshot in Figure 9.27 doesn't precisely match what you see on your screen, don't worry. Online software and their websites are often updated without notice.

Because all of the customization options on Windows Live and its various services (Hotmail, Messenger, etc.) are entirely optional, I won't cover any of them in this book. Feel free to nose around a bit and set any preferences about your Windows Live experience that you might have.

If you feel skittish about entering any personal information as part of your SkyDrive sign-up process and you plan to use SkyDrive only to share your OneNote notebooks across your own computers and mobile devices, you don't have to give your real name or real birth date. However, if you use fictional information, make sure you write down your login information somewhere so you can authenticate your account again if it's ever compromised (for example, if you forget to log off at an Internet café). If you'll be using your shared note-books on SkyDrive with clients and other people who will look for your name as confirmation that your interaction with the site is legitimate, I would strongly recommend using at least your real name or the name of your company.

At the time this book was written, a free SkyDrive account included a generous 25GB of storage for all of your files, including shared notebooks. As is the custom for most online storage providers, Microsoft may adjust this allowance over time, so be sure to check your Windows Live account now and then for any important announcements about the service.

Files you store on SkyDrive work in a similar fashion as they would on your com-puter's hard drive. For example, although you can use OneNote 2010 to create a notebook on SkyDrive, you can also do so right in SkyDrive and then simply open that notebook in OneNote 2010.

Remember that the Office Web Apps on SkyDrive have limited functionality com-pared with the full versions of OneNote 2010, Word 2010, PowerPoint 2010, and Excel 2010. For this reason, I typically recommend creating new shared notebooks on SkyDrive from within OneNote 2010 so you can learn the interface properly. If you later prefer to do all of your shared notes housekeeping from your SkyDrive home page, that choice is entirely yours.

Like most cloud-based software and services, Windows Live, SkyDrive, and the Office Web Apps are continually updated and enhanced, sometimes without notice. By the time you read this book, some of the online interface elements that you see in our screenshots may have changed, as may some of the steps in our procedures. Take care never to breeze past any new or changed options and commands too quickly (especially when setting or changing folder permissions) until you've had a chance to experiment with how they work.

 **LET ME TRY IT**

Creating a SkyDrive-Based Shared Notebook

Until you become familiar with how OneNote 2010 on your computer and your SkyDrive account interact with each other, I recommend using the OneNote 2010 interface to create and maintain your shared notebooks and staying signed in to your SkyDrive home page in your web browser so you can see how your files show up.

Let's first create a brand-new notebook on SkyDrive. This is actually a pretty simple undertaking, but I'll break this procedure into a few more steps to give you some context along the way about what's happening.

Follow these steps:

1. In OneNote 2010, click the Share tab. In the Shared Notebook group, click New Shared Notebook. (You can also get here by clicking the File tab and then clicking New.)

2. Under the heading 1. Store Notebook On, click Web.

3. Under the heading 2. Name, type a meaningful description for the notebook (for example, *Holiday Travel Planning*). Remember that the name of the notebook should make sense to all participants if you plan on sharing this notebook with other people.

4. Under the heading 3. Web Location, click the Sign In button and then either sign in with your Windows Live, Hotmail, or Xbox LIVE account (see Figure 9.28). Depending on the speed of your Internet connection, you might see a progress indicator for several seconds while OneNote 2010 establishes a secure connection to the SkyDrive servers (see Figure 9.29).

Figure 9.28 *When you click the Sign In button during the web notebook creation process in OneNote 2010, you'll be prompted to enter your Windows Live account credentials. If you don't want to see this screen every day, click the Sign Me In Automatically check box before clicking OK.*

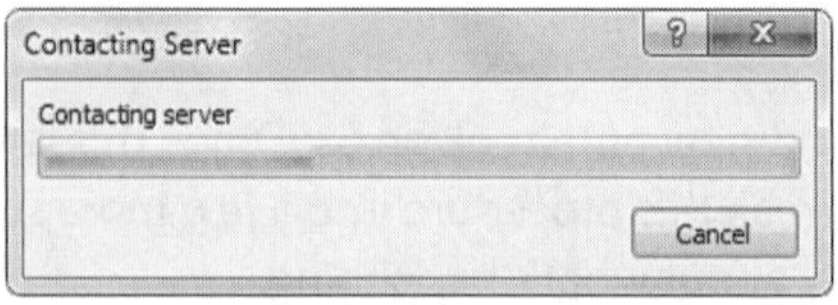

Figure 9.29 *A progress bar might appear briefly while OneNote 2010 establishes a secure connection with the SkyDrive server over the Internet. If you see this indicator for a long time, verify that you're still connected to the Internet.*

5. When you're successfully signed in, your default SkyDrive folder (My Documents) will appear with an orange highlight under the 3. Web Location heading (see Figure 9.30). The orange color means that this SkyDrive folder is selected and, if you proceed, the notebook will be created here. Because we'll want to later share this particular notebook with other people, let's create a new folder whose permissions you can manage separately from your personal My Documents folder. To do so, click the New Shared Folder button (see Figure 9.30).

6. OneNote 2010 switches to SkyDrive in your web browser and displays the Create a Folder interface. In the Name field, type a meaningful name for the new folder (for example, *My* Shared Notebooks), and then click Next (see Figure 9.31).

7. When the folder has been created on SkyDrive, it will appear empty. Switch back to OneNote 2010. (If necessary, click the File tab and then click New to return to the place you were at.) Here, you might see a prompt to refresh your shared folder list. Click the Refresh button if it appears (see Figure 9.32). Even if you're not prompted to do so, refreshing your SkyDrive contents in OneNote 2010 before working with the files in any of your folders is a good habit to get into.

8. In the refreshed folders list, click the new *My Shared Notebooks* folder (see Figure 9.33). This is where you'll create the new notebook. OneNote confirms your selection by highlighting the folder in orange.

9. Click Create Notebook to create the new notebook in the selected SkyDrive folder.

10. When prompted to invite others to the notebook via e-mail (see Figure 9.10 earlier in this chapter), click No, Thanks. You can invite others to the notebook later, when you have set the appropriate notebook permissions and have created the basic notebook structure.

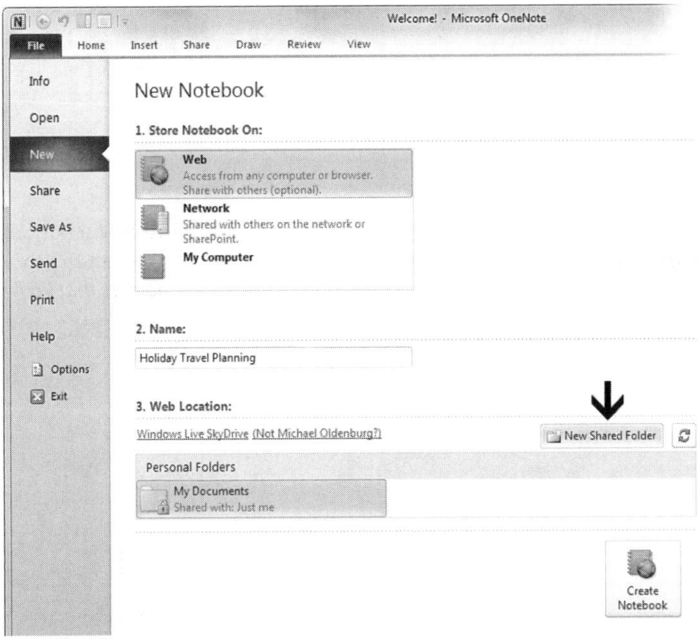

Figure 9.30   *Once you're signed in to your SkyDrive account, your name and your personal folders will appear under the Web Location heading. It's best to keep all of your notebooks that you plan to share with other people in a separate, new folder. To create this new folder, click the New Shared Folder button.*

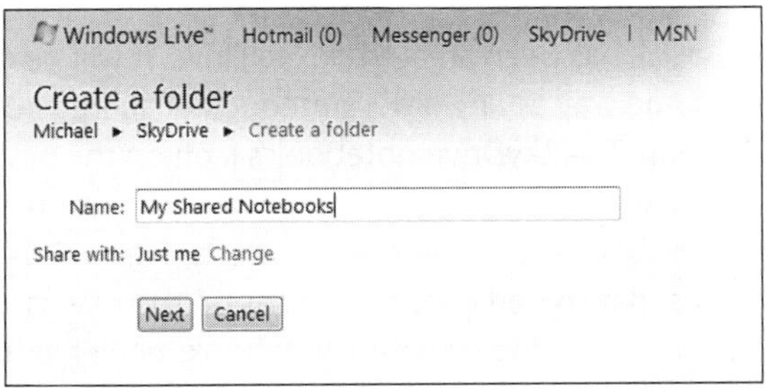

Figure 9.31   *When OneNote 2010 switches to the SkyDrive interface to create a new folder to which you can later apply specific permissions for other people, type a folder description into the Name field and then click Next. When the folder has been created on SkyDrive, return to OneNote 2010 to finish creating a new shared notebook in this folder.*

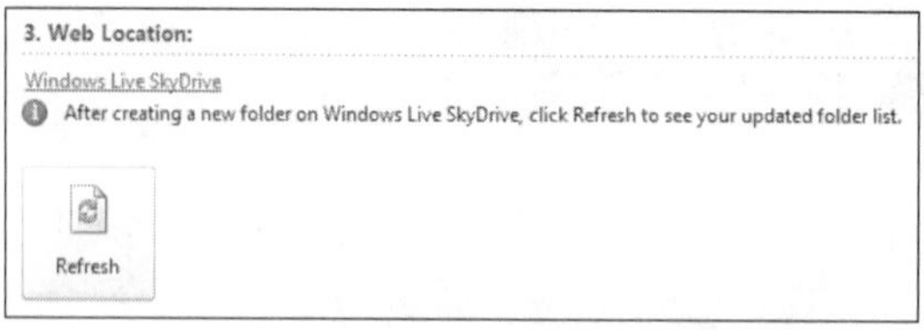

3. Web Location:

Windows Live SkyDrive

ℹ After creating a new folder on Windows Live SkyDrive, click Refresh to see your updated folder list.

Refresh

Figure 9.32   *Whenever OneNote 2010 detects that the SkyDrive folder list has changed, it might prompt you to refresh the folder display in the Backstage View (to return here, click the File tab and then click New). Click the Refresh button to display any folders that you've created or modified on SkyDrive.*

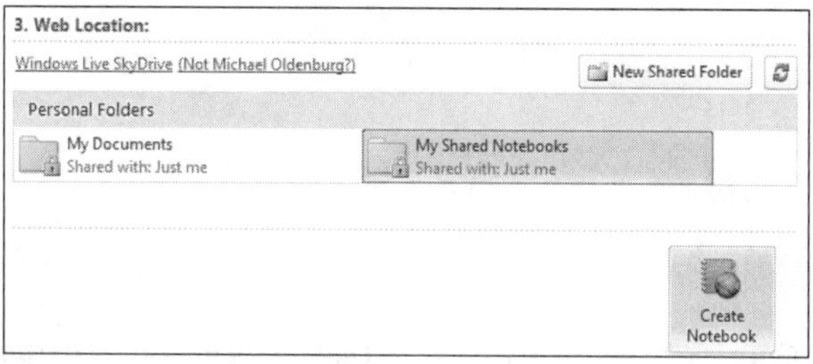

3. Web Location:

Windows Live SkyDrive (Not Michael Oldenburg?)   🗐 New Shared Folder   ⟳

Personal Folders

My Documents
Shared with: Just me

My Shared Notebooks
Shared with: Just me

Create
Notebook

Figure 9.33   *When you've refreshed your Personal Folders list in OneNote 2010, click to select the new My Shared Notebooks folder that you created. It will appear highlighted in orange to let you know it has been selected. If you need to refresh your folders list at any time, click the small button with the two blue arrows. When you're ready to create the new notebook in the selected folder, click the Create Notebook button.*

After the new notebook has been created on SkyDrive, it will be displayed in OneNote 2010 the same way as any other notebook or shared notebook you create, with one exception: The SkyDrive notebook's icon on the navigation bar reminds you that you're working in a web-based notebook by placing a globe symbol (for World Wide Web) over the notebook icon (see Figure 9.34). For a reminder about the other clues that shared notebook icons on the navigation bar can indicate, refer back to "Synchronizing a Shared Notebook," earlier in this chapter.

Although a SkyDrive-based notebook will always be referred to as a "shared notebook," this does not mean that other people can necessarily see it. In the previous procedure, when you created the new Shared Notebooks folder, you saw that I didn't have you change the access permissions. I did this on purpose for two reasons.

For one, it's important that you understand the difference between a *shared notebook*, where *shared* indicates that you can share the information it contains with

Figure 9.34   *When a globe symbol (for World Wide Web) appears over a notebook icon, it means that notebook is shared on a web server such as SkyDrive. As with normal shared notebooks on your network, you generally don't need to do anything to keep a SkyDrive notebook in sync. If a red, slashed circle appears over the icon, it means your connection has been broken. See "Synchronizing a Shared Notebook" earlier in this chapter to learn more about shared notebook icons and the actions they suggest.*

yourself from various points of access, such as OneNote 2010 on your desktop computer, the OneNote Web App on your laptop, and even from your cell phone in OneNote Mobile (more about that in Chapter 11, "Using OneNote on Your Mobile Phone"). In this scenario, the notebook isn't shared with other people and your information is secure and kept confidential.

The second reason we didn't set access permissions for the Shared Notebooks folder you created on SkyDrive is because I want you to know how to do this after the fact. As I mentioned earlier in this chapter (in the section "Creating a New Shared Notebook"), it's a good idea to first set up the new notebook's sections structure before inviting other authors to view and edit your shared notebook. You can even include a brief welcome page with instructions about how others should use, navigate, and add information to the notebook. This provides useful guidance to people who aren't yet very familiar with the OneNote Web App or with shared notebooks in OneNote 2010.

Although there's no reason not to use your full version of OneNote 2010 to view and edit your shared notebooks on SkyDrive, let's take a look at how you can open such notebooks in a web browser with the OneNote Web App. This will also show you how your notes might appear slightly differently than they do in the full version of OneNote and how other people might see those notes.

 **LET ME TRY IT**

Opening a SkyDrive Notebook in the OneNote Web App

The simplest way to open a shared notebook in the OneNote Web App is to log into your SkyDrive account and then open the notebook from within the online folder in which it is stored.

To open a notebook, do the following:

1. In your web browser, open http://www.skydrive.com and sign into your Windows Live account, if necessary.

2. Under My Files, click the folder that contains the shared notebook you want to open. To stay with our previous example, click the folder called My Shared Notebooks.

3. When the contents of the My Shared Notebooks folder are displayed, click the OneNote icon of the notebook you want to open. (In this case, click the notebook called *Holiday Travel Planning*.)

4. OneNote opens the notebook in the OneNote Web App in your web browser (see Figure 9.35).

> If you decide you want to continue editing the SkyDrive notebook in the full version of OneNote 2010, click the Open in OneNote icon near the right side of the Home tab on the ribbon. If you're prompted for credentials, enter your Windows Live account ID and password.

When you're done viewing or editing your shared notebook in the OneNote Web App, you can return to the SkyDrive home screen by clicking the blue SkyDrive text link over the Web App ribbon near the top of your browser screen.

If you want to quickly view or edit a SkyDrive-based shared notebook in the OneNote Web App (for example, to make sure that new content you've added to the notebook with OneNote 2010 shows up as you expect it to), you can copy and paste the direct link to the notebook by doing the following:

1. In OneNote 2010, click the File tab and then click Info.

2. In your list of notebooks, look for the title of your shared notebook on SkyDrive (*Holiday Travel Planning*).

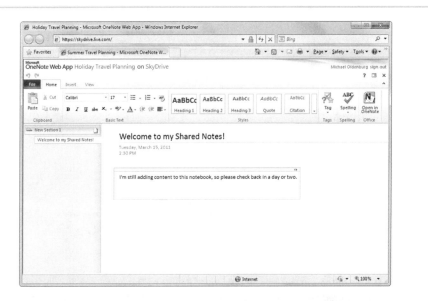

Figure 9.35   *When you open a shared notebook in the OneNote Web App, it resembles what you see in the full version of OneNote 2010. The page tabs appear on the left side to simulate an expanded navigation bar, showing the structure of your notebook. The commands that are available on the ribbon indicate the OneNote 2010 features that the Web App supports. If in doubt, right-click items for additional options (for example, page and section tabs). If you make a mistake while exploring by clicking commands and icons, click the Undo button over the File tab.*

3. Move the mouse pointer over the URL shown under the notebook name and then click the left mouse button once to select the text (see Figure 9.36).

4. When the URL turns blue to confirm that it has been selected, press Ctrl+C on your keyboard to copy the address.

5. Switch to your web browser, click in its Address box, and then press Ctrl+V to paste the copied URL.

6. Press Enter to open the shared notebook in the OneNote Web App.

Remember to treat your SkyDrive account the same way you would your personal e-mail account. If you access your private files from a shared computer, take care to always properly log out of your Windows Live account when you're done working with your SkyDrive files!

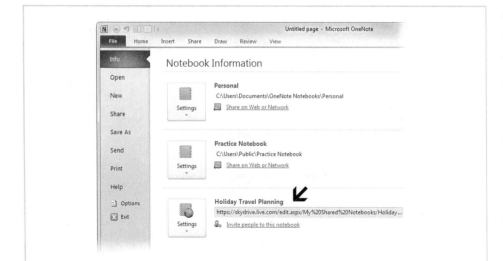

Figure 9.36   *Although you can click the Invite People to This Notebook link underneath the name of a shared notebook, the URL shown under the title of a SkyDrive notebook can be copied and pasted into your web browser if you want to quickly view or edit this notebook in the OneNote Web App.*

 LET ME TRY IT

Allowing Others to View or Edit Your SkyDrive Notebook

When you've created a basic notebook structure of sections and pages in your shared notebook and have perhaps added some welcome text or instructions for others, you can assign specific permissions to let others view or edit the shared notebook.

Do the following:

1. While signed in to your Windows Live account, go to http://www.skydrive.com.

2. When your list of folders appears, click the folder whose permissions you want to change.

3. When the contents of the folder appear, click the Edit Permissions link in the navigation bar on the far right of the screen (see Figure 9.37).

Figure 9.37   *As you navigate through your files and folders on SkyDrive, keep an eye on the contextual navigation bar near the right side of your screen. Here, you can look up and change things about your selected folder or file.*

4. When Windows Live displays the Edit Permissions screen (see Figure 9.37), click and drag the vertical slider upward to select the group of people for whom you want to set permissions. The higher you go, the more people can potentially see or use your files.

5. Next to each level of access that you've included, click the drop-down menu to set the specific level of authorization. This lets you specify whether you want certain people to only view your notebooks in a web browser without the ability to edit your notes, or if you want to give them full author's rights.

6. To set permissions for specific people, either click the Select From Your Contact List link or enter single e-mail addresses one at a time and then press Enter to add them to the permissions list.

7. When the permissions have been set to your liking, click Save. If you don't click the Save button before leaving this screen, your settings will not take effect.

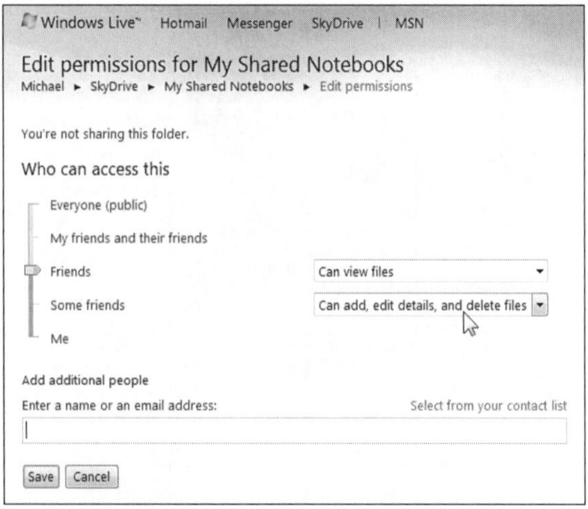

Figure 9.38   *By clicking and dragging the slider to the appropriate position and then selecting the level of access for the people on your Windows Live friend list, you can control who can see or use the files in the selected SkyDrive folder. You can also select specific people from your Windows Live contact list by clicking the blue link in the lower right or entering the e-mail addresses of people you want to authorize to view and use your files.*

Remember to check the permissions list for your SkyDrive folders now and then, especially as you add more and more files to the same folders and the information (and perhaps the intended level of sensitivity) in your notebooks changes over time. The security of your personal files on SkyDrive is only as strong as your password. A strong password includes a mix of numbers and letters, a mix of uppercase and lowercase letters, and a symbol or two (such as a dash or underscore).

After you've set the permissions for your *My Shared Notebooks* folder (or any other SkyDrive folder you want), you can invite people to access your shared notebook. If you have Microsoft Outlook 2010 or another e-mail program installed, OneNote can generate the invitation e-mail message for you.

To invite people to access your shared notebook, do the following:

1. In OneNote 2010, click the File tab and then click Info.

2. Next to any listed notebook whose Settings button shows a globe symbol over the notebook icon, click the Invite People to This Notebook link (see Figure 9.36) and then send the e-mail message to the people with whom you want to share your notebook.

3. If you don't have Outlook 2010 or another e-mail program installed or properly configured, or if you use a web-based e-mail program, select the *https://* link shown under the notebook title by clicking it once.

4. Press Ctrl+C to copy the link, switch to a new e-mail message, and then press Ctrl+V to paste the link into your message.

If you're away from the computer that has the full version of OneNote 2010 installed, you can still invite others to your shared notebook on SkyDrive by doing the following:

1. In your web browser, open http://www.skydrive.com.

2. Navigate to the SkyDrive folder in which the shared notebook is stored.

3. Near the far right side of the screen, click Get a Link.

4. On the Get a Link screen, press Copy above the link that SkyDrive provides for you.

5. Create a new e-mail message in Hotmail or whichever program or service you're using, and then press Ctrl+V to paste the copied link to the shared notebook folder you want the mail recipient to know about.

 LET ME TRY IT

Downloading a Copy of Your SkyDrive Notebook

If you want to download a copy of any notebook currently stored on SkyDrive, you can do so from the notebook list in the SkyDrive folder that the notebook is stored in.

Do the following:

1. In your web browser, open http://www.skydrive.com.

2. Navigate to the SkyDrive folder in which the shared notebook is stored.

3. Move the mouse pointer over the notebook you want to download. When a round "i" icon appears at the far right, click this icon to display a Download link in the navigation bar on the far right side of your browser.

4. Click the Download link and then, when the File Download dialog box appears, click Save.

Saving a Zip file of your SkyDrive notebooks provides an easy way for you to make manual backups of your notes on occasion. This is especially useful after you or one of the other authors has made significant additions or changes to a notebook. Although the OneNote Web App supports the Page History feature previously covered for the full version of OneNote 2010, sometimes it might just be easier to create a quick manual backup file.

Another use for saving a SkyDrive notebook as a Zip file is that you can quickly share this file with others who don't have access to your SkyDrive folder but who still want or need to see the information in the notebook. Although sharing a notebook in this way does not keep its information up-to-date with what's online, this lets you share a snapshot of a set of notes without the need to add that person or a group of people to your SkyDrive folder permissions list.

 **LET ME TRY IT**

Deleting a SkyDrive Notebook

To delete a notebook from SkyDrive, do the following:

1. In your web browser, open http://www.skydrive.com.

2. Navigate to the SkyDrive folder in which the shared notebook is stored.

3. Move the mouse pointer over the notebook you want to delete. When a round "i" icon appears at the far right, click this icon to display a Delete link in the navigation bar on the far right side of your browser. (Note that if you don't first select a notebook to delete by clicking the "i" icon, clicking the Delete link that appears in the right navigation bar of the current folder deletes the entire folder.)

4. Carefully heed the warning that appears. If you haven't yet warned the other authors that you're deleting the notebook, click Cancel. If you're absolutely certain that you don't care about the information in the selected shared notebook, click OK to permanently erase the notebook.

It is strongly recommended that you first make a reliable backup copy of any notebook that you're considering erasing. In addition, if the notebook was shared with other people, you should first warn the other authors that the notebook will no longer be available after a certain date and time. That way, no one will lose work by adding or editing information that will be deleted shortly after they've completed the work. You cannot undo deleting a notebook on SkyDrive.

Displaying Content from Features Not Supported by the OneNote Web App

SkyDrive and your Windows Live account have a lot of other tricks up their sleeves, so be sure to explore all of the tools that are available to you while you are logged into the service.

Before concluding this chapter, I did want to reiterate something I previously mentioned. Although the OneNote Web App is a wonderful way to view and edit your shared notebooks on the Web from anywhere in the world, browser-based clients typically offer only a subset of features compared with their full desktop versions. OneNote is no exception. The full OneNote 2010 desktop client is the only version that contains every feature that OneNote has to offer.

If you use the OneNote Web App to view and edit a notebook that was originally created with the full version of OneNote 2010, some of its pages might contain content that the OneNote Web App cannot display. Examples of such content include handwriting from a Tablet PC, drawing objects, and custom formatting.

When such pages are viewed in the OneNote Web App, it will warn you with an orange alert message over the top of the page (see Figure 9.39) that it cannot show you all of the page content.

Figure 9.39   *When using the OneNote Web App to view notebook pages originally created in the full version of OneNote 2010, a warning will appear at the top of any page that contains objects or content that the Web App can't understand or display, such as handwriting or drawing objects. If you must see the complete version of the page, click the Open in OneNote button on the Web App ribbon.*

In Chapter 11, you'll learn how you can access your SkyDrive notebooks with the OneNote Mobile apps that are available for Windows Phone 7 and the iPhone—or from mobile browsers on other cell phones and devices.

Though nothing matches the full functionality of OneNote 2010 on your computer, keeping your notes on SkyDrive gives you the most flexibility in accessing, searching, and using your information from virtually anywhere in the world, no matter if you're merely sharing your notes across devices with yourself or if you're sharing them with other people.

This chapter summarizes how OneNote and some of your other applications work better together.

10

Using OneNote with Other Programs

One of the reasons OneNote is one of my favorite programs is that it has reached a level of integration into my life that has made my goal of going paperless without sacrificing convenience more and more of a reality.

My choices as a consumer are based on my personal experiences with technology that manages to delight me by offering me what I care about or by doing something for me that I didn't know it could do. Though it took me a while to warm up to electronic note-taking and really commit to leaving my trusted notepad and pen on my desk whenever I went to meetings, the benefits of OneNote were immediately clear to me when I first began using it. It's a rare example in which a product can so seamlessly introduce itself into one's life and become a part of it.

How we allow different technology into our lives—from the choices we make between brands, features, and price—depends on our mood as much as on our need to get something done. Our preferences can change on a dime and we often reach for a familiar solution just because it's the only thing we know. Have you ever performed a mail merge in Microsoft Word? When you tried it again six months later, did you figure out a better way of doing it, or did you find the task to be as arduous as it was the first time?

As I often remind friends and co-workers, computers were meant to save us time and to help us work smarter, but I see missed opportunities every day, either because we're completely unaware that the technology we already own and use can help us do even better things or because we almost perpetually claim that we're "too busy" to learn anything new—like the time-saving features in the software we use every day. The irony of this only hits us when we really stop and think about what we originally wanted technology to do for us.

Along the lines of discovery and understanding what's really under the hood in OneNote 2010, I want to briefly highlight some of the features that quietly become available when you install OneNote 2010 on your computer—either as the standalone version or as part of a Microsoft Office 2010 suite. Many of OneNote's integration features are overlooked by the very people who could most benefit from them.

Because this book is aimed at beginners, I hope that highlighting some of OneNote's coolest features in this way will inspire you to learn and use them right from the start. The smallest time savings can really add up and make you appreciate OneNote even more.

A Quick Note About Interface Differences

OneNote 2010 comes in two different versions—the standalone edition that includes only the OneNote program, and the version that is included with all editions of the Microsoft Office 2010 suite. Office includes other programs such as Microsoft Word, Excel, Outlook, and PowerPoint, among others.

Technically speaking, the two versions of OneNote are identical, but certain features will click on and off, depending on the other programs you have installed, which version of Microsoft Windows you are using, and what kind of computer you have. Some of these differences are more obvious than others.

For example, Figure 10.1 shows what the right half of the Home tab on the OneNote ribbon looks like when no other Office programs are present.

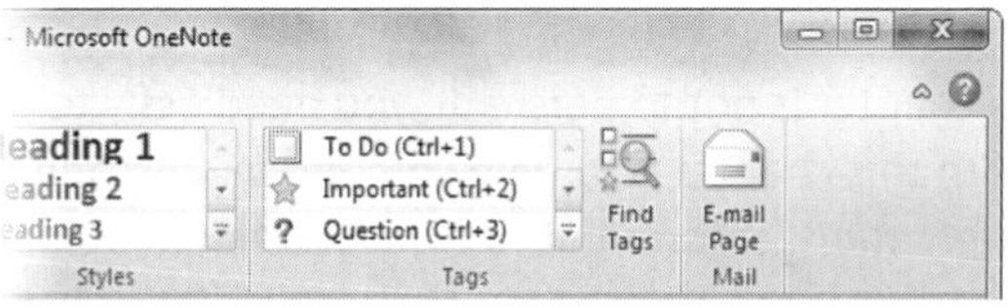

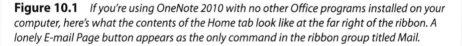

Figure 10.1   *If you're using OneNote 2010 with no other Office programs installed on your computer, here's what the contents of the Home tab look like at the far right of the ribbon. A lonely E-mail Page button appears as the only command in the ribbon group titled Mail.*

Figure 10.2 shows how the same area of the Home tab on the OneNote ribbon appears when Microsoft Outlook 2010 is detected.

Subtle differences in appearance and functionality can also occur if you're using OneNote or Office on an older version of Microsoft Windows, such as Windows XP or Windows Vista, or if you're using OneNote or Office on a computer that offers handwriting, drawing, or Multi-Touch capabilities.

For example, as I pointed out in Chapter 9, "Sharing Notes with Other People," clicking the E-mail Page button in the standalone version of OneNote 2010 on Windows

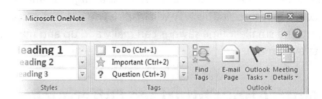

Figure 10.2   *When OneNote 2010 detects Outlook 2010, the contents of the Home tab at the far right of the ribbon change slightly. The ribbon group that was called Mail is renamed to Outlook and the lonely E-mail Page button is now accompanied by two additional command buttons. Likewise, the appearance of some ribbon tabs in Outlook 2010 will change when Outlook detects OneNote.*

Vista will generate an e-mail message with a notes attachment. That's because Windows Vista included its own e-mail client, called Windows Mail, which was the successor to Outlook Express on Windows XP. On Windows 7, the newest operating system in the Windows family, clicking the E-mail Page button in OneNote does nothing because the built-in functionality was removed. This wasn't an oversight but a deliberate decision due to the ever-increasing rise in popularity of web-based mail programs. It's an interesting example of how different flavors and versions of software, when used together, can exceed or fall short of our individual expectations.

The point of this chapter is not to persuade you needlessly to upgrade your software. My goal with this chapter is to help you understand and decide which Office and Windows integration features in OneNote you might actually care about, after you discover them and learn more about their capabilities. Spotting them without a guided tour of sorts can be difficult, as many of them are tucked away in hidden places. Knowing what you have—or don't have—can help you better understand how the choices you've already made might affect the functionality you have available to you, compared with the functionality you might expect.

Enough introductions! Let's get the tour started.

OneNote Integration with Windows

No matter what version of Windows you're using, installing OneNote 2010 adds a useful feature called the Send to OneNote print driver.

A device driver is a software program that allows your operating system or a software program to "talk" to a device connected to your computer, such as a printer or a scanner. The OneNote print driver can intercept the information other programs send to your printer and, instead of committing the information to paper and ink, print it out electronically on a OneNote page instead.

SHOW ME Media 10.1—Integrating OneNote with Windows
Access this video file through your registered Web Edition at
my.safaribooksonline.com/9780132182447/media.

If you read Chapter 6, "Collecting and Researching Information," you already learned how to insert files as printouts into your notes. The Send to OneNote print driver works the same way, just in the opposite direction. Instead of importing printed content from other programs into OneNote, the Send to OneNote print driver lets you "push" information from other programs to OneNote. It also lets you use the quick filing dialog box to select the exact destination in your notebook where you want the printout to appear.

 LET ME TRY IT

Printing from Any Windows Program to OneNote

To print to a page in OneNote instead of a page in your printer, do the following:

1. In the program you want to print from, click the Print command.

2. In the Print options that your program displays, select the Send to OneNote 2010 print driver (see Figure 10.3).

3. Select any other options you want, such as page range, and then click Print.

4. In the Select Location in OneNote dialog box that appears, click to select the notebook section where you want the page with the printout to be added and then click OK.

Different Windows programs have different-looking Print options. In most cases, clicking the Print command on a menu or ribbon-type interface will display a screen or dialog box where you can temporarily override your default printer. If you want to always print to OneNote, you can make the OneNote print driver your default printer. In Windows Control Panel, open Devices and Printers (Windows 7) or Printers (Windows Vista). In the list of printers and print drivers, right-click the Send to OneNote 2010 icon and then click Set as Default Printer (see Figure 10.4). Now all of your print jobs will automatically go to OneNote, unless you override this choice for specific print jobs by selecting your real printer in the Print dialog box.

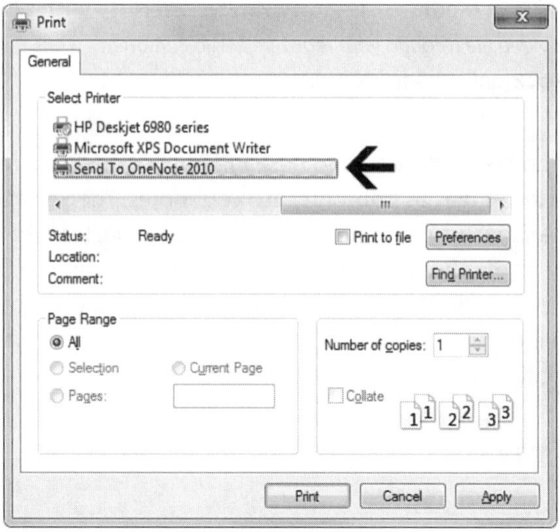

Figure 10.3   *In any Windows program, selecting the Send to OneNote 2010 print driver as your "printer" will print out the pages from your program to a new page in OneNote instead of using ink and paper on your real printer. This lets you capture important information without wasting paper or having to worry about finding the information again. OneNote's search features can instantly find information in your printouts.*

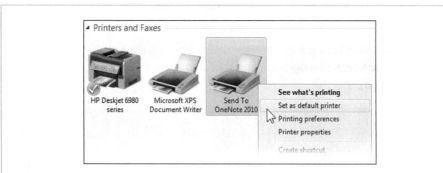

Figure 10.4   *In Windows Control Panel, your list of available printers includes the Send to OneNote 2010 print driver. The green check mark over the icon of your real printer indicates what Windows uses as your default printing choice. If you make the Send to OneNote 2010 print driver your default printer, all of your printouts will be sent to their own OneNote pages. You can still choose to use your real printer whenever you need to print something on a sheet of paper.*

Remember what else you learned in Chapter 6: You can right-click a printout when it appears in OneNote and click Copy Text from this Page of the Printout (or Copy Text from All Pages of the Printout) whenever you want to use the text for editing in your notes. If you have picture search enabled, OneNote will also find words in printouts when you search for them. These features are another benefit of printing to OneNote instead of to paper.

Using the OneNote Screen Clipper and Launcher in the Windows Notification Area

I already covered this nifty feature in Chapter 6 (see the section, "Meet the OneNote Screen Clipper and Launcher"), so I won't repeat all of the information about this little OneNote icon here, which appears on the Windows taskbar, in the notification area near the clock display (see Figure 10.5).

Figure 10.5   *The OneNote Screen Clipper and Launcher icon as it appears when displayed in the notification area of the Windows taskbar. When the icon is visible here, the keyboard shortcut combinations shown next to the commands on the shortcut menu provide instant access to those commands, even when OneNote 2010 isn't running.*

However, I do want to remind you of it in this chapter as it can be an even more useful Windows integration feature than the OneNote print driver.

The detailed step-by-step procedures in Chapter 6 tell you more about how this special icon works, how to configure and unhide it, and how to use it.

Next, let's look at how OneNote improves the Windows Internet Explorer web browser.

OneNote Integration with Internet Explorer

If you use Internet Explorer as your web browser, you can use the integration features that OneNote 2010 offers. If you use a different web browser, these features are not available.

 SHOW ME   Media 10.2—Integrating OneNote with Internet Explorer
Access this video file through your registered Web Edition at
my.safaribooksonline.com/9780132182447/media.

 LET ME TRY IT

Displaying the OneNote Command Buttons in Internet Explorer 8

If you're using Internet Explorer 8, the OneNote command buttons might be hidden from view (see Figure 10.6).

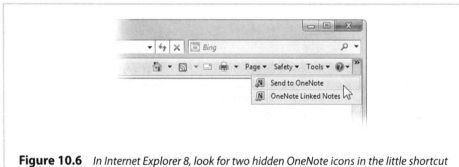

Figure 10.6   *In Internet Explorer 8, look for two hidden OneNote icons in the little shortcut menu that appears when you click the button with the chevron arrows, located just to the right of the circled blue Help (?) button. If you frequently use these commands in Internet Explorer, you can permanently unhide these icons by customizing the Internet Explorer toolbars.*

To use them, do the following:

1. Start Internet Explorer 8.

2. Near the upper-right corner of the Internet Explorer program window, underneath the Search field, click the double-arrow button to the right of the circled blue Help (?) button.

3. On the shortcut menu that appears, do either of the following:

   • To send the current web page in your browser to a OneNote notes page, click Send to OneNote. When the quick filing dialog box appears, click the section of the notebook in which you want the page to appear.

   • To begin a linked note-taking session in Internet Explorer, click OneNote Linked Notes.

 LET ME TRY IT

Displaying the OneNote Command Buttons in Internet Explorer 9

At the time that this book went to print, Microsoft released Internet Explorer 9, the newest version of its web browser. Although its user interface has been dramatically updated compared with previous versions, its integration with OneNote works the same.

Finding the OneNote command icons in Internet Explorer 9 is a bit trickier because the interface was purposely simplified.

To display the OneNote command buttons in Internet Explorer 9, do the following:

1. Start Internet Explorer 9.

2. Near the upper-right corner of the Internet Explorer program window, right-click in a blank area of the title bar and then click Menu Bar on the shortcut menu that appears.

3. When the menu bar appears near the upper left of the program window, click Tools and then, at the bottom of the menu, do either of the following:

   • To send the current web page in your browser to a OneNote notes page, click Send to OneNote. When the quick filing dialog box appears, click the section of the notebook in which you want the page to appear.

   • To begin a linked note-taking session in Internet Explorer, click OneNote Linked Notes.

If you'd prefer to use these commands as icons, do the following instead:

1. Near the upper-right corner of the Internet Explorer program window, right-click in a blank area of the title bar and then click Command Bar on the shortcut menu that appears.

2. When the two OneNote icons appear on the command bar near the upper left (see Figure 10.7), do either of the following:

    - To send the current web page in your browser to a OneNote notes page, click Send to OneNote. When the quick filing dialog box appears, click the section of the notebook in which you want the page to appear.

    - To begin a linked note-taking session in Internet Explorer, click OneNote Linked Notes.

Figure 10.7   *In Internet Explorer 9, you can unhide the two OneNote icons by right-clicking in a blank area near the upper right of the program window and then clicking Command Bar on the shortcut menu that appears. This places the command bar underneath the Address box near the upper left of the browser window.*

The two OneNote icons are very small and might be hard to distinguish, but if you hover the mouse pointer over either icon for a second or two, a ToolTip appears that will tell you the OneNote command that each icon represents.

If you prefer to leave the Internet Explorer 9 user interface uncluttered, you can hide the command bar again and use the Ctrl+T shortcut instead, which brings up the Tools menu, from which you can choose either of the two OneNote commands.

Sending a web page to OneNote is a great way to capture information that may frequently change at the source. For example, you could send the results list of a web search to OneNote to capture the results information there. If you were to perform the same web search again in a week's or a month's time, you'd likely see very different results. By capturing a snapshot of temporary or changing information, you can refer to it again later.

Sending web pages to OneNote can be a useful alternative to screen clippings because most of the information from a sent web page can be edited in OneNote, whereas a screen clipping is a static image that can't be changed. That said, sometimes a screen clipping is the only way to capture the layout of a web page exactly as it appears. Understanding these choices lets you capture information you care about in the format you prefer.

Taking linked notes in Internet Explorer lets you do research online across several web pages and sites. As you take notes in a docked OneNote window in this mode, OneNote automatically keeps track of the web addresses to the pages you visited and took notes on, so you can return to them again later. Without OneNote, you don't have this functionality in your web browser.

To learn more about (or brush up on) sending web pages to OneNote or how to take linked notes in Internet Explorer, see Chapter 6.

Next, let's see how OneNote integrates with some of the other programs in the Microsoft Office 2010 suite.

OneNote Integration with Word

As a tool for giving life to ideas and plans, I find OneNote to be without equal. However, there might be times when you need to present the information in your notes to someone else in a more formal manner, such as a report for your boss or a paper for a teacher.

The following procedures highlight how you can send notes from OneNote 2010 to Word 2010 in any of three different ways.

 LET ME TRY IT

Saving Notes as a Word Document

When you're ready to move a selection of notes to a Microsoft Word document for more advanced formatting and word processing features, OneNote provides a direct path to its Microsoft Office counterpart.

To save notes to Word, do the following:

1. Navigate to the notes that you want to save as a Word document.

2. Click the File tab and then click Save As.

3. Under the heading 1. Save Current, choose what you want to include (the current page, or the current section and its pages). Note that you cannot save an entire notebook as a Word document.

4. Under the heading 2. Select Format, click either the Word Document (*.docx) option to save the file in a newer format that can be used by Word 2010 and Word 2007, or click the Word 97–2003 Document (*.doc) option to save the file in an older format that can be read by Microsoft Word 97, Word 2000, Word XP (2002), and Word 2003.

5. Click Save As.

6. In the Save As dialog box that opens, navigate to the folder on your computer where you want to save the file containing the notes you selected, type a name into the File name field (for example, *Curriculum Vitae*), and then click Save.

Because OneNote does not by default use page dimensions typically used by a word processor, you might want or need to adjust the margins and the selected view in Microsoft Word after opening a document that was created from your OneNote notes.

 LET ME TRY IT

Sending a Notes Page to Word as a Printout

When you merely want a quick way to include the information from a single notes page in a Word document, you can send the notes from OneNote to Word without using the Save As dialog box by doing the following:

1. Navigate to the page that you want to save as a Word document.

2. Click the File tab and then click Send.

3. In the list, click Send to Word.

OneNote starts Word 2010 on your computer and inserts a formatted copy of your notes in a new document. Formatting that is exclusive to OneNote (for example, note tags) is not shown in the version of the page that appears in Word.

After the notes have been sent to a new Word document, you can move them to another location in the document or, if you prefer, cut and paste the notes into a Word document that you've already created.

 LET ME TRY IT

Creating a Blog Post from Your Notes with Word

Word 2010 includes functionality that lets you use your Word documents as blog posts. Word does this by providing a custom blogging interface that can be used with some of the leading blog sites. After you set up your blog account with Word, the integration can be a seamless document management and publishing experience.

Rather than duplicating all of this functionality, OneNote 2010 instead provides a bridge to Word 2010 so you can extend its blog publishing functionality to your OneNote pages.

To create a blog post from a page of your notes, do the following:

1. Navigate to the page that you want to send to Word as a blog post.

2. Click the File tab and then click Send.

3. In the list, click Send to Blog.

OneNote starts Word 2010 in blog mode with a custom Blog Post ribbon tab (see Figure 10.8). If you haven't yet registered Word with your blog hosting provider, follow the onscreen prompts or tell Word that you'll set up your account later. You can further format the notes in Word before publishing them to your blog, or you can publish your notes as they are.

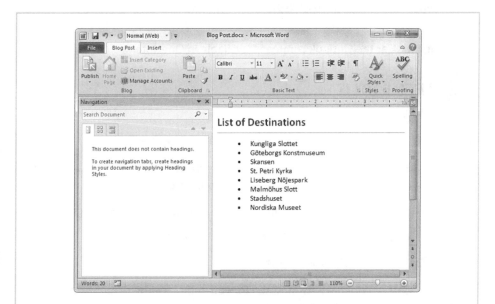

Figure 10.8 *When you send a page of your notes to Word as a blog post, OneNote opens Word in blog mode, where you can register with your blog hosting provider, further format your notes with Word's formatting features, and publish the page to your blog by using the commands on the Blog Post ribbon tab.*

Finally, though I won't duplicate the information here, I want to remind you that Word is one of the supported Office programs that you can use with OneNote's linked notes feature.

To learn more or to remind yourself about this feature, see "Doing Research with Linked Notes" in Chapter 6.

Next, you'll learn more about OneNote's rich integration with Outlook.

OneNote Integration with Outlook

Out of all of the other Microsoft Office programs, Outlook 2010 enjoys the richest integration with OneNote 2010. The two programs complement each other so well because the partnership goes both ways. OneNote enriches the functionality of Outlook, and Outlook enriches the functionality of OneNote.

SHOW ME Media 10.3—Integrating OneNote with Outlook 2010
Access this video file through your registered Web Edition at
my.safaribooksonline.com/9780132182447/media.

Let's first look at the Outlook command available in OneNote.

 LET ME TRY IT

Sending Notes in an Outlook Message

When Outlook 2010 is installed on the same computer as OneNote 2010, sending a copy of a notes page is as simple as clicking a button on the ribbon.

To send a copy of a notes page in an Outlook message, do the following:

1. In OneNote, navigate to the page you want to send.

2. On the Home tab, click E-mail Page.

Outlook 2010 will open a new message for you and place the contents of the notes page into the body of the message. It will also use the page title and place it into the Subject field of the message, which you can keep or modify as needed.

> If you want to attach a copy of the notes you're sending as either a OneNote file attachment or as a Web Page attachment, or both, see "Sending Notes as an Outlook Attachment" in Chapter 9.

 **LET ME TRY IT**

Inserting Outlook Meeting Details into Your Notes

If you frequently take notes based on meetings or appointments that you schedule with Outlook 2010, you probably already know that every notes page starts with the rather dreary task of filling out the same information every time: the subject and location of the meeting, its date and time, the names of the attendees, and the contextual notes that the meeting facilitator might have included in the meeting invitation.

An easier way is to have OneNote 2010 read your Outlook 2010 calendar and automatically insert all of the pertinent information from a meeting invitation into your notes. Do the following:

1. In OneNote, navigate to the page on which you'll take notes about a meeting that's already on your Outlook calendar and then click the cursor near the top of the page under the page title.

2. On the Home tab, click Meeting Details.

3. Under Today's Meetings, click to select the meeting you want.

At the location of your cursor, OneNote will insert all available meeting details in an easy-to-skim table. You can delete any information that you don't want or need to keep as part of your notes. Similarly, you can delete the names of people who were invited but didn't attend.

The word *Notes:* appears under your inserted meeting details so you can click the cursor in the line below and start taking notes when the meeting begins.

Using the Meeting Details command provides a convenient way to consistently format all of your meeting notes with the correct information about the meeting and its attendees.

If the meeting you want isn't shown on the Today's Meeting list that appears when you click the Meeting Details button, you can look up any other meeting in OneNote and insert its information into your notes without having to switch to Outlook by doing the following:

1. On the page on which you'll take notes about a meeting, click the cursor near the top of the page under the page title.

2. On the Home tab, click Meeting Details.

3. At the bottom of the menu that appears, click Choose a Meeting from Another Day.

4. In the Insert Outlook Meeting Details dialog box that appears (see Figure 10.9), do any of the following:

   - To display all available meetings on your Outlook calendar from a few days before or after the present day, click the round arrow buttons in the upper-left corner of the dialog box. The left arrow displays the previous day, and the right arrow displays the next day.

   - To display all available meetings on your Outlook calendar for a specific day, click the small calendar icon in the upper-right corner of the dialog box and then click the specific day you want. Use the Back and Next arrows at the top of the pop-up calendar to change months.

   - To select a specific meeting whose details you want to insert into your notes, click it once in the list.

   - To insert details about the meeting you have selected, click the Insert Details button.

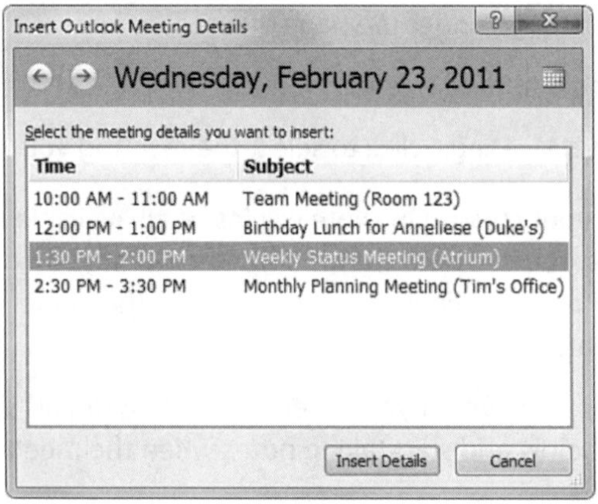

Figure 10.9 *If the meeting details you want to insert into your notes don't show up in the Today's Meetings list, clicking the Choose a Meeting from Another Day command displays this dialog box. Use the navigation buttons in the upper-left corner or the calendar control in the upper-right corner to access information for any Outlook meeting from any day of any month of any year.*

OneNote can look up information about your Outlook meetings even when Outlook 2010 isn't running. This works as long as you have a connection to your Microsoft Exchange mail server at the time you use the Meeting Details button on the OneNote ribbon.

 **LET ME TRY IT**

Flagging Important Notes as Outlook Tasks

Although OneNote includes a wealth of note tags that you can place next to important notes to help you search for and categorize them, none of the note tags offer the ability to flag notes for follow-up so you'll be reminded when they come due.

When you use Outlook 2010 together with OneNote 2010, OneNote inherits Outlook's Tasks features that let you flag important notes and action items. The benefit of this marriage of features is that you can create OneNote-based tasks much faster than if you were to go through the Outlook interface for creating new tasks. You still have the option to open Outlook tasks in Outlook, where you can set additional options, but this is optional.

To flag a line of notes as an Outlook task, do the following:

1. Click anywhere on the line of text that you want to flag as an Outlook task. For example, on a page of meeting notes, you could click all of the line items that represent important action items for you that you want to be reminded about.

2. On the Home tab, click Outlook Tasks.

3. From the menu that appears, click any of the preconfigured due dates (for example, Tomorrow or Next Week). OneNote places an Outlook task flag next to the selected line of notes (see Figure 10.10) and silently creates a task for this text in the Outlook Tasks view.

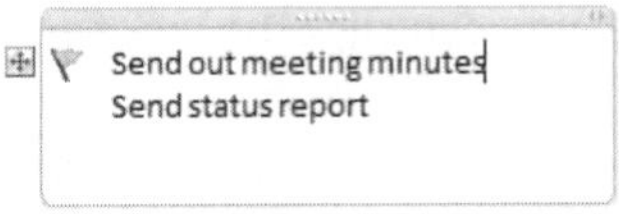

> Send out meeting minutes
> Send status report

Figure 10.10 *When you flag a line or paragraph of notes with an Outlook task, OneNote displays the task flag icon next to the note and creates an Outlook task behind the scenes. The next time you switch to Outlook and look at your Tasks list, this task will appear in the list. To edit the task to add a reminder or additional information, either right-click the task flag in OneNote and then click Open Task in Outlook or open it directly from your Outlook Tasks list.*

As long as you have a connection to your Microsoft Exchange mail server at the time you assign the task in your notes, OneNote will communicate the new task to Outlook, even when Outlook 2010 isn't running. If OneNote cannot reach your Exchange Server, it will attempt to create the task the next time you start Outlook 2010.

To open the task in Outlook, right-click the task flag on your notes page and then click Open Task in Outlook. Outlook will open the task in its regular window, where you can set additional options for the task (for example, to add a reminder to go off at a specific time).

If you want to associate a note with an Outlook task for a specific date, do the following:

1. Click anywhere on the line of text that you want to flag as an Outlook task.

2. On the Home tab, click Outlook Tasks.

3. From the menu that appears, click Custom. OneNote places an Outlook task flag next to the selected line of notes.

4. Wait for the Outlook Task window to open and then select the Start Date, Due Date, Status, Priority, % Complete, and Reminder you want. When the task has been updated, click Save & Close.

You'll notice that when you open an Outlook task that was created in OneNote, Outlook includes a OneNote page icon in the body of the task (see Figure 10.11). This is to make it easy for you to consistently switch between the Outlook task and the OneNote page to which the task is linked.

Because each program is completely aware of the other, you can open related OneNote items while in Outlook and related Outlook items in OneNote, without first having to switch from either program to the other.

To mark a task as complete, you can click the task flag on your OneNote page, right-click the flag and click Mark Complete, or mark it complete in your Outlook Tasks list. To remove pending or completed tasks that you no longer want or need, right-click the task flag on your notes page and then click Remove Tag.

This concludes the Outlook-related commands on the OneNote ribbon. Let's continue by looking at other places in Outlook where the presence of OneNote adds functionality.

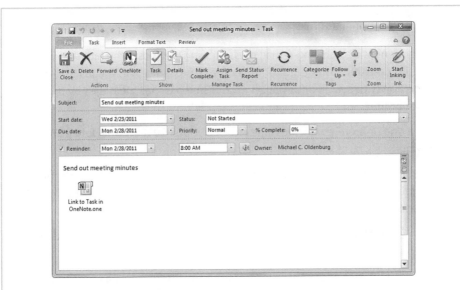

Figure 10.11 *When editing a task in Outlook 2010 that was created in OneNote 2010, Outlook includes a OneNote file icon in the body of the task. Double-clicking this icon will open the page that this task is linked to in OneNote. This is instantaneous, meaning you don't need to ever manually search for the page on which this task appears. Similarly, you can create a new task in Outlook and then click the OneNote icon on the task window ribbon to associate the task with one of your notes pages.*

 LET ME TRY IT

Archiving Outlook E-mail Messages in OneNote

In this age of ever-increasing litigation, most companies now have document retention policies in place that automatically expire and delete e-mail messages after a period of time. Although this is important for e-mail concerning official business, most of us from time to time receive personal messages in our Inbox at work, either from a friend or family member, an associate at another company, or from a co-worker.

If you have personal messages which contain important information that you don't want to lose when the message is deleted by your administrator, you can send such messages to OneNote, where they will not expire. In addition, by storing selected Outlook e-mail messages in your notebooks, you can use OneNote's Instant Search to find specific information in the messages. Search in OneNote also works generally faster than in Outlook because OneNote does not have to retrieve its information from a server.

Another benefit of archiving e-mail messages in OneNote is the fact that it pre-serves the date and time stamp of the original messages. This means that you don't lose the ability to search information in your saved e-mail messages by their origi-nal date or time.

To send one or more e-mail messages from Outlook 2010 to OneNote 2010, do the following:

1. In OneNote, create a notebook section that you want to use specifically as your repository for saved e-mail messages. This makes it easier for you to know where all of your archived mail will be saved. (This step is optional.)

2. In Outlook 2010, go to your Inbox or the mail folder from which you want to send messages to OneNote.

3. Click to select one or more messages in the list. To select a range of mes-sages, click to select the first message, hold the Shift key, and click to select the last message in the range. To select multiple messages that are not next to each other in the list, hold the Ctrl key while you click the mes-sages you want to include.

4. When you've selected the messages you want to send to OneNote, click the Home tab in the main Outlook program window (not a message window) and then, in the Move group, click the OneNote button (see Figure 10.12).

Figure 10.12 *If you have one or more e-mail messages selected in your Outlook Inbox or in any Outlook folder, clicking the Send to OneNote button in the Move group on the Home tab of the Outlook ribbon sends each message to OneNote on its own page, while fully retaining the information in each message envelope.*

5. In the Select Location in OneNote dialog box that appears, click to select the notebook section you created in step 1, and then click OK.

OneNote copies each Outlook e-mail message on its own page in OneNote and saves each page in the notebook section you selected. The Subject field of the e-mail message is used as the page title. Although each page holding an e-mail message includes the page creation date and time under the page header, OneNote retains the date that the message was sent or received on the page so you can search for specific dates when looking for information that originated in your e-mail correspondence.

> To quickly send a single e-mail message from Outlook to OneNote, right-click the message in your Inbox or mail folder and then click OneNote on the short-cut menu that appears.
>
> If you want to first read a message to make sure that you want to save it to OneNote, double-click to open the message, and then, in the Move group on the ribbon, click the OneNote icon to send the message you're viewing to OneNote.

A friendly word of warning: Though this feature is extremely handy for archiving personal information that you may receive at work, it is not intended to bypass any part of your company's or organization's document retention policies and legal requirements. It is entirely your own responsibility to comply with such rules and to know and understand whether or not your company permits archiving of mail in this fashion.

If you're not entirely sure, it's best not to place your job in unnecessary jeopardy by assuming anything. Ask your manager, your Human Resources or legal representative, or your Outlook administrator before you use OneNote to save your e-mail messages.

 **LET ME TRY IT**

Linking Outlook Meetings to OneNote Meeting Notes

If you're in the habit of creating separate notes for meetings you have already scheduled on your Outlook calendar, you could save time by getting in the habit of creating linked meeting notes (not to be confused with the linked notes feature that I previously discussed in Chapter 6). When a notes page in OneNote is linked to an Outlook meeting, you can click a OneNote button in the meeting window to instantly open the associated notes page, no matter where it is saved. Similarly, the linked OneNote page includes an automatic link back to the original appointment, which means you'll never have to search for a specific meeting in your Outlook calendar again.

To link Outlook meetings to OneNote meeting notes, do the following:

1. In your Outlook 2010 Calendar view, open an existing appointment or meeting.

2. On the Appointment or Meeting tab, click the OneNote icon (see Figure 10.13).

Figure 10.13 *Clicking the OneNote icon in the Actions group on the ribbon of an Outlook appointment or meeting notice automatically links that appointment or meeting to the notes page that is created in this way. No matter which program you're in, you can instantly look up a meeting and its related meeting notes without any manual searching in either application.*

3. In the Select Location in OneNote dialog box that opens, select the section where you want to create the meeting notes page that will be linked to this appointment or meeting.

When you click OK, OneNote creates a new notes page in the section you selected. The details of the appointment or meeting will be automatically copied over for you. Underneath this information, you'll see a blue underlined text link called Link to Outlook item. Clicking this link will automatically fetch the associated appointment or meeting on your calendar and display it in Outlook. The linked relationship between the notes page and the appointment or meeting notice from which you create it will not expire unless either or both linked items are deleted.

 **LET ME TRY IT**

Linking Outlook Contacts to OneNote Pages

If you use the Contacts view in Outlook 2010 to manage personal information about your clients and associates, you may have found the Notes field in the Contact form quite limiting.

When you have OneNote 2010 and Outlook 2010 installed together, you can replace the small Notes field and instead take all of your notes about each of your Outlook Contacts in OneNote. When a notes page in OneNote is linked to an Outlook contact, you can click a OneNote button in the Contact window to instantly open the associated notes page, no matter where it is saved. Similarly, the linked notes page includes an automatic link back to the original Contact form, which means you'll never have to search for a specific person again in your Outlook Contacts list.

To link Outlook contacts to a OneNote notes page, do the following:

1. In your Outlook 2010 Contacts view, open an existing contact.

2. On the Contact tab, click the OneNote icon (see Figure 10.14).

Figure 10.14   *Clicking the OneNote icon in the Actions group on the ribbon of an Outlook Contact form automatically links that person's information to the notes page that is created in this way. No matter which program you're in, you can instantly look up an Outlook contact without any manual searching in either application.*

3. In the Select Location in OneNote dialog box that opens, select the section where you want to create the notes page that will be linked to this Outlook contact.

When you click OK, OneNote creates a new notes page in the section you selected. The person's name will become the page title and any available contact information and a photo (if available) will be automatically placed on the page.

Underneath this information, you'll see a blue underlined text link called Link to Outlook item. Clicking this link will automatically fetch the associated Outlook contact and display it in Outlook. The linked relationship between the notes page and the associated Outlook contact from which you create it will not expire unless either or both linked items are deleted.

Although Outlook could be considered overkill to use as an e-mail program at home, you might consider using it there, if you find these features as invaluable as I do. I hope that seeing how OneNote and Outlook complement each other gives you a better idea about how the value of each program greatly increases when they are used together.

OneNote Integration with PowerPoint

Though PowerPoint 2010 is not as tightly integrated with OneNote as Word and Outlook are, there's nevertheless a handy tip I wanted to share with you for printing PowerPoint presentations to OneNote.

 LET ME TRY IT

Printing a PowerPoint Presentation to OneNote

Typically, when you send information from other programs to OneNote, each printout image is placed on a separate page. For documents and such, this is fine. However, PowerPoint 2010 has some nifty print options that you can use to influence how your slide printouts appear when you send them to OneNote 2010.

To print a PowerPoint presentation to OneNote, do the following:

1. In PowerPoint 2010, open or create the slide presentation that you want to send to OneNote.

2. Click the File tab and then click Print.

3. Under Printer, select the Send to OneNote 2010 print driver.

4. Under Settings, change the Print Layout from Full Page Slides (Print 1 Slide per Page) to any of the other available options (see Figure 10.15).

5. Click Print.

6. In the Select Location in OneNote dialog box that opens, click to select the section or page where you want the presentation printout to appear and then click OK.

If you use the File Printout command on OneNote's Insert tab to import a PowerPoint presentation, you're stuck with the one slide per page default setting. However, by printing a presentation from PowerPoint to OneNote instead, you can control how the slides, your slide notes, or your presentation outline will appear in your notes.

Did you know you can easily annotate a PowerPoint presentation after it's been printed to OneNote? Right-click any of the pages of the printout on which you want to type or write notes, and then click Set Picture as Background. This lets you click over a printout image and then take notes over it. For example, you could print a slide presentation to OneNote before a meeting and annotate the printout pages by typing questions and ideas you have about the content right over the slides in red text. During the meeting, you can further annotate each slide by jotting down the answers to your questions with green text. This way, you have a clear record of your train of thought before, during, and after an important presentation.

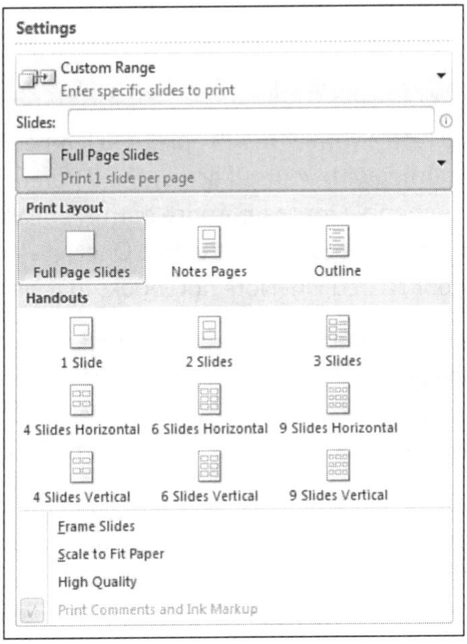

Figure 10.15 *PowerPoint 2010 has some pretty unique print layout options that you can use to your advantage when you want to send the information in a busy slide deck for safekeeping in OneNote.*

Finally, though I won't duplicate the information here, I want to remind you that PowerPoint is also one of the supported Office programs that you can use with OneNote's linked notes feature.

To learn more or to remind yourself about this feature, see "Doing Research with Linked Notes" in Chapter 6.

I hope this chapter has given you a better idea about some of OneNote's less-visible features that either lurk under the hood or quietly jump into action whenever OneNote is combined with the functionality of other programs. Although I think you'll agree that OneNote stands perfectly well on its own, there are definitely many situations in which OneNote makes other programs better and, in turn, inherits some useful functionality of its own from its big brothers in Microsoft Office.

The basics of using OneNote Mobile on your cell phone are described in this chapter.

11

Using OneNote on Your Mobile Phone

In Chapter 9, "Sharing Notes with Other People," you learned about the benefits of sharing notebooks—either with yourself across the different computers you may be using, or with other people for the purpose of truly collaborating on a project together. I also briefly introduced you to the free OneNote Web App, which lets you view and even edit your shared OneNote notebooks in a web browser.

If you purchased a smartphone in recent months, you have an additional option for using OneNote on the go, especially when you don't have access to a computer or you don't want to lug a laptop around with you. It's called OneNote Mobile (see Figure 11.1), and it's currently available on Windows Phone 7 and on the iPhone.

Attempting to document something like an ever-changing mobile phone app in a book might seem counterproductive, considering that the development and release cycles of such apps are dramatically faster than that of the full-featured desktop apps in Microsoft Office. Indeed, by the time you read this chapter, the features in the two flavors of OneNote Mobile are likely to have evolved and improved. Nevertheless, I wanted to briefly cover basic OneNote Mobile functionality in this overview to give you an understanding of how the various flavors of OneNote may suit your needs and fit into your life. You can learn more about OneNote Mobile on Windows Phone 7 at http://www.microsoft.com/windowsphone, and more information about OneNote Mobile for iPhone is available by searching for Microsoft OneNote in the iTunes AppStore at http://www.itunes.com.

OneNote Mobile on Windows Phone 7

Not surprisingly, probably the best way to experience any Microsoft Office mobile app is on Microsoft's own smartphone platform, called Windows Phone 7. Although the individual devices that support this operating system vary with different North American cell phone providers, the complete version of Office Mobile—including OneNote Mobile—is included for free on all Windows Phone 7 devices.

Figure 11.1 *The OneNote Mobile app offers yet another choice for managing all of the information in your busy life on the go. OneNote Mobile is currently available for your Windows Phone 7 smartphone or your iPhone.*

The following procedures outline the basic tasks for getting started with this version of OneNote Mobile.

 LET ME TRY IT

Starting OneNote Mobile on Windows Phone 7

On your Windows Phone 7 device, do the following:

1. Near the upper right on your phone's Start screen, click the circled arrow pointing to the right. Alternately, you can swipe your finger across the screen from the right side to the left.

2. In the list of installed apps that appears, swipe your finger upward to scroll down to the app named Office.

3. With your finger, tap the Office app. The Microsoft Office hub appears, giving you access to OneNote Mobile, Excel Mobile, Word Mobile, and PowerPoint Mobile.

You might notice that the Office hub displays OneNote right on its home screen. This allows fast access to all of your notes, making capturing and accessing your information on the go less cumbersome.

 LET ME TRY IT

Exploring the OneNote Mobile Guide

The square, orange tiles on the Office home screen represent individual notes that you've created or opened in OneNote Mobile. To open a note, tap its orange tile.

If you don't have any of your own notes there yet, take a moment to read the short OneNote Mobile Guide, which is included as a OneNote note. It briefly outlines the features that are available in OneNote Mobile on Windows Phone 7.

To explore the OneNote Mobile Guide, do the following:

1. On the Office Mobile home screen, tap the orange tile labeled "Explore OneNote." This is how you open any of your OneNote Mobile notes for viewing or editing.

2. When the note opens, read the information provided. Swipe your finger upward across the screen to scroll down and display the rest of the page.

3. To return to the Office Mobile hub, tap the Back button at the bottom of your phone or device.

 LET ME TRY IT

Creating a New Note

To create your first note in OneNote Mobile on your Windows Phone 7, follow these steps:

1. On the Office home screen, under the OneNote app heading, tap the New Note button (see Figure 11.2).

2. When the note opens and the onscreen keyboard appears, tap the words *Enter title* at the top of the screen.

3. Type a page title to describe the note. This page title will appear on the note's orange tile on the home screen and it will also be used as the page title when you view the note in the OneNote Web App or in the full version of OneNote 2010 on your computer.

Figure 11.2 *Tapping the New Note button on the home screen of the Office hub launches OneNote Mobile on Windows Phone 7. Each note you create will be shown as an orange tile on the home screen, giving you easy access to all of your mobile notes.*

4. Tap below the line that appears under the page title and then use the onscreen keyboard to type notes.

As with the full version of OneNote 2010, you don't need to explicitly save your work when you're done taking notes in OneNote Mobile. It will save your notes as soon as you've written them, which means you can tap the Back button or the Start (Windows logo) button at the bottom of your phone or device at any time to quit your session of OneNote Mobile. The next time you return to the Office hub, you'll see your note on the OneNote home page.

OneNote Mobile on Windows Phone 7 supports landscape mode, allowing you to use a wider onscreen keyboard and see more of your notes horizontally. To use landscape mode, tilt your phone 90 degrees to the left until the user interface changes to a widescreen layout. You can change back to portrait mode at any time by tilting your phone back into its normal upright position.

 LET ME TRY IT

Correcting Text in a Note

If you're using any Microsoft Office program on your computer, you're already familiar with the convenient spell-checking feature, which underlines potentially misspelled or unknown words with a red squiggly line. In OneNote Mobile, this feature works, too. Given that the onscreen keyboards on cell phones are much more

error-prone than using a real, physical keyboard, this is a welcome and useful feature, allowing you to make corrections easily, especially if you'll be sharing your
mobile notes with others.

To check spelling in a mobile note, do the following:

1. Open or create a new note.

2. Look for text that is underlined with a red, squiggly line.

3. Tap the questionable word once with your finger to select it and then
    inspect the word list that's displayed just above the onscreen keyboard.

4. To substitute a misspelled word with a word that appears in the list, tap to
    select the correct word. To substitute a misspelled word with a new word that
    doesn't appear in the word list, type the correct word.

> Although misspelled text in the page header won't appear marked with a red,
> squiggly underline, the word replacement feature works the same here as for
> normal text. Tap a misspelled word once in your page header to select it, and
> then tap the correct word when it appears in the word list above the onscreen
> keyboard.

 LET ME TRY IT

Formatting Text in a Note

Excluding the page title, OneNote Mobile on Windows Phone 7 supports basic text
formatting that you might already be used to from any of the programs in the full
version of Microsoft Office on your computer.

You can format any part of your notes text in any of the following styles:

- Bold text

- Italic text

- Underline text

- Strikethrough text

- Yellow highlighted text

To apply text formatting to any part of your notes, do the following:

1. Open or create a note whose text you want to format.

2. Tap the text you want to format to select it. If you want to extend the selection, tap and hold either of the two small arrows that appear underneath the selection highlight and then drag them to include all of the text you want to format. If you make a mistake, either start over or format the remaining text separately.

3. At the bottom of the screen, to the right of the round command icons, tap the More (...) icon to display the action menu.

4. At the bottom of the menu that appears, tap Format.

5. In the Format menu, tap the formatting style you want. Because the text will stay selected, you can easily apply any additional formatting style to the selected word or paragraph. To do so, repeat steps 3–5 in this procedure to apply the additional formatting.

> To remove any formatting style that you've applied, reselect the text in your notes and then apply the same formatting style again. Doing so removes that style from the selected text.

 LET ME TRY IT

Creating Lists in a Note

Besides text formatting, you can format lines or paragraphs of text in your note as lists. OneNote Mobile supports numbered lists and bulleted lists. You can also use text indentation for creating a basic text outline without any list formatting or to create additional levels of detail in a numbered or bulleted list. No matter which format you choose, list formatting can be applied to any blank line in your note or to a selection of existing text.

Numbered lists are best for showing items in sequential order (for example, the steps in a list of driving directions). To start a numbered list, do the following:

1. Open or create a note.

2. Place the cursor on a new, blank line, and then tap the round Numbered List command icon at the lower left of the screen.

3. When 1. appears as the start of the list, type the first list item by using the onscreen keyboard.

4. Tap the Enter key (the L-shaped arrow on the lower right of the onscreen keyboard) to continue the list with the next item. To end the list, tap the Enter key twice.

To format existing text as a numbered list, do the following:

1. In your note, tap the line of text that should become the first item in a numbered list.

2. Tap the round Numbered List command icon at the lower left of the screen.

3. Tap to select any additional lines of text underneath the current line and then repeat step 2.

Bulleted lists are best for showing items that belong together but don't require a logical order (for example, a shopping list). To start a bulleted list, do the following:

1. Open or create a note.

2. Place the cursor on a new, blank line.

3. At the bottom of the screen, to the right of the round command icons, tap the More (...) icon to display the action menu.

4. On the menu that appears, tap Bulleted List.

5. When the first bullet symbol appears, type the first list item by using the onscreen keyboard.

6. Tap the Enter key (the L-shaped arrow on the lower right of the onscreen keyboard) to continue the list with the next item. To end the list, tap the Enter key twice.

To format existing text as a bulleted list, do the following:

1. In your note, tap the line of text that should become the first item in a bulleted list.

2. At the bottom of the screen, to the right of the round command icons, tap the More (...) icon to display the action menu.

3. On the menu that appears, tap Bulleted List.

4. Tap to select any additional lines of text underneath the current line and then repeat steps 2–3.

To add one or more levels of detail to any list, you can increase the indentation of any list item. To do this, select the list item by tapping any of its text. Tap the More (...) icon at the bottom of the screen, and then tap Increase Indent on the action menu. You can do this multiple times, if needed. Indented numbered list items will change their numbering style the deeper you go, whereas bulleted items will stay with the same bullet style (additional bullet styles can be applied if you open the note in the full version of OneNote 2010 on your computer).

To demote any list item in level, you can use the Decrease Indent menu command on any selection, and you can repeat this command to return a list item back to its normal level.

Aside from controlling list levels, you can also use the Increase Indent and Decrease Indent commands to create unformatted lists in your notes. This can be useful when you want to create a basic outline structure in your notes to organize your thoughts and ideas.

If you want, you can easily switch back and forth between numbered and bulleted list styles by selecting the list text and then choosing the new style you want. Similarly, you can remove list formatting altogether by selecting the formatted list text and then applying the same list style that's currently applied. This removes the selected list formatting.

 LET ME TRY IT

Adding a Picture to a Note

If you want to insert a picture into your notes, do the following:

1. In your note, tap to activate the cursor where you want the picture to be inserted.

2. At the bottom of the screen, tap the round Picture (+) icon.

3. From the Choose Picture screen that appears, do either of the following:

   - To use an existing picture, tap any of your existing photo albums and then tap to select the picture you want to insert into your notes.

   - To take a new picture, tap the round Camera icon at the bottom of the screen, take a new picture, and then tap Accept to insert it into your notes.

To delete a picture that you've inserted, tap outside and to the right of it and then tap the Backspace/Delete key on the onscreen keyboard.

 **LET ME TRY IT**

Adding an Audio Recording to Your Note

Inserting an audio recording into your notes is a great way to capture spoken information on the go when you can't or don't want to type. For example, you could record a spoken lecture in class or record an interview that you're conducting as part of a research project.

To add an audio recording to your note, do the following:

1. In your note, tap to activate the cursor where you want the audio clip to be inserted.

2. At the bottom of the screen, tap the round Audio (microphone) icon.

3. Start speaking or recording.

4. When you're done, tap the Stop button. OneNote inserts an audio clip icon in your notes. You can play the audio again by tapping this icon.

To delete an audio clip that you've inserted, tap to the right of it and then tap the Backspace/Delete key on the onscreen keyboard.

 LET ME TRY IT

Sending a Note in E-mail

To quickly send a snapshot of your note in e-mail, do the following:

1. On the Office home screen, tap the note you want to send.

2. At the bottom of the screen, tap the round Email icon.

3. Tap the name of the e-mail account you want to use.

4. Add one or more recipients to the To line and, if necessary, modify the Subject line and message body.

5. For additional options, tap the More (...) icon before sending the message.

6. When ready, tap the round Send icon.

If you open a OneNote file that was attached to an e-mail message you received, you can only view that file; you won't be able to save or edit it on your phone. To truly keep your mobile notes in sync with your other notes, sync your mobile notes with your SkyDrive account.

 **LET ME TRY IT**

Synchronizing Your Notes with SkyDrive

When you first begin to use OneNote Mobile on your Windows Phone 7, it creates your notes on the phone.

To synchronize your default notebook on Windows Live SkyDrive (see Chapter 9 for more information) for the first time, do the following:

1. On the Office home screen, tap All (see Figure 11.3).

Figure 11.3 *The All button provides access to all of your mobile notes, including notes that might not be listed as orange tiles on the Office home screen. This command also provides access to the option of synchronizing your notes with Windows Live SkyDrive.*

2. At the bottom of the screen, tap the round Refresh icon.

3. When the Sync with SkyDrive? prompt appears, tap Yes.

4. Watch the very top of your screen for status messages. When OneNote has finished signing in and synchronizing your account, a personal notebook named "Personal (Web)" will be created in your My Documents folder on SkyDrive. Notes you create or edit here will be automatically synchronized with SkyDrive.

To view the contents of your "Personal (Web)" notebook on SkyDrive, tap All on the Office home screen and then, at the top of the screen, tap Notebooks.

To open any page in your "Personal (Web)" notebook, tap the notebook in the Notebooks list and then tap the page you want to open. Any changes you make to the page will be automatically synchronized with your SkyDrive account.

If you don't want your mobile notes to be automatically synchronized with your SkyDrive account for some reason, you can turn this option off. On the Office home screen, tap All, and then tap the More (...) icon. On the menu that appears, tap Settings. Tap the Automatic Sync switch from On to Off.

You should never rename or delete the "Personal (Web)" notebook or the Unfiled Notes section within it while a sync relationship between your Windows Phone 7 and SkyDrive exists. Doing so may result in the loss of some of your notes.

If you want to open a different OneNote notebook that you've stored on SkyDrive, do the following:

1. On your Windows Phone 7 device, tap the Internet Explorer icon on your phone's Home screen.

2. At the bottom of the screen, tap the More (...) icon and then tap Settings.

3. On the Settings page, under Website Preference, make sure the Mobile Version option is selected (tap it, if necessary).

4. Tap the Back button at the bottom of your phone or device to return to the previous screen.

5. Tap the Address bar in Internet Explorer, type http://office.live.com, and then tap the Go button (the right-facing arrow on the onscreen keyboard).

6. On the Windows Live sign-in screen, enter your Windows Live ID and password and then tap Sign In.

7. In your folder list, tap the folder containing the notebook you want to open and then tap the name of the notebook.

8. When the notebook properties are displayed, tap the big OneNote icon to open the notebook and then tap any page to view or edit its notes.

 **LET ME TRY IT**

Searching Your Notes

OneNote's wonderful Instant Search feature that you've likely come to appreciate in the full version of OneNote 2010 is also available on Windows Phone 7.

To find specific text in any of your notes pages, do the following:

1. On the Office home screen, tap All (see Figure 11.3).

2. While in the Pages list, tap the Search button at the bottom of your phone or device.

3. In the Search box that appears at the top of the page, type a word or phrase for which to search your notes.

4. Tap any of the pages that appear in the results list to go to the note containing the occurrence.

To cancel searching without going to a note, tap the Back button at the bottom of your phone or device.

 **LET ME TRY IT**

Deleting Notes

To erase notes you no longer need, do the following:

1. On the Office home screen, tap All (see Figure 11.3).

2. In the Pages list, tap and hold the title of the page you want to delete.

3. When the pop-up menu appears, tap Delete.

4. When the confirmation prompt appears, tap Yes to delete the note.

Deleting pages on your phone permanently destroys the information they contain. You cannot undo page deletions, so be sure not to rush through the deletion steps.

LET ME TRY IT

Checking for Updates

OneNote Mobile is part of Office Mobile, which is installed and updated as part of the Windows Phone 7 operating system.

To make sure you're alerted of occasional software updates, do the following:

1. Near the upper right on your phone's Start screen, click the circled arrow pointing to the right. Alternately, you can swipe your finger across the screen from the right side to the left.

2. In the list that appears, scroll down and then tap Settings.

3. On the Settings screen, scroll down and then tap Phone Update.

4. If necessary, tap the check boxes here to enable the update notification option.

5. Tap the Start (Windows logo) key at the bottom of your phone or device to save your settings.

If you're notified of updates to your Windows Phone 7 operating system (which might or might not include functionality changes and updates for Office Mobile), connect your phone or device to the Windows Phone 7 software installed on your computer and follow the upgrade prompts.

This covers the basic features of OneNote Mobile on your Windows Phone 7. Mobile apps and platforms change continuously, so if the instructions in this chapter don't exactly match the version you're using by the time you read this chapter of the book, be sure to look online for the latest documentation for your version and device. As is the case with the OneNote Web App discussed in Chapter 9, the OneNote Mobile apps do not support all of the features that are available in the full version of OneNote 2010 on your computer, but they're a great way to keep basic versions of your notes in sync, no matter where in the world you may find yourself.

OneNote Mobile on iPhone

OneNote Mobile for iPhone marks the first time Microsoft has released an Office 2010 application on another company's mobile operating system. This is wonderful news for OneNote users because it's just another example of how you can integrate OneNote into your life, even if you decide to adopt a mix of different technologies and devices to suit your lifestyle.

Though the features available in OneNote Mobile differ somewhat between the Windows Phone 7 and the iPhone versions, the basics of accessing and using your shared notebooks on SkyDrive are supported equally. However, whereas OneNote Mobile is already built in to Windows Phone 7 devices, you first must download it and install it on your iPhone. Depending on your region, there may also be an App Store fee for purchasing the app.

The following procedures aim to outline the basic tasks for downloading OneNote Mobile for iPhone and how to get started with the app after you have it installed. Please keep in mind that the features and design of this app have been rapidly changing, so if the information here does not precisely match the version of the app that you're using, remember to search online for the latest documentation—either in the iTunes App Store or on Microsoft's Office.com website.

 LET ME TRY IT

Downloading OneNote Mobile for iPhone

Before you can use OneNote Mobile for iPhone, you must download the app from Apple's iTunes App Store and install it on your iPhone by doing the following:

1. On your iPhone, tap the App Store icon.

2. At the bottom of the screen, tap the Search icon.

3. Tap the Search box at the top of the screen, type Microsoft OneNote, and then tap Search.

4. In the results list, tap Microsoft OneNote.

5. On the details screen, tap the Price button and then tap Install.

At the time this book went to print, OneNote Mobile for iPhone was supported on any iPhone or iPod Touch running Apple iOS 4.2 or later. Because mobile apps are frequently updated, you should always carefully read the system requirements of any later versions of OneNote Mobile for iPhone.

Although the iPhone version of OneNote Mobile can be used on the iPad in compatibility mode, a native iPad app had not yet been developed when this book was released.

The following procedures and screenshots are based on OneNote Mobile for iPhone version 1.2, which was the current version when this book was released. If you're using a newer version of OneNote on your iPhone, the basic steps should remain the same, but you might need to poke around the interface a bit more to find commands and interface elements that were moved, changed, or deprecated in the newer version.

 **LET ME TRY IT**

Starting OneNote Mobile for iPhone

You can run OneNote Mobile for iPhone as soon as it has finished installing. Do the following:

1. Tap the OneNote app icon when it appears on your iPhone.

2. When the title screen appears (see Figure 11.4), sign in using your Windows Live SkyDrive account (see Chapter 9 for more information). If you didn't create one, you can tap Learn More on this screen to sign up. You must sign in before you can use OneNote Mobile on the iPhone.

Figure 11.4 *Before you can use OneNote Mobile for iPhone, you must sign in with your Windows Live account so that the app knows with which SkyDrive notebooks you want to synchronize your notes.*

3. When you're signed in, OneNote creates a "Personal (Web)" mobile notebook. The Home screen that appears displays all of your available notes and notebooks that will be synchronized between your iPhone and your Windows Live SkyDrive account.

> You should never rename or delete the "Personal (Web)" mobile notebook or the Unfiled Notes section within it while a sync relationship between your iPhone and your SkyDrive account exists. Doing so may result in the loss of some of your notes.

 LET ME TRY IT

Creating a New Note

To quickly create a new note, do the following:

1. In the lower-right corner of the Home screen, tap the New Page icon.

2. When the note opens and the onscreen keyboard appears, tap the words *Add title* at the top of the screen.

3. Type a page title to describe the note. This page title will appear in the page list when you view the contents of notebooks on your iPhone and it will also be used as the page title when you view the note in the OneNote Web App or in the full version of OneNote 2010 on your computer.

4. Tap below the line that appears under the page title and then use the onscreen keyboard to type notes.

As with the full version of OneNote 2010, you don't need to explicitly save your work when you're done taking notes in OneNote Mobile. It will save your notes as soon as you've written them, which means you can exit the current page or the OneNote Mobile app at any time without manually saving your work.

> OneNote Mobile for iPhone supports landscape mode, allowing you to use a wider onscreen keyboard and see more of your notes horizontally. To use landscape mode, tilt your iPhone 90 degrees to the left until the user interface changes to a widescreen layout. You can change back to portrait mode at any time by tilting your iPhone back into its normal upright position. If you have Portrait orientation locked (an optional feature in iOS 4.2 and later), you must first unlock it before tilting your iPhone will display OneNote in landscape mode.

LET ME TRY IT

Creating Lists in a Note

With OneNote Mobile for iPhone, you can format text in your note as bulleted lists, which is useful for creating groups of unordered items that belong together, such as the items on a shopping list.

To start a bulleted list, do the following:

1. Open or create a note.

2. Place the cursor on a new, blank line.

3. On the command bar above the onscreen keyboard, tap the List icon.

4. When the first bullet symbol appears, type the first list item by using the onscreen keyboard.

5. Tap Return to continue the list with the next item. To end the list, tap the Return key twice.

To format existing text as a bulleted list, do the following:

1. In your note, tap the line of text that should become the first item in a bulleted list.

2. Tap the List icon.

3. To add additional items to this list from existing text, tap to select any additional lines of text underneath the current line and then repeat step 2.

To remove list formatting, tap the text whose formatting you want to remove, and then tap the List icon again.

 **LET ME TRY IT**

Adding a Picture to a Note

If you want to insert a picture into your notes, do the following:

1. In your note, tap to activate the cursor where you want the picture to be inserted.

2. Tap the Camera icon.

3. From the menu that appears, do either of the following:

   - Tap the Camera button to take a new picture that you can then insert into your notes.

   - Tap the Photo Library button to choose an existing image on your iPhone that you can then insert into your notes.

To view a full-screen version of the picture that you've inserted, tap it once in your notes. Use the return button in the upper-left corner of your screen to return to the notes page containing the picture.

To delete a picture that you've inserted, tap outside and to the right of it, and then tap the Backspace/Delete key on the onscreen keyboard. When prompted, tap Delete.

 **LET ME TRY IT**

Sending a Note in E-mail

To quickly send a snapshot of your note in e-mail, do the following:

1. Open or create the note you want to send.

2. If the onscreen keyboard is visible while you view the page, hide it by tapping the keyboard icon.

3. In the upper-right corner of the screen, tap the Action button (arrow icon), and then tap Email This Page.

> If you have no e-mail accounts configured on your iPhone, this option will not be displayed.

 **LET ME TRY IT**

Synchronizing Your Notes with SkyDrive

Because you must sign in to a Windows Live SkyDrive account to begin using OneNote Mobile for iPhone, your notes are automatically kept in sync from the very first time you use OneNote on your iPhone.

To check when the last synchronization occurred, or to force a manual sync after you've typed or changed a lot of notes, do the following:

1. On the Home screen in OneNote Mobile, tap the Settings button in the upper-right corner of the screen.

2. At the very top of the Settings screen, note the "Last sync" date and time. This indicates when OneNote Mobile last synchronized your notes automatically.

3. If you want to manually sync your notes for any reason, tap the Sync Now button.

4. If you encounter any temporary sync errors (for example, if you lose your cellular or wireless signal while OneNote attempted synchronization), they will be displayed underneath the Sync Now button on the Settings screen. To try and resolve temporary sync errors, tap the Sync Now button to force a manual sync when your signal has been restored.

5. If you like, explore any of the other options on this screen. To exit the Settings page, tap the Close button in the upper-right corner of the screen.

 LET ME TRY IT

Searching Your Notes

OneNote Mobile for iPhone version 1.2 or later includes the wonderful Search function in OneNote, which lets you quickly find the information you need. This is extremely useful in a variety of situations, especially if you take full advantage of keeping all your notes uploaded to your free SkyDrive account.

To find specific text in any of your notes pages, do the following:

1. On the Home screen, tap Search.

2. On the Search Results screen, type a word or phrase for which to search your notes, and then tap Search.

3. Tap any of the pages that appear in the results list to go to the note containing the match.

To cancel searching without going to a note, tap the Close button in the upper-right corner of the screen.

LET ME TRY IT

Deleting Notes

To delete mobile notes on your iPhone, do the following:

1.   Open the note you want to delete.

2.   If the onscreen keyboard is visible while you view the page, hide it by tap-
     ping the keyboard icon on the far right of the command bar.

3.   In the upper-right corner of the page, tap the Action button (arrow icon), and
     then tap Delete This Page. There is no confirmation prompt for this action, so
     take care not to tap this button too quickly.

Deleting notes pages on your iPhone permanently destroys the information
they contain. You cannot undo this, so be sure not to rush through the deletion
steps.

LET ME TRY IT

Checking for Updates

Because it's still a new development effort, OneNote Mobile for iPhone may be
updated more frequently than typical mobile apps.

To make sure you're alerted of occasional software updates, do the following:

1.   On your iPhone, tap the App Store icon.

2.   At the bottom of the screen, tap the Updates icon.

3.   If Microsoft OneNote appears in the results list, tap it to display the results
     screen. Here, you can read about what's been added and changed in the
     app.

4.   To update OneNote Mobile for iPhone to the newer version, tap the
     Update button on the details screen. If prompted, enter your iTunes pass-
     word (not to be confused with your OneNote Mobile sign-in password).

5. When the app has been updated, tap the OneNote icon on your iPhone to restart the app. You might need to sign in to your Windows Live account again.

This covers the basic features of OneNote Mobile for iPhone. As is the case with the OneNote Web App discussed in Chapter 9, the OneNote Mobile app does not support all of the features that are available in the full version of OneNote 2010 on your computer, but it's a great way to keep basic versions of your notes in sync, no matter where in the world you may find yourself.

Customizing OneNote 2010

Throughout this book, you've read the words *default* or *default settings* a few times in reference to any number of OneNote (or Windows) features or their behaviors. Although the word default typically has a negative connotation (defaulting on a loan, for example), it can also refer to the initial factory settings with which a product is shipped.

For example, when you buy a toaster, its 1-through-10 heat dial will probably be set to 5 at the factory. This initial, middle-of-the-road setting is likely the best choice for most people. If you buy the toaster, but you happen to prefer a type of bread that burns easily, you're free to change the heat setting from 5 to something lower. This lets you toast your choice of bread to perfection. If you also wanted to toast bagels once in a while, you could temporarily increase the heat setting to accommodate the higher density of the bread. Your toaster gives you this control by letting you indicate a preference that you can set and easily change to something else at any time.

In software, it's quite similar. For example, when you install Windows on your computer (or when you buy a PC with Windows already installed), certain features are turned on, even though you might not ever need or want them, and others are turned off, even though you happen to be someone who could benefit from them. This isn't done to annoy you; it's simply not possible for the author of the software to guess which features you'll care about and which you'll never use. By providing an interface for optional settings (just like the dial on your toaster), the person or company releasing the software lets you tweak these settings so that the software and its features are tailored to better meet your needs (see Figure 12.1).

The only pity about software customization is how relatively seldom the average user seems to take advantage of it. Although some tweaks might be nothing more than a cosmetic change, such as choosing a different background picture on your computer or selecting a new ring tone on your cell phone, some settings can dramatically change the way your software performs or how it controls the device on which it runs. For example, the power management control panel in Windows 7 lets you decide whether you want to get the most processing power out of your computer or whether you care more about getting every last minute out of a battery charge on your laptop. By changing these settings at the right times, you can tell Windows how it should adjust its performance to fit your situation—no matter if you're about to embark on a processor-hungry task at your desktop such as video editing or database crunching, or if you need to have enough juice in your laptop battery to last you through a day full of meetings.

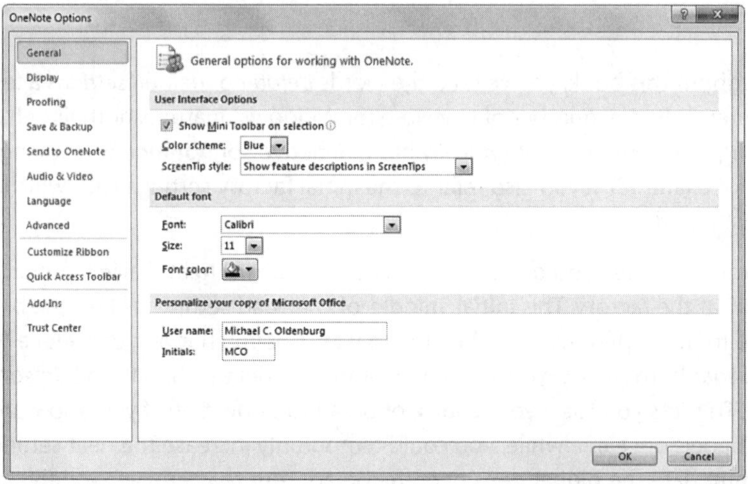

Figure 12.1 *In the OneNote Options dialog box, you can click any of the categories listed on the left to inspect, customize, or override any of the initial or current settings shown on the right. If necessary, you can resize this dialog box by clicking and dragging its lower-right corner.*

Although you don't have to change all (or any) of the default settings of your software programs, knowing about these options and understanding what they do can have a profound effect on your time, productivity, and the enjoyment that you get out of your computer. OneNote 2010 has a marvelous range of preferences that you can take advantage of. Many of these settings work together with others, giving you a much wider array of program customization than what other programs might offer.

Unless self-explanatory, I'll provide examples of why and how the following preferences can be useful when selected or changed. I'll also omit here any settings that I've already discussed in context in any of the previous chapters, unless there's more to be said about them.

If ever you're not sure whether you need to change a particular feature preference in OneNote, it's probably best to leave its default setting in place. As soon as you've gotten more comfortable with the basics of using OneNote 2010 and you're ready to fine-tune the specific features that you use the most often, you can return to the information here.

Setting Display Preferences

In OneNote, display preferences include optional settings that let you show or hide certain parts of the OneNote interface or control how and where such elements appear.

 LET ME TRY IT

Showing or Hiding the Ribbon

In OneNote 2010, the ribbon defaults to a minimized state, with only its tabs visible (see Figure 12.2). As I explained in Chapter 3, "A Tour of the OneNote Workspace," this setting allows for more of your screen space to remain visible while taking or reading notes. This is especially useful if you're using OneNote on a laptop or net-book computer with a small screen. To use the ribbon in this minimized state, click any ribbon tab to temporarily reveal all of the commands available on that tab. As soon as you click a command, the ribbon hides itself again.

| File | Home | Insert | Share | Draw | Review | View |

Figure 12.2   *The ribbon in OneNote 2010, as it appears with only its tabs visible in the default view.*

If you work on a desktop computer with a large monitor, or if your laptop computer has a decent-sized screen, you can opt to keep the full ribbon visible at all times (see Figure 12.3).

Figure 12.3   *The ribbon in OneNote 2010, expanded to full view.*

To toggle the ribbon display, do either of the following:

- Hold the Ctrl key and then press F1.

- At the far right of the ribbon tabs, next to the circular blue Help (?) button, click the Expand the Ribbon (or Minimize the Ribbon) button (see Figure 12.4).

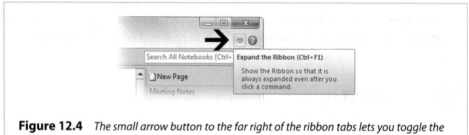

Figure 12.4   *The small arrow button to the far right of the ribbon tabs lets you toggle the ribbon display between minimized and expanded view. You can also use the Ctrl+F1 keyboard shortcut to toggle the ribbon view in the same way.*

Aside from showing or hiding its contents, you can fully customize the ribbon, including its commands, groups, and tabs. See "Customizing the OneNote Workspace" later in this chapter.

 **LET ME TRY IT**

Changing the Current Page View

The commands in the Views group let you change the appearance and dimension of the OneNote program window.

To change the current page view, do the following:

1. Click the View tab.

2. In the Views group (see Figure 12.5), do any of the following:
   - Click the Full Page View button (or press the F11 key) to remove most interface elements from the OneNote program window. This gives you the most amount of available screen space for reading and editing notes. The Quick Access Toolbar and the ribbon tabs are still available, and keyboard shortcuts that you know still work in this mode. To exit this view, click the View tab and then click Normal View (or press F11 again).

- Click the Dock to Desktop button (or press Ctrl+Alt+D) to shrink OneNote down to a narrow vertical window that docks to the right side of the Windows desktop. This view is useful for taking notes on something else you're looking at. To exit this view, click the View tab and then click Normal View (or press Ctrl+Alt+D again).

- Click the Normal View button whenever you want to return the OneNote program window to its original appearance and dimensions.

Figure 12.5   *On the ribbon, the Views group on the View tab lets you switch between Normal view, Full Page view, and a window docked to the Windows desktop. The button that appears orange is the view you currently have selected.*

If you choose to work in the Dock to Desktop view, OneNote will automatically turn on Linked Notes mode. If you take notes while looking at information in other windows (for example, a web page in Internet Explorer or another Microsoft Office document), OneNote will keep links to such information so you can revisit it again later. For more information about Linked Notes, see Chapter 6, "Collecting and Researching Information." To turn off automatic Linked Notes mode when entering the Dock to Desktop view, see "Disabling Linked Notes Creation in a Docked Window" later in this chapter.

 **LET ME TRY IT**

Displaying Rule Lines or Gridlines on All New Pages

In Chapter 4, "Notebooks, Sections, and Pages," you learned how to change the appearance of your notebook pages by applying a color background or adding rule lines or gridlines to the page. If you want all new pages that you create to have rule lines or gridlines, you can tell OneNote to apply them automatically by doing the following:

1. Open or create a blank, new page.

2. Click the View tab.

3. In the Page Setup group, click the Rule Lines drop-down arrow and then click the style of rule lines or gridlines you want to use for the current page.

4. Click the Rule Lines drop-down arrow again, but this time, click Rule Line Color and then select a color if you want the rule lines or gridlines style you chose to appear differently from the default color of Light Blue. If you don't like a color selection you made, repeat this step with another choice until you find a color you like, or reselect the Light Blue setting at the top of the list.

5. After you've selected the line style and color in steps 3–4, click the Rule Lines drop-down arrow once more and then click Create New Pages with Rule Lines.

OneNote will now apply the rule line or gridline style and color you selected in steps 3–4 and automatically apply them to all future new pages when they are created.

If you want to turn this setting off again, you can repeat step 4 in the previous procedure, which will toggle the option off again. Alternately, you can also turn this option off in the OneNote Settings dialog box. Click the File tab and then click Options. Click the Display category on the left of the dialog box and then uncheck the Create All New Pages with Rule Lines option on the right. Be sure to click OK to save your changes.

Note that if you want any existing pages in your notebook to have the same look, you'll need to go back to those pages and manually apply the same rule line or gridline style.

One question that I'm sometimes asked is why OneNote doesn't provide a similar setting for automatically applying a specific color to all new pages. One way to achieve this is to create a blank, new page, applying your preferred background color to the page (View tab, Page Setup group, Page Color button) and then saving that page as a template. You then can have OneNote automatically use that simple template as your default page appearance for all of the new pages you'll create from then on. For more information, see "Automatically Applying a Template to All New Pages" in Chapter 4.

 **LET ME TRY IT**

Zooming the Page Display

Much like in other Microsoft Office programs, you can increase or decrease (zoom) the magnification of a page to either get a closer look at a part of your notes or to see more of the entire page layout all at once. Zooming in and out lets you change the size of your notes text and any other objects on the page without changing the formatting of the content itself. You can return to the 100% view setting again at any time to restore the normal appearance of the page.

To zoom in or out of your notes, do the following:

1. Open the page you want to zoom.

2. Click the View tab.

3. In the Zoom group, do any of the following:

   • Click Zoom In (either once or repeatedly) to increase the level of magnification of the current page.

   • Click Zoom Out (either once or repeatedly) to decrease the level of magnification of the current page.

   • Click the 75% button to decrease magnification by 25%.

   • Click the 100% button to restore the current page view to its normal appearance.

   • Click the Zoom box drop-down arrow to select a specific level of magnification (see Figure 12.6).

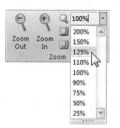

Figure 12.6   *To zoom in and out of a page, either click the buttons provided in the Zoom group on the View tab, or select a specific level of magnification from the Zoom drop-down menu.*

You're not limited to the choices you see on the Zoom drop-down menu. Click to activate the cursor in the Zoom field (see where the cursor is shown in Figure 12.6), replace the percentage shown there by typing over it with your own preferred value and then press Enter.

 LET ME TRY IT

Opening Additional OneNote Windows

Typically, working in a single OneNote window will suffice. However, if you frequently need to switch between different pages without losing your place (for example, when comparing notes in different locations on the page or in different locations in a notebook), you can open any number of additional OneNote windows and navigate to a different place in your notes in each of them.

To open additional OneNote windows, do the following:

1. On the View tab, in the Window group, click New Window. OneNote opens a duplicate of your current OneNote program window. To open additional windows, click the New Window button again.

2. In any new window, navigate to any page you want—either in the same notebook or in a different one.

3. Use the Windows Alt+Tab shortcut to switch between all of your open OneNote windows.

You can use the window management commands in Windows 7 to arrange all of your open OneNote windows on the desktop. Start by minimizing all open windows so you see only your desktop. Next restore the OneNote windows you opened. Now, right-click in a blank area of the Windows taskbar and then click Show Windows Side by Side on the shortcut menu (see Figure 12.7).

When you no longer need any of the additional OneNote windows you've opened, simply close them.

Figure 12.7 *If you have multiple OneNote windows open and you want to see their contents all at once, you can choose to arrange them across your Windows desktop in equal tiles. Click in a blank area of the Windows 7 taskbar and then click the Show Windows Side by Side command on the shortcut menu. To change things back to the way they were, return to this menu and then click the Undo Show Windows Side by Side command that will now appear.*

 LET ME TRY IT

Displaying a New Docked Window

Because we've already covered the Dock to Desktop command in the Views group on the ribbon, the command called New Docked Window in the Window group might seem redundant.

The difference is that while the Dock to Desktop command docks the current OneNote window to the right side of the Windows desktop, the New Docked Window command opens an additional OneNote window, which it docks to the desktop while leaving your original OneNote window the same.

This is mainly useful if you want to take notes about another notes page—either elsewhere in the same notebook or in another notebook, such as a SkyDrive-based notebook.

To display a new docked window, do the following:

1. Click the View tab.

2. In the Window group, click the New Docked Window button. OneNote doesn't change your current OneNote window but instead opens a second OneNote window, which it then docks to the Windows desktop (see Figure 12.8).

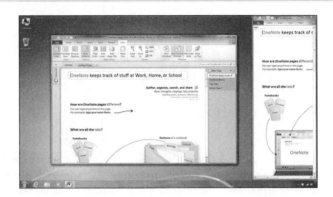

Figure 12.8 *If you use the New Docked Window command on the View tab, OneNote opens a secondary OneNote window that's docked to the side of your desktop. You can then create a new page in the docked window to take notes on any pages that you're viewing in the normal OneNote window.*

By default, any new docked OneNote window you create will automatically start in Linked Notes mode (for more information about Linked Notes, see Chapter 6). If you don't want this to happen, you can turn this behavior off. To turn off automatic Linked Notes mode when entering the Dock to Desktop view, see "Disabling Linked Notes Creation in a Docked Window" later in this chapter.

 LET ME TRY IT

Docking New Side Notes to the Desktop

In Chapter 6, you learned about side notes, the small OneNote windows that resemble the yellow sticky notes you might still be in the habit of pasting all over your computer's monitor. Because side notes are a great way to take notes on top of other documents or programs, you might prefer to have OneNote automatically dock new side note windows to the desktop.

To dock new side notes to the desktop, do the following:

1. Click the File tab and then click Options.

2. In the OneNote Options dialog box, click the Display category on the left side.

3. On the right side, under the Display heading, select the Dock New Side Note Windows to the Side of the Desktop check box.

4. Click OK to save your changes.

Now when you open a new side note by clicking the New Side Note button on the View tab, OneNote will automatically dock it to the side of your Windows desktop. Though docked side notes don't look like little yellow sticky notes, they'll still work the same as side notes that aren't docked.

As with any other kind of docked window, choosing to dock your side notes will automatically start them in Linked Notes mode (for more information about Linked Notes, see Chapter 6). If you just want to jot down notes in side notes normally, see "Disabling Linked Notes Creation in a Docked Window" later in this chapter.

 LET ME TRY IT

Keeping OneNote Visible over Other Windows

If you're taking notes on information displayed in other windows (such as documents or web pages), you can choose to have OneNote stay on top of such other windows so you can still see your notes even when you switch control to any of your other open windows.

To keep OneNote visible over other windows, do the following:

1. Click the View tab.

2. In the Window group, click Keep on Top. The button turns orange, letting you know that this window will now stay pinned on top of other windows.

3. To restore normal window behavior at any time, click the Keep on Top button again.

The Keep on Top option is a separate control for each OneNote window you have open. This way, you can control which window should always appear over the other windows. For example, if you're taking notes in your main OneNote window but need to reference information in a side note, you could pin the side note to the top so that this information remains visible even while you're typing your notes in the main window.

LET ME TRY IT

Displaying Page Tabs on the Right or Left

By default, the page tabs column appears to the right side of the OneNote program window. If you want to display your page tabs on the left side instead, do the following:

1. Click the File tab and then click Options.

2. In the OneNote Options dialog box, click the Display category on the left side.

3. On the right side, under the Display heading, select the Page Tabs Appear on the Left check box.

4. Click OK to save your changes.

If you frequently work in both the full version of OneNote 2010 (which displays the page tabs on the right) and the OneNote Web App (which displays the page tabs on the left), you can use this option to match the appearance of the page tabs between the full version and the Web App.

LET ME TRY IT

Turning the Floating New Page Button On or Off

In previous versions of OneNote, if you wanted to insert a new page between two existing pages, you would first have to create the new page and then drag it from the end of your page tabs list to the position where you wanted it.

In OneNote 2010, you can move the mouse pointer over any existing page tabs and then click the small New Page icon that appears just to the left of your position (see Figure 12.9). OneNote will then insert a blank page between those pages.

If you don't want this shortcut icon to be displayed when you move the mouse pointer over your page tabs, you can turn it off by doing the following:

1. Click the File tab and then click Options.

2. In the OneNote Options dialog box, click the Display category on the left side.

3. On the right side, under the Display heading, uncheck the Show the Floating New Page Button Near Page Tabs check box.

4. Click OK to save your changes.

Figure 12.9 *Whenever you move the mouse pointer between page tabs, a small New Page icon appears just to the left of the page tabs, with a small arrowhead indicating where OneNote will create a new, blank page if you click the icon. If you don't want the shortcut icon to be displayed for some reason, you can turn this option off.*

 LET ME TRY IT

Displaying the Navigation Bar on the Left or Right

Much like you can switch the side on which the page tabs appear, you can swap the position of the navigation bar (the area on the side of the OneNote program window that shows the notebooks that you currently have open) from the left side of the OneNote program window to the right side.

Do the following:

1. Click the File tab and then click Options.

2. In the OneNote Options dialog box, click the Display category on the left side.

3. On the right side, under the Display heading, uncheck the Navigation Bar Appears on the Left check box. This will place it on the right side instead.

4. Click OK to save your changes.

LET ME TRY IT

Displaying the Vertical Scrollbar on the Left or Right

As any notes page fills up with notes past the bottom edge of your OneNote program window, a vertical scrollbar appears to the left of the page tabs. This lets you quickly scroll through the contents of long notes pages, the same way scrollbars work elsewhere in Windows.

If you don't want the scrollbar so close to the page tabs (for example, if you tend to accidentally click a random page tab instead of the scrollbar), you can swap its position.

To display the vertical scrollbar on the left, do the following:

1. Click the File tab and then click Options.

2. In the OneNote Options dialog box, click the Display category on the left side.

3. On the right side, under the Display heading, select the box labeled Vertical Scroll Bar Appears on the Left.

4. Click OK to save your changes.

When active, the vertical scrollbar will now appear to the left of the page.

 LET ME TRY IT

Changing the Microsoft Office Color Scheme

Though you can freely change the colors of your notebook icons, your sections, and the background of your pages, the default color scheme of certain elements of the OneNote interface (for example, the surface of the ribbon) will appear as light blue. If this clashes with your other Windows color preferences or you'd simply prefer something more neutral, you can choose from two other Microsoft Office color schemes that are built in to OneNote 2010.

To change the Microsoft Office color scheme in OneNote, do the following:

1. Click the File tab and then click Options.

2. In the OneNote Options dialog box, click the General category on the left side.

3. On the right side, under the User Interface Options heading, click the Color Scheme drop-down menu.

4. From the list, select Silver to change the user interface from light blue to a more neutral light gray. Alternately, select Black to choose a dark gray contrast color scheme.

5. Click OK to save your changes.

Though most of the controls that you see in the OneNote Options dialog box apply only to OneNote 2010, any change you make to the user interface color scheme will automatically apply to any other Microsoft Office 2010 programs that you have installed. For example, if you change your OneNote color scheme from Blue to Silver and then open Microsoft Word 2010, the ribbon and other interface elements in Word will also appear Silver. Similarly, if you change the color scheme in any other Office 2010 program and then return to OneNote, you'll see your last color scheme preference applied to OneNote as well.

 LET ME TRY IT

Turning the OneNote Taskbar Icon On or Off

In Chapter 6, you learned about the OneNote 2010 Screen Clipper and Launcher—the small OneNote icon that appears in the notification area of the Windows taskbar (see Figure 12.10). If you previously dismissed this icon and want it back, or if you want to turn it off temporarily, you can set the appropriate option by doing the following:

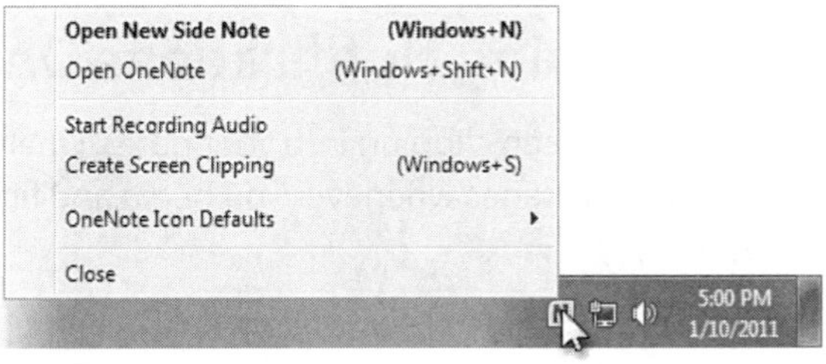

Open New Side Note	(Windows+N)
Open OneNote	(Windows+Shift+N)
Start Recording Audio	
Create Screen Clipping	(Windows+S)
OneNote Icon Defaults	▶
Close	

5:00 PM
1/10/2011

Figure 12.10 *The small OneNote icon on the taskbar provides access to additional OneNote functionality as well as some useful keyboard shortcuts. Note that Windows might hide this icon after some time, in which case you'll need to first expand your notification icons by clicking a small arrow that will appear near your Windows clock display.*

1. Click the File tab and then click Options.

2. In the OneNote Options dialog box, click the Display category on the left side.

3. On the right side, under the Display heading, click the Place OneNote Icon in the Notification Area of the Taskbar check box.

4. Click OK to save your changes.

The ability to turn this feature off is provided in case you're using other programs that use the same Windows keyboard shortcuts, in which case you can resolve the conflict by removing the OneNote taskbar icon.

If you have no keyboard shortcut conflicts, turning this icon off is not recommended. Doing so will disable several useful features and keyboard shortcuts. For more information, see "Meet the OneNote Screen Clipper and Launcher" in Chapter 6.

On rare occasions, it's possible that the check box mentioned in step 3 of the previous procedure appears selected, but the Screen Clipper and Launcher icon isn't available. This can happen if the program was manually terminated in the Windows Task Manager, either by you or someone else using your computer. In this case, you can easily restore the correct setting by repeating steps 1–4 in the previous procedure twice in a row—first deselecting the check box and clicking OK and then reselecting the check box and clicking OK. This action restores the icon on your Windows taskbar and puts it back in sync with the option check box.

 LET ME TRY IT

Turning Screen Clipping Notifications On or Off

Whenever you insert a new screen clipping into your notes, OneNote offers guidance by displaying helpful messages whenever you begin and finish a new screen clipping (see Figure 12.11).

Although these messages are quite helpful while you're learning OneNote, you might eventually prefer not to display them once you've gotten the hang of working with screen clippings.

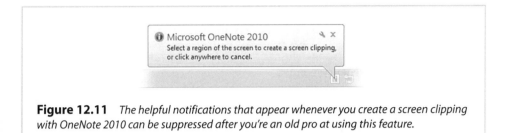

Figure 12.11 *The helpful notifications that appear whenever you create a screen clipping with OneNote 2010 can be suppressed after you're an old pro at using this feature.*

To turn off the notifications, do the following:

1. Click the File tab and then click Options.

2. In the OneNote Options dialog box, click the Display category on the left side.

3. On the right side, under the Display heading, click the Disable Screen Clipping Notifications check box.

4. Click OK to save your changes.

 LET ME TRY IT

Turning Linked Notes Thumbnails On or Off

Whenever you work in Linked Notes mode (see Chapter 6), OneNote keeps track of any documents, presentations, or websites you look at and it automatically links to this information from your notes. To help you quickly distinguish between multiple types of information, it includes a small thumbnail image for each link so you can recognize its content (see Figure 12.12).

Though generally useful, these thumbnail images can sometimes prove distracting—for example, when you're going through your linked notes to format them and the pop-ups get in the way of your text.

To suppress the thumbnail images that may repeatedly appear, do the following:

1. Click the File tab and then click Options.

2. In the OneNote Options dialog box, click the Advanced category on the left side.

3. On the right side, scroll down to the Linked Notes heading, and then uncheck the Save Document Snippets and Page Thumbnail for Better Linking to the Right Place in the Document check box.

4. Click OK to save your changes.

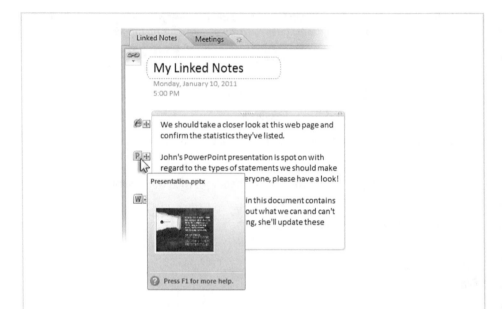

Figure 12.12   *Resting the mouse pointer over any of the program icons that appear to the left of notes from a Linked Notes session will trigger the display of a thumbnail image of the page or file with which the notes are associated. If these thumbnail images get in the way of other tasks, such as formatting your notes, you can suppress their display.*

Changing the thumbnail display option will apply to your next new Linked Notes session that you initiate in OneNote 2010. If you turn this option off, then create a new set of Linked Notes, and then turn this option back on again, you will not see any thumbnail images for the linked notes you previously created in that session. To ensure that you'll always have page previews available from your Linked Notes, remember to turn this option back on before you start your next Linked Notes session.

 **LET ME TRY IT**

Customizing or Hiding the OneNote E-mail Signature

Whenever you send a notes page in e-mail, OneNote appends a signature at the bottom of the last page (see Figure 12.13). If you don't like the default text or you want to disable the signature altogether, do the following:

1. Click the File tab and then click Options.

2. In the OneNote Options dialog box, click the Advanced category on the left side.

3. On the right side, under the E-mail Sent from OneNote heading, do one of the following:

   - To change the signature text, type over the existing text with new text that you want to use for your signature.

   - To turn off the signature, uncheck the Add the Following Signature to E-mail Messages and Web Pages Created in OneNote check box.

4. Click OK to save your changes.

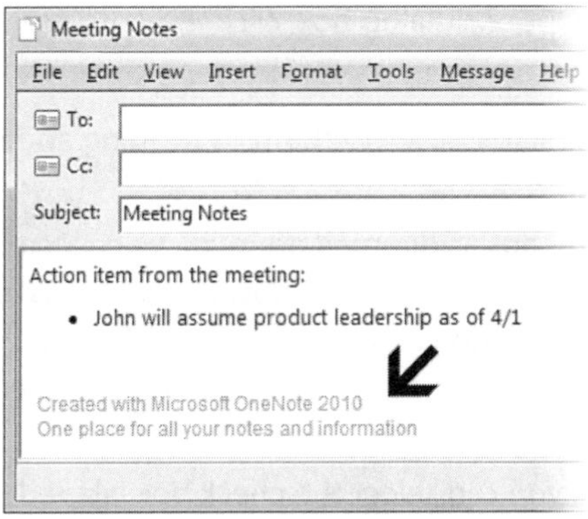

Figure 12.13   *OneNote automatically appends its default signature to pages sent in e-mail or as a web page. Depending on your preference, you can customize or disable this text.*

If you frequently distribute your notes to other people in e-mail, consider changing your e-mail signature text to something useful, such as reminding people of the time and location for your recurring meetings, or providing contact information for follow-up questions. Similarly, if you want to mark all notes you send out with a copyright notice or a disclaimer of some sort, setting your OneNote signature text will ensure that you'll never forget to mark your notes accordingly.

 **LET ME TRY IT**

Changing How Tagged Notes Are Displayed on a Tags Summary Page

When you tag notes to categorize them or to mark them for follow-up, they will typically appear in your notes and in your tag search results the same way they appeared when you created them.

If you frequently tag notes for follow-up and you use the Create Summary Page option in the Tags Summary task pane, you can effectively mark tags as read by making them appear dimmed once you've collected them on a summary page.

To do this, follow these steps:

1. Click the File tab and then click Options.

2. In the OneNote Options dialog box, click the Advanced category on the left side.

3. On the right side, scroll down to the Tags heading and then do the following:

   - To show note tags as dimmed after you've collected them in a summary page, click the option labeled Show Original Tags as Dimmed. Unless you check the next option as well, the dimmed original versions of the tags will not appear in subsequent tag searches in order to avoid duplicate search results.

   - Additionally, you can select the check box labeled Show Dimmed Tagged Notes in the Tags Summary Task Pane. This will include any previously searched (and now dimmed) note tags in your next search. With this option, their dimmed state will be your only reminder that you've already searched for these tags previously and that your Tags Summary search results list may contain duplicates.

4. Click OK to save your changes.

For more information about note tags, see Chapter 7, "Organizing and Searching Notes."

Customizing the OneNote Workspace

OneNote 2010 is the first version of OneNote to include the Microsoft Office ribbon interface and the Quick Access Toolbar. Aside from providing convenient access to the most popular commands available in OneNote, these interface elements also provide an unprecedented level of customization, allowing you to precisely fine-tune the OneNote interface to your preferences and needs.

I encourage you to try out these options without fear of messing anything up. You can easily reset any customizations you experiment with if you don't want to keep the result or if you want to start over.

 LET ME TRY IT

Changing the Location of the Quick Access Toolbar

The Quick Access Toolbar is a small row of frequently used command icons (see Figure 12.14). Although it typically appears to the left of the title bar in the OneNote program window, you can choose to display it underneath the ribbon instead. You can make this change as a purely cosmetic preference or to increase the amount of space available for toolbar customization.

Figure 12.14   *The fully customizable Quick Access Toolbar leaves frequently used commands visible at all times, no matter which ribbon tab you've selected. By default, it appears in the upper-left corner of the OneNote program window. However, if that's too far to move the mouse every time, you can opt to display this toolbar underneath the ribbon instead.*

To change the location of the Quick Access Toolbar, do the following:

1. Click the small drop-down arrow to the right of the Quick Access Toolbar.

2. On the menu that appears, click Show Below the Ribbon. The toolbar now appears on its own row between the ribbon and the top of the section tabs in the current notebook.

When displayed underneath the ribbon, the Quick Access Toolbar has a bit more space available for adding additional command buttons (see "Adding or Removing Quick Access Toolbar Commands" in the procedure that follows).

> To restore the original location of the Quick Access Toolbar after you've moved it, repeat the preceding steps. The option in step 2 will now appear as Show Above the Ribbon.

LET ME TRY IT

Adding or Removing Quick Access Toolbar Commands

After you first install OneNote 2010, it will display the following four preset commands on the Quick Access Toolbar:

- Back
- Undo
- Dock to Desktop
- Full Page View

The first two buttons are good to have available at all times, as you may frequently want to navigate back to the previous notes page that you looked at or you might need to undo an unintentional change that you made to your notes. If you find the Dock to Desktop and Full Page View options useful, you can keep them around; otherwise you can remove them from the Quick Access Toolbar and replace them with commands you tend to use more often.

To turn any preset commands on or off, do the following:

1. Click the small drop-down arrow to the right of the Quick Access Toolbar.

2. On the menu that appears, do either (or both) of the following:
   - To add a new command to the Quick Access Toolbar, click it in the list. For example, Chapter 9, "Sharing Notes with Other People," suggested that if you frequently print notes, adding the Print command to the Quick Access Toolbar will make this task more convenient. While you rest the mouse pointer over the Print command in the list, a ToolTip appears to confirm what will happen when you click it (see Figure 12.15).

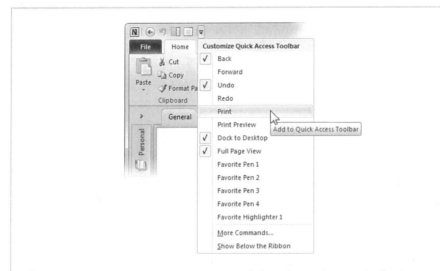

Figure 12.15 *Adding or removing commands from the Quick Access Toolbar is as easy as clicking them in this menu. A check mark appears next to commands you've already added. Resting the mouse over any of the commands listed tells you if you'll be adding or removing the command if you click it in the list.*

- To remove a command from the Quick Access Toolbar, click it in the list. Commands that are currently on the toolbar will appear with an orange-highlighted check mark icon to the left of the command's name.

> The customization menu disappears as soon as you make a selection. If you want to make additional customizations from the presets on the Quick Access Toolbar menu, just repeat the previous steps for each additional command.

If the command you want to add to the Quick Access Toolbar isn't listed on the customization presets menu but you see it on one of the ribbon tabs, you can just as quickly add the commands you want by doing the following:

1. Navigate to the ribbon tab that contains the command you want to add to the Quick Access Toolbar.

2. Move the mouse pointer over the command button and then right-click it.

3. On the shortcut menu that appears, click Add to Quick Access Toolbar (see Figure 12.16). OneNote will instantly append the command to the end of the Quick Access Toolbar.

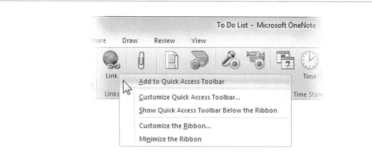

Figure 12.16   *If the command you want to add to the Quick Access Toolbar appears somewhere on the ribbon (such as the Link command in this example), you can right-click its icon and then click Add to Quick Access Toolbar.*

If the commands you want to add to the Quick Access Toolbar appear neither on the customization presets menu nor on the ribbon, you can display the advanced interface for the customization of the toolbar (see Figure 12.17). Here, you can find and add just about any command that's available in OneNote 2010.

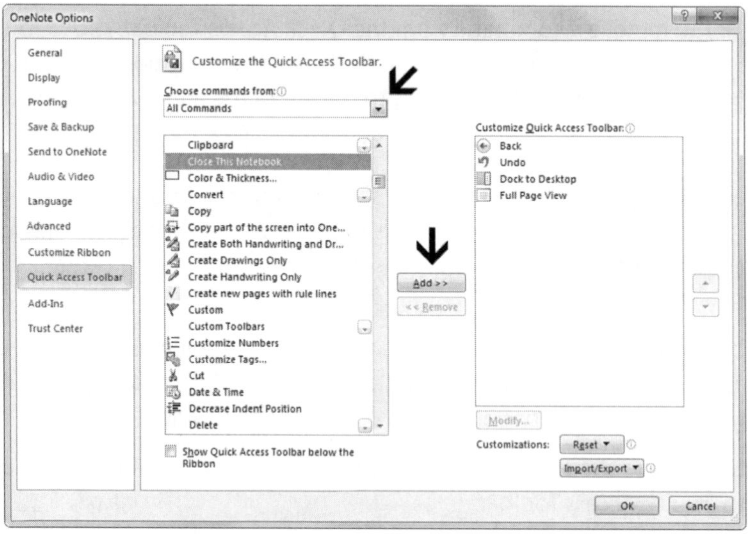

Figure 12.17   *Though it might seem a bit daunting at first, the advanced customization screen for the Quick Access Toolbar is actually quite easy to use. In the list of icons and commands on the left, click the specific command that you want to add, and then click the Add button in the middle. When all of the commands you want have been added to the list on the right, you can organize their order of appearance.*

Do the following:

1. Click the small drop-down arrow to the right of the Quick Access Toolbar.

2. On the menu that appears, click More Commands.

3. In the OneNote Options dialog box that appears, the Quick Access Toolbar will appear selected. Under Choose Commands From, click the drop-down arrow and then select All Commands (see Figure 12.17).

4. Scroll through the alphabetical list to browse commands.

5. To add a command to the Quick Access Toolbar, click to select it in the list on the left and then click the Add button between the two lists (see Figure 12.17).

6. When the commands you want appear in the list on the right, you can select individual commands and then click the Up and Down arrow buttons on the far right of the dialog box to organize the commands in the order you want them to appear.

7. To save your changes, click OK.

 LET ME TRY IT

Exporting Your Quick Access Toolbar Customizations for Use on Other Computers

If you've spent a fair amount of time making significant customizations to the Quick Access Toolbar and you want to duplicate these settings on another computer where you have a second copy of OneNote 2010 installed (or if you want to share your settings with a friend who uses OneNote 2010), you can export your settings to a file.

To do this, do the following:

1. Click the File tab, click Options, and then, in the OneNote Options dialog box that appears, click Quick Access Toolbar in the list of categories on the left.

2. At the bottom of the list on the right, click the Import/Export button, and then click Export All Customizations on the shortcut menu that appears (see Figure 12.20 later in the chapter).

3. In the File Save dialog box, accept or change the filename that is provided and then click Save.

4. Click OK.

By importing this settings file into OneNote 2010 on another computer, your Quick Access Toolbar customizations will be applied to that installation of OneNote.

By clicking the Import/Export button (see Figure 12.17) and then clicking Export all Customizations on the shortcut menu that appears (see Figure 12.20), you can save all of your customizations. On the computer that is to receive your saved settings, you can use this same button to then select the Import Customization File command and apply the stored settings. Note that these settings files contain any custom settings for both the Quick Access Toolbar as well as any ribbon customizations that you might have made (see "Adding Commands to the Ribbon" later in this chapter).

Resetting Your Quick Access Toolbar Customizations

If you've made extensive customizations to the Quick Access Toolbar that you no longer want to keep, or if you made a mistake and you want to restore the Quick Access Toolbar to its initial settings, do the following:

1. Click the File tab, click Options, and then, in the OneNote Options dialog box that appears, click Quick Access Toolbar in the list of categories on the left.

2. At the bottom of the list on the right, click the Reset button (see Figure 12.17) and then click Reset Only Quick Access Toolbar.

3. Click OK.

 LET ME TRY IT

Adding Commands to the Ribbon

Although the Quick Access Toolbar is intended to provide access to your most frequently used commands at all times, it's important to understand that it does not replace the ribbon, which is your main and most important toolbox in OneNote

2010. For this reason, Microsoft has included the same sophisticated customization interface for ribbon commands, ribbon groups, and ribbon tabs.

To create your own custom ribbon tab with a ribbon group of commands, do the following:

1. Click the File tab, click Options, and then, in the OneNote Options dialog box that appears, click Customize Ribbon in the list of categories on the left.

2. Near the top middle, under Customize the Ribbon, click the Choose Commands From drop-down and then select All Commands (see Figure 12.18).

3. Scroll through the list on the left to look for your first command. In this example, scroll down to commands beginning with the letter R and then click to select the Rotate Left 45° command.

4. In the list on the right, click to select Home in the Main Tabs list, and then click the New Tab button at the bottom of the list. OneNote creates a new ribbon tab called New Tab (Custom) and it creates on that tab a new ribbon group called New Group (Custom).

5. Right-click New Tab (Custom) and then click Rename on the shortcut menu that appears. In the Rename dialog box that appears, replace the selected text by typing Rotation as the new name for this tab, and then click OK.

6. Right-click New Group (Custom) and then click Rename on the shortcut menu that appears. In the Rename dialog box that appears, replace the selected text by typing Rotate Object as the new name for this group, and then click OK (see Figure 12.18).

7. With the Rotate Left 45° command still selected in the list on the left, click the Add button between the two lists. OneNote adds the command to the new ribbon group on the new tab you just created.

8. In the list on the left, click to select the Rotate Left 90° command and then click the Add button between the two lists.

9. In the list on the left, click to select the Rotate Right 45° command and then click the Add button between the two lists.

10. In the list on the left, click to select the Rotate Right 90° command and then click the Add button between the two lists.

11. When all four rotation commands appear in the new ribbon group under the new tab you created (see Figure 12.18), click OK to save your changes.

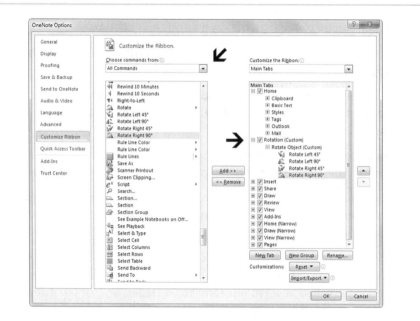

Figure 12.18   *In this example, we're adding a new tab called Rotation to the ribbon. This tab will contain one ribbon group called Rotate Object, and that group will contain four command buttons for the four rotation commands that are available in OneNote.*

The tab you just created now appears where it was shown in the list (see Figure 12.18)—between the Home and the Insert tabs. If you click the new Rotation tab, you'll see the four commands you added to it, which are in the ribbon group that you called Rotate Object (see Figure 12.19).

To try out the commands you just added, do the following:

1. Create a new, blank page and then click the Draw tab.

2. In the Insert Shapes group, click the rectangle shape.

3. When the mouse pointer changes to a crosshair icon, click and drag a rectangle on the blank page.

4. Click the Rotation tab you created. Because your drawing object is still selected, all four rotation commands should now be available.

5. Click any of the four commands to see the rotation angle of your selected rectangle change.

As with the Quick Access Toolbar customizations, I encourage you to experiment with these settings as soon as you feel comfortable with using OneNote.

Figure 12.19 *Shown here are the results from following the previous steps. The newly created tab that now appears between the Home and Insert tabs is called Rotation. It contains one ribbon group called Rotate Object, and this group contains four commands that control the rotation of a selected picture or drawing object. If no object on the page is selected, these four commands will appear dimmed.*

 LET ME TRY IT

Removing Commands from the Ribbon

To remove commands from the ribbon, you can either hide the tab that contains the commands, or you can delete custom commands as well as custom groups or entire custom tabs.

To hide a ribbon tab, do the following:

1. Click the File tab, click Options, and then, in the OneNote Options dialog box that appears, click Customize Ribbon in the list of categories on the left.

2. In the list on the right, clear the check mark next to the tab you want to hide, and then click OK.

The tab and its associated groups and commands will no longer appear on the ribbon. It's still available, however, so whenever you want to turn it back on, repeat the previous steps and then click the check box next to the tab you want to restore.

To remove a custom command or a custom ribbon group from its associated ribbon tab, do the following:

1. Click the File tab, click Options, and then, in the OneNote Options dialog box that appears, click Customize Ribbon in the list of categories on the left.

2. In the list on the right, click the + sign next to the name of the custom ribbon tab that contains the ribbon group or the commands you want to remove.

3. Do one of the following:

   • To remove an entire custom ribbon group, click to select it in the list.

   • To remove a specific command, click the + sign next to the name of the ribbon group containing that command, and then click to select the command in the list.

4. Click the Remove button between the two lists to remove either the selected ribbon group or the selected command.

5. Click OK to save your changes.

Restoring deleted ribbon groups cannot be easily done. You must re-create the groups and their commands the same way you initially created them. For this reason, don't breeze by these features while you're still learning them and take care when deciding which ribbon customizations you want to delete.

 LET ME TRY IT

Renaming Ribbon Tabs or Groups

There might be times when you want or need to rename existing tabs or ribbon groups. For example, if you're customizing a ribbon group with new commands, these commands might no longer fit their group or tab label. Rather than creating a new tab or group, you can rename the existing one.

To rename ribbon tabs or groups, do the following:

1. Click the File tab, click Options, and then, in the OneNote Options dialog box that appears, click Customize Ribbon in the list of categories on the left.

2. In the list on the right, click to select the tab or ribbon group you want to rename. If necessary, click the + signs next to the name of the tabs containing the groups you want to rename.

3. At the bottom of the list, click the Rename button.

4. In the Rename dialog box that opens, type a new name for the tab or group and then click OK.

5. Click OK to save your changes.

 **LET ME TRY IT**

Exporting Your Ribbon Customizations for Use on Other Computers

If you've made any customizations to the OneNote interface—either just to the Quick Access Toolbar, just to the ribbon, or to both—you can save your custom settings in a file that you can then transfer to another computer that has OneNote 2010 installed.

To export your OneNote 2010 interface customizations, do the following:

1. Click the File tab, click Options, and then, in the OneNote Options dialog box that appears, click Customize Ribbon in the list of categories on the left.

2. At the bottom of the list on the right, click the Import/Export button, and then click Export All Customizations on the shortcut menu that appears (see Figure 12.20).

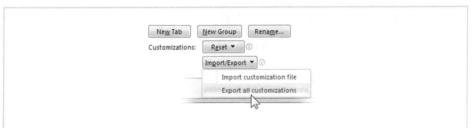

Figure 12.20   *The Export All Customizations command lets you save all of your OneNote 2010 interface customizations to a single file, which you can then import on any other computer that also has OneNote 2010 installed. This way, your time-consuming customizations to the ribbon and to the Quick Access Toolbar can be instantly duplicated for use on other computers or for other OneNote users.*

3. In the File Save dialog box, accept or change the filename that is provided and then click Save.

4. Click OK.

By importing this settings file into OneNote 2010 on another computer, your ribbon customizations will be applied to that installation of OneNote.

LET ME TRY IT

Resetting Your Ribbon Customizations

If you've made extensive customizations to the ribbon that you no longer want to keep, or if you made a mistake and you want to restore the ribbon to its default settings, do the following:

1. Click the File tab, click Options, and then, in the OneNote Options dialog box that appears, click Customize Ribbon in the list of categories on the left.

2. To restore only a specific ribbon tab, click it in the list on the right.

3. At the bottom of the list on the right, click the Reset button (see Figure 12.18) and then click Reset Only Selected Ribbon tab. Alternately, if you want to reset all ribbon customizations, click the Reset button and then click Reset All Customizations.

4. Click OK.

Setting Preferences for Editing and Searching

OneNote 2010 also includes several optional settings that affect the way you take notes, import and edit content, and how you link to and search for information.

 LET ME TRY IT

Setting the Default Font

Typed text in OneNote 2010 defaults to 11-point Calibri—a very legible screen font that's included with all Microsoft Office 2010 applications. If you have a different preference for how new text should appear in your notes, you can specify a different font, font size, and font color to be used as the initial setting for text on new pages.

To set the default font, do the following:

1. On the File tab, click Options.

2. In the OneNote Options dialog box that opens, look for the Default Font section.

3. Select your preferences from the Font, Size, and Font Color drop-down menus, and then click OK. Your preferences will be applied to all new text that you create in your notes.

 LET ME TRY IT

Changing the Default Measurement Unit

If you frequently print notes and you need to work with specific paper sizes, you can change the unit of measure from inches to a different preference by doing the following:

1. On the File tab, click Options.

2. In the OneNote Options dialog box, click the Advanced category on the left side.

3. On the right side, scroll down to the Other heading at the very bottom and then select the unit of measure you want from the Measurement Units drop-down menu.

4. Click OK to save your changes.

5. Click the View tab.

6. In the Page Setup group, click Paper Size.

7. In the Paper Size task pane, verify that the paper size or print margins you want are shown with the new units of measure.

 LET ME TRY IT

Turning Note Containers On or Off

As you type in OneNote, a small gray frame appears around the text you type (see Figure 12.21). These frames are called note containers. They are only visible while you type or format the text within them, or while you move the mouse over them.

Think of note containers as little helpers that make it easier for you to line up text and objects on your page. They don't show up when you print a page or share a page with someone over e-mail.

A note inside of a note container.

Figure 12.21   *Unless you choose to hide them, note containers containing text or objects can be resized and repositioned by interacting with them on the page. When note containers are hidden, you can still move the mouse over a line of text and then click and drag the four-headed arrow icon that appears next to the text to reposition it on the page.*

If you don't ever need to resize or move blocks of text on your page, you can hide the note containers around text by doing the following:

1.   On the File tab, click Options.

2.   In the OneNote Options dialog box, click the Display category on the left side.

3.   On the right side, under the Display heading, uncheck the Show Note Containers on Pages check box.

4.   Click OK to save your changes.

 LET ME TRY IT

Showing or Hiding the Mini Toolbar when Selecting Text

Whenever you select text on a page, the Mini toolbar appears, giving you quick access to the formatting commands that you can also find on the ribbon (see Figure 12.22). Though it gives you convenient shortcuts to your formatting commands, there might be times when you want to disable the Mini toolbar.

Figure 12.22   *The Mini toolbar appears whenever you select text on a page. Its formatting commands and buttons work the same as they do on the ribbon. If this frequently covers up what you want to select on a page, you can temporarily or permanently turn the Mini toolbar display off.*

To hide the Mini toolbar when selecting text, do the following:

1. On the File tab, click Options.

2. In the OneNote Options dialog box, click the General category on the left side.

3. On the right side, under the User Interface Options heading, uncheck the Show Mini Toolbar on Selection check box.

4. Click OK to save your changes.

 LET ME TRY IT

Turning Automatic Spell Checking On or Off

Like most Microsoft Office programs, OneNote 2010 automatically checks your spelling as you type text, underlining misspelled or questionable words with a red, squiggly line.

If you want to disable automatic spell-checking for some reason (for example, if you're temporarily typing notes in a different language), do the following:

1. On the File tab, click Options.

2. In the OneNote Options dialog box, click the Proofing category on the left side.

3. On the right side, under the When Correcting Spelling in OneNote heading, uncheck the Check Spelling as You Type check box.

4. Click OK to save your changes.

 **LET ME TRY IT**

Viewing or Editing the Word List in Your Custom Dictionary

Whenever you encounter misspelled or questionable words during a spell-check, you have the option of adding such words to your custom dictionary. This is useful when you want to add legitimate words and names to your dictionary so that OneNote doesn't question them again in the future.

To view or edit the word list in your custom dictionary, do the following:

1. On the File tab, click Options.

2. In the OneNote Options dialog box, click the Proofing category on the left side.

3. On the right side, under the When Correcting Spelling in Microsoft Office Programs heading, click the Custom Dictionaries button.

4. In the Custom Dictionaries list, select the dictionary you want (typically, you'll only see CUSTOM.DIC in the list) and then click the Edit Word List button.

5. In the dialog box that opens, you can review words on the list, add new ones by clicking Add, or delete existing words by selecting them and then clicking Delete.

6. Click OK to save your changes.

7. Click OK to exit the Custom Dictionaries dialog box.

8. Click OK to close the OneNote Options dialog box.

 LET ME TRY IT

Setting AutoCorrect Options

Like most Microsoft Office programs, OneNote 2010 can automatically replace words or phrases that you frequently misspell and correct them on the spot. For example, if you type the misspelled word *adn* in OneNote, it will automatically correct it to *and*.

You can also use this feature to assign text codes for long or complex phrases that you need to frequently type. For example, you could have OneNote automatically change "fmi" to the phrase "for more information" if this is something you must frequently type.

To view or edit your AutoCorrect options, do the following:

1. On the File tab, click Options.

2. In the OneNote Options dialog box, click the Proofing category on the left side.

3. On the right side, under AutoCorrect Options, click the AutoCorrect Options button.

4. In the AutoCorrect Options dialog box that opens, set the options you want. In the double column list at the bottom, you can view the text replacements that are currently in effect, and you can add new ones by filling in the Replace and With fields and then clicking Add.

5. To delete any entry that you no longer want to use, click to select it in the list and then click Delete.

6. If you want to view or change the default AutoCorrect options for Math equations, click the Math AutoCorrect tab.

7. Click OK to save any changes you made in either dialog box tab.

 **LET ME TRY IT**

Showing or Hiding the Paste Options Button when Pasting

Whenever you paste text on a page in OneNote, the Paste Options button automatically appears (see Figure 12.23), letting you choose how the pasted text should be formatted.

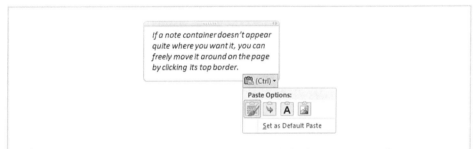

Figure 12.23 *When you paste copied text into OneNote, the Paste Options button appears. You can click this button or press the Ctrl key to open the Paste Options menu, which lets you specify how pasted text should be formatted. Rest the mouse pointer over each of the available buttons for a more detailed explanation.*

Although a convenient and useful feature, the Paste Options button can sometimes partially hide or obscure text. If you find this annoying, or if you don't care how copied text appears in your notes, you can temporarily or permanently turn off the Paste Options button by doing the following:

1. On the File tab, click Options.

2. In the OneNote Options dialog box, click the Advanced category on the left side.

3. On the right side, under Editing, uncheck the Show Paste Options Button When Content Is Pasted check box.

4. Click OK to save your changes.

 LET ME TRY IT

Including or Suppressing Source Links when Pasting from the Web

Whenever you paste content from a web page or you insert a screen clipping, OneNote includes a web link back to the source page underneath the pasted content (see Figure 12.24). This lets you easily return to the source content if you need to find the original information again.

Figure 12.24 *OneNote automatically generates a clickable link underneath pasted text, pictures, or screen clippings that you've imported from the Web. This lets you easily return to the source of the information you've included in your notes.*

If you don't find this information useful or if you don't want to reveal it to people with whom you share your notes, you can suppress the automatic inclusion of links by doing the following:

1. On the File tab, click Options.

2. In the OneNote Options dialog box, click the Advanced category on the left side.

3. On the right side, under Editing, uncheck the Include Link to Source when Pasting from the Web check box.

4. Click OK to save your changes.

 **LET ME TRY IT**

Automatically Applying Numbers or Bullets to Lists

Though you can click the Numbering or Bullets buttons on the Home tab to start either type of list, OneNote can also automatically recognize when what you type resembles a list.

For example, if you start a new line by typing 1. followed by space and some text, OneNote will assume you want to start a numbered list. Likewise if you type an asterisk (*) followed by a space and some text, OneNote will assume that you want to start a bulleted list. Typically, this is very helpful. However, if you don't want list formatting to be applied for you automatically, you can turn this feature off by doing the following:

1. On the File tab, click Options.

2. In the OneNote Options dialog box, click the Advanced category on the left side.

3. On the right side, under Editing, do either of the following:

   - Uncheck the Apply Numbering to Lists Automatically check box.
   - Uncheck the Apply Bullets to Lists Automatically check box.

4. Click OK to save your changes.

 **LET ME TRY IT**

Automatically Calculating Mathematical Expressions in Notes

OneNote includes a handy little feature that's affectionately called "napkin math." When enabled, OneNote will attempt to solve any simple mathematical expressions that you type out on a page.

For example, if you type 1+1= and then type a space or press Enter, OneNote will correctly place the number 2 after the equal sign. You can solve additions, subtractions, multiplications, and divisions in this way, and you can combine any amount of numbers and operators for slightly more complex calculations.

If you frequently type out figures and you don't want OneNote to solve anything that looks like a math problem, you can turn this feature off by doing the following:

1. On the File tab, click Options.

2. In the OneNote Options dialog box, click the Advanced category on the left side.

3. On the right side, under Editing, uncheck the Calculate Mathematical Expressions Automatically check box.

4. Click OK to save your changes.

 LET ME TRY IT

Enabling or Disabling Automatic Wiki Link Creation

As you learned in Chapter 7, OneNote supports automatic wiki link creation. If you type the name of a page or section within double brackets (for example, [[Meeting Notes]]), OneNote will automatically link to the section or page with that title, allowing you to click the link and jump to that part of your notes without having to manually navigate to it.

If you use wiki links for pages that don't yet exist, OneNote will automatically create a blank new page in the current section to remind you that you wanted to link to such a page later on. If you'd prefer to do this manually instead, you can turn off automatic wiki link creation by doing the following:

1. On the File tab, click Options.

2. In the OneNote Options dialog box, click the Advanced category on the left side.

3. On the right side, under Editing, uncheck the Enable Link Creation by Typing [[ ]] Around a Phrase check box.

4. Click OK to save your changes.

 **LET ME TRY IT**

Disabling Linked Notes Creation in a Docked Window

By default, OneNote will assume that you want to begin a Linked Notes session whenever you dock the OneNote program window to your Windows desktop (see "Changing the Current Page View" earlier in this chapter) or whenever you choose to open a new docked window (see "Displaying a New Docked Window" and "Docking New Side Notes to the Desktop" earlier in this chapter).

If you prefer to take notes in a docked window without starting a Linked Notes session, do the following:

1. Click the File tab, and then click Options.

2. In the OneNote Options dialog box, click the Advanced category on the left side.

3. On the right side, scroll down to the Linked Notes heading, and then uncheck the Allow Creation of New Linked Notes check box.

4. Click OK to save your changes.

Once you've followed these steps, you will not be able to use the Linked Notes feature in any new docked OneNote windows. To remind you of this, the Linked Notes icon in the upper-left corner of the docked window will be shown with a red, slashed circle over it (see Figure 12.25).

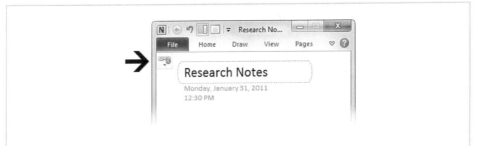

Figure 12.25 *Whenever the Linked Notes icon in the upper-left corner of a docked OneNote window appears with a red, slashed circle over it, the Linked Notes feature is turned off. You can still type notes normally in the docked window, the same way you would in a normal OneNote window.*

To restore Linked Notes functionality in your docked OneNote windows or your docked side notes, repeat the steps in the previous procedure, but be sure to select the check box option in step 3. Click OK to save your new preference.

Once Linked Notes functionality has been restored, the red, slashed circle over the link icon will disappear. You can then click the icon for additional options.

> If you previously created Linked Notes by opening a docked window and you don't want to keep these link relationships between your notes and the source files you looked at during your note-taking session, you can delete the links. See "Removing Links from Linked Notes" in the procedure that follows.

 LET ME TRY IT

Removing Links from Linked Notes

If you no longer need the information that OneNote saves about the source documents and pages for linked notes, or you started a Linked Notes session unintentionally and want to remove the links it created, do the following:

1. Click the File tab and then click Options.

2. In the OneNote Options dialog box, click the Advanced category on the left side.

3. On the right side, scroll down to the Linked Notes heading, and then uncheck the Save Document Snippets and Page Thumbnail for Better Linking to the Right Place in the Document check box.

4. Click OK to save your changes.

> Only use this option if you're certain that you will no longer need the link relationship between the content in your notes and the source of that content. If you're changing this setting in a shared notebook, consider how the removal of these links might affect other notebook authors. Removing the links from Linked Notes cannot be undone.

 **LET ME TRY IT**

Turning the Scratch-out Gesture On or Off

If you're using the handwriting features in OneNote 2010 on a Tablet PC or Touch-compatible device, you can choose whether you want to use the scratch-out gesture for removing ink strokes while taking notes.

By default, this option is disabled. To turn it on, do the following:

1. Click the File tab and then click Options.

2. In the OneNote Options dialog box, click the Advanced category on the left side.

3. On the right side, scroll down to the Pen heading, and then uncheck the Disable the Scratch-out Gesture While Inking check box.

4. Click OK to save your changes.

To disable the options again, repeat the previous steps but click to select the check box in step 3.

 **LET ME TRY IT**

Turning Pen Pressure Sensitivity On or Off

If you're using the handwriting features in OneNote 2010 on a Tablet PC or Touch-compatible device, you can choose whether you want to use variable pen pressure, the way ink might flow when you rest or press the pen on the paper in different ways. Using this feature can give your handwritten or drawn notes a more natural appearance, but it can also increase the file size of your OneNote notebooks.

By default, this option is disabled. To turn it on, do the following:

1. Click the File tab and then click Options.

2. In the OneNote Options dialog box, click the Advanced category on the left side.

3. On the right side, scroll down to the Pen heading and then click to select the Use Pen Pressure Sensitivity (Increases File Size) check box.

4. Click OK to save your changes.

To disable the options again, repeat the previous steps but be sure to clear the check box in step 3.

 **LET ME TRY IT**

Automatically Switching Between Inking, Selecting, Typing, and Panning

If you're using the handwriting features in OneNote 2010 on a Tablet PC or Touch-compatible device, OneNote automatically switches its selection mechanism when you switch between inking and typing and when selecting and panning content.

If you frequently work with mixed content on a page and you want OneNote to stay in the mode you selected, you can turn this option off by doing the following:

1. Click the File tab and then click Options.

2. In the OneNote Options dialog box, click the Advanced category on the left side.

3. On the right side, scroll down to the Pen heading, and then uncheck the Automatically Switch Between Inking, Selecting, Typing and Panning check box.

4. Click OK to save your changes.

The use of "panning" here is in reference to the Panning Hand, a page navigation command that you learned about in Chapter 5, "Taking and Formatting Notes" (see Figure 12.26).

Figure 12.26   *Using the Panning Hand tool, you can bring other parts of the page into view without accidentally deselecting any handwriting objects on the current page. The Select & Type command at the far left of the Draw tab is activated automatically, unless you turn the automatic mode switching option off.*

Enabling or Disabling Text Recognition in Pictures

When you search your notes for a specific word or phrase, OneNote will try to find them not just in typed text but also in pictures that contain the word or phrase (for example, in a scanned business card image). If you don't want OneNote to recognize text in pictures in your notes, you can disable this feature by doing the following:

1. Click the File tab and then click Options.

2. In the OneNote Options dialog box, click the Advanced category on the left side.

3. On the right side, scroll down to the Text Recognition in Pictures heading and then click to select the Disable Text Recognition in Pictures check box.

4. Click OK to save your changes.

If you find that searching through unusually large notebooks is happening more slowly than you would like, you can temporarily disable the text recognition feature for your pictures. To restore this feature again later, repeat the previous steps but uncheck the check box in step 3.

 LET ME TRY IT

Enabling or Disabling Word Recognition in Audio and Video Clips

When you search your notes for a specific word or phrase, OneNote is capable of finding them in the sound recording in audio or video files that you imported in your notes. This is especially useful if you frequently take audio or video notes and need to find specific information that does not appear typed out on a page.

Because this feature takes additional system resources to work, it is turned off by default. If you want to enable it, do the following:

1. Click the File tab and then click Options.

2. In the OneNote Options dialog box, click the Audio & Video category on the left side.

3. On the right side, scroll down to the Audio Search heading and then click to select the Enable Searching Audio and Video Recordings for Words check box.

4. Click OK to save your changes.

Search performance will be noticeably slower with this option turned on than when you do a normal search. The rate of success for finding spoken words in audio clips or the audio portions of video clips in your notes greatly depends on the quality of the recording, the volume of the speaker, and the amount of ambient noise. If necessary, you can experiment with the audio recording settings and the video recording settings on the Audio & Video page in the OneNote Options dialog box until you find the right configuration for the type of audio you frequently record and that you want to include when searching for spoken words.

Adjusting OneNote Performance Settings

Though mostly self-explanatory, I do want to include the following pointers to some of OneNote's performance tweaks that you might find useful. As with most of the settings discussed in this chapter, it is typically not necessary to change these settings unless you have a specific reason or preference for doing so.

 **LET ME TRY IT**

Modifying the Default Location of New Notebooks

Typically, new notebooks that you create on your hard drive are stored in the OneNote Notebooks folder in your Documents (or My Documents) folder.

If you want all future new notebooks to be created in a different location, you can tell OneNote your preferred new default location by doing the following:

1. Click the File tab and then click Options.

2. In the OneNote Options dialog box, click the Save & Backup category on the left side.

3. On the right side, under the Save heading, click the Default Notebook Location path in the list, and then click Modify.

4. Navigate to the new location where you want notebooks to be created and then click Select.

5. In the list, verify that the new file path now shows up next to Default Notebook Location.

 LET ME TRY IT

Modifying the Location of Unfiled Notes

If you want to change the default location of your Unfiled Notes section, do the following:

1. Click the File tab and then click Options.

2. In the OneNote Options dialog box, click the Save & Backup category on the left side.

3. On the right side, under the Save heading, click the Unfiled Notes Section path in the list and then click Modify.

4. Navigate to the new location where you want your Unfiled Notes to be stored from now on and then click Select.

5. In the list, verify that the new file path now shows up next to Unfiled Notes Section.

 LET ME TRY IT

Modifying the Location of Your Backups

If you want to change the default location of automatic backups that OneNote creates for you (or the default location of any manual backups that you create), do the following:

1. Click the File tab and then click Options.

2. In the OneNote Options dialog box, click the Save & Backup category on the left side.

3. On the right side, under the Save heading, click the Backup Folder path in the list and then click Modify.

4. Navigate to the new location where you want your OneNote backups to be stored and then click Select.

5. In the list, verify that the new file path now shows up next to Backup Folder.

 LET ME TRY IT

Modifying the Default Locations of Notes, Outlook Items, and Screen Clippings Sent to OneNote

If you frequently use any of the Send to OneNote commands that may appear in other programs that you have installed, you can more specifically control where such items should automatically be filed by doing the following:

1. Click the File tab and then click Options.

2. In the OneNote Options dialog box, click the Send to OneNote category on the left side.

3. On the right side, for any of the items you see listed, click the drop-down arrow next to the items whose default location you want to change, and then make a selection from the available options.

4. Click OK to save your changes.

> You might need to restart OneNote for these settings to take effect.

 LET ME TRY IT

Changing Office Language Preferences

Microsoft Office 2010 is available in over 30 world languages. In addition to your native language for which you have configured Windows and Office, you can purchase and install optional language packs that provide additional proofing tools and spelling capabilities in your copy of OneNote or Office.

To install, verify, and troubleshoot such optional language packs after you have purchased them, do the following:

1. Click the File tab and then click Options.

2. In the OneNote Options dialog box, click the Language category on the left side.

3. On the right side, choose the appropriate settings for your editing languages and for your display and Help languages for OneNote or for Office.

4. If you need assistance with these features, click the Help links provided on this screen or visit www.office.com and search the Microsoft Office website for information about language packs.

5. If you make changes on this screen, click OK to save them.

 LET ME TRY IT

Optimizing OneNote for Laptop Battery Life

OneNote typically decides automatically how often to run a variety of housekeeping activities in the background while you take notes, such as search and audio indexing, text and handwriting recognition, and notebook synchronization.

If you're using OneNote on a laptop with a short battery charge, you can tell OneNote to minimize such activities to extend your battery life by a bit.

To optimize OneNote for laptop battery life, do the following:

1. Click the File tab and then click Options.

2. In the OneNote Options dialog box, click the Advanced category on the left side.

3. On the right side, scroll down to the Battery Options heading and then choose the option you want from the Optimize for the Following Battery Life drop-down list.

4. Click OK to save your changes.

It's impossible to accurately predict how much battery life you will save by setting this option to any of the battery-saving options. It depends on the size of your notebook, the types of notes you've written, how often you navigate through your notebook, the speed of your computer, the type of hard drive in use, and the capabilities and age of your battery. If you want to determine how dramatically these settings may or may not affect your specific computer, keep track of the time it takes to fully discharge your battery on the two configuration settings most opposite to one another and then compare the results.

Customizing OneNote Installation Options

Depending on the choices that were made when you (or someone else) first installed OneNote, you can change certain installation settings at any time.

 **LET ME TRY IT**

Personalizing Your Copy of OneNote 2010

If you use shared notebooks with OneNote 2010, it's highly recommended that you tell OneNote your full name and your initials so that your edits can be properly identified in the author information which will be visible to others may be working in a shared notebook with you.

To verify or update your personalization, do the following:

1. Click the File tab, and then click Options.

2. In the OneNote Options dialog box, click the General category on the left side.

3. On the right side, under Personalize Your Copy of Microsoft Office, type your full name into the User Name box, and then type your initials into the Initials box.

4. Click OK to save your changes.

 LET ME TRY IT

Changing OneNote 2010 Setup Options

To view or change Setup options in your standalone copy of OneNote 2010 or in your edition of Microsoft Office 2010 that contains OneNote 2010, do the following:

1. Exit OneNote and any other Office programs that you may be running.

2. In Windows 7, click the Start button and then click Control Panel.

3. In Control Panel under Programs, click the blue Uninstall a Program link.

4. In the Uninstall or Change a Program list that appears, find either Microsoft OneNote 2010 or Microsoft Office 2010 and then click its entry once to select it in the list.

5. Near the top of the list, click Change.

6. In the window that appears (see Figure 12.27), click Add or Remove Features, and then click Continue.

Figure 12.27 *When you click the Change button in Control Panel while OneNote or Office is selected in your installed programs list, OneNote or Office will display the maintenance menu where you can view, add, or remove features, repair your installation of OneNote or Office, uninstall the product from your computer, or enter a different product key to activate your version of OneNote or Office.*

7. On the next screen, click the control buttons to the left of specific features that you want to enable or disable.

8. If you make any changes in this list, click Continue and then follow any instructions that appear.

9. If no changes are necessary, click the Close button (the red X) in the upper-right corner of the window.

10. When prompted if you want to cancel Setup, click Yes and then click Close.

LET ME TRY IT

Repairing Your OneNote 2010 Installation

If any particular feature in OneNote 2010 does not work as you expect it to, or as it's been described here in the book, it's possible that you or someone else who is using your computer might have inadvertently changed something. If you don't know what's changed and you can't use the preferences in the OneNote Options dialog box to fix the problem, you can try repairing your installation of OneNote 2010 or Office 2010 by doing the following:

1. Exit OneNote and any other Office programs that you are running.

2. In Windows 7, click the Start button and then click Control Panel.

3. In Control Panel under Programs, click the blue Uninstall a Program link.

4. In the Uninstall or Change a Program list that appears, find either Microsoft OneNote 2010 or Microsoft Office 2010 and then click its entry once to select it in the list.

5. Near the top of the list, click Change.

6. In the window that appears, click Repair and then click Continue.

7. Follow any instructions that appear.

It's a good idea to restart your computer after you repair a program. This frees up any files that might have been in use and it gives you a fresh start with the newly restored settings.

 **LET ME TRY IT**

Checking for OneNote 2010 Software Updates

If you don't have Windows Update configured to automatically check for OneNote 2010 and Office 2010 updates for some reason, you can manually check for software updates right in OneNote by doing the following:

1. Click the File tab and then click Help.

2. Under Tools for Working with Office, click Check for Updates.

It's a good idea to keep all of your software programs updated so you'll have all of the latest feature enhancements and security updates.

 **LET ME TRY IT**

Setting Preferences for the OneNote Taskbar Icon

In Chapter 6, you learned all about the OneNote taskbar icon, also called the OneNote 2010 Screen Clipper and Launcher. Although its default behavior is suitable for most occasions, you can set some options for this small program that runs in the background and gives you access to OneNote features even when OneNote isn't running.

To set preferences for the OneNote taskbar icon, do the following:

1. On the Windows taskbar, right-click the OneNote icon in the notification area near the Windows clock (see Figure 12.28).

Figure 12.28   *Clicking the OneNote Icon Defaults option on the shortcut menu of the OneNote taskbar icon lets you choose what should happen when you left-click the icon. The option that appears in bold on this menu is the default selection that's currently active.*

2. Click OneNote Icon Defaults and then choose the default command that OneNote should use when you left-click the icon. For example, if you want to open OneNote by clicking this icon instead of creating a new side note (the initial setting), click Open OneNote. Your new preference is saved as soon as you make a selection.

LET ME TRY IT

Displaying OneNote 2010 Version Information

Lastly, if you should ever need to troubleshoot OneNote, you might be asked what specific version of OneNote 2010 you're running. To display this information, do the following:

1. Click the File tab and then click Help.

2. At the far right, under About Microsoft OneNote, you'll see a long string of numbers that indicates the exact version of the program that you are currently running. In parentheses after that, you can see whether you're running the 32-bit or the 64-version of OneNote 2010 or Office 2010 (this might also be important information for troubleshooting).

3. To obtain product support from Microsoft, click the Microsoft Customer Services and Support link on this screen and then follow the instructions that are displayed. Alternately, you can visit http://www.office.com to learn more about your Support options for your Microsoft Office 2010 programs—including OneNote 2010. You can also visit the official Microsoft product support forums on the Web by visiting http://answers.microsoft.com.

Make sure that you have a legally obtained copy of OneNote or Office before attempting to obtain product support and make sure that your product was properly activated after installation. You can view your product activation status by clicking the File tab, clicking Help, and then looking at the activation status information underneath the Microsoft Office logo at the far right of the screen.

Thank You!

This concludes *Using Microsoft OneNote 2010*. Thanks for giving this book your attention. No matter if you were brand-new to OneNote or you wanted to brush up on your OneNote skills, I sincerely hope that you have found the information in this book to be helpful.

I encourage you to "play" with OneNote 2010 to your heart's content by experimenting with the various features that you learned about in the preceding chapters. Remember that you can't do much damage if you're using your practice notebook until you figure things out a bit more. Besides, as I've pointed out numerous times along the way, the Undo command is your best friend while learning any new computer program.

If there are features I've described that feel a bit more technical than you're comfortable with, remember to take advantage of the many "Show Me" media links that appear throughout the chapters. If you purchased this book, you're eligible to view the many free videos that are associated with each of the walkthroughs in this book.

My final reminder and encouragement about OneNote is this: When in doubt, right-click something. Whether it's text, a picture, a file, an object, a part of the interface, or anything else, you're sure to discover something new.

I wish you much fun and success in your continued exploration and use of OneNote 2010!

Michael C. Oldenburg
Redmond, Washington

index